P9-AFN-635

GOLDEN GULAG

AMERICAN CROSSROADS
EDITED BY EARL LEWIS, GEORGE LIPSITZ, PEGGY PASCOE, GEORGE SÁNCHEZ, AND DANA TAKAGI

DISCARD

GOLDEN GULAG

PRISONS, SURPLUS, CRISIS, AND OPPOSITION IN GLOBALIZING CALIFORNIA

RUTH WILSON GILMORE

UNIVERSITY OF CALIFORNIA PRESS
BERKELEY   LOS ANGELES   LONDON

365.9794
G4889

University of California Press, one of the most distinguished university presses in the United States, enriches lives around the world by advancing scholarship in the humanities, social sciences, and natural sciences. Its activities are supported by the UC Press Foundation and by philanthropic contributions from individuals and institutions. For more information, visit www.ucpress.edu.

University of California Press
Berkeley and Los Angeles, California

University of California Press, Ltd.
London, England

© 2007 by
The Regents of the University of California

Library of Congress Cataloging-in-Publication Data

Gilmore, Ruth Wilson, 1950–.
    Golden gulag : prisons, surplus, crisis, and opposition in globalizing California / Ruth Wilson Gilmore.
        p.   cm—(American crossroads ; 21).
    Includes bibliographical references and index.
    ISBN-13: 978-0-520-22256-4 (cloth : alk. paper)
    ISBN-10: 0-520-22256-3 (cloth : alk. paper)
    ISBN-13: 978-0-520-24201-2 (pbk. : alk. paper)
    ISBN-10: 0-520-24201-7 (pbk. : alk. paper)
    1. Prisons—California.   2. Prisons—Economic aspects—California.   3. Imprisonment—California.
    4. Criminal justice, Administration of—California.
    5. Discrimination in criminal justice administration—California.
    6. Minorities—California.   7. California—Economic conditions.
    I. Title.   II. Series.

HV9475.C2G73   2007
365'.9794—dc22   2006011674

Manufactured in the United States of America

15   14   13   12   11   10   09   08   07
11   10   9   8   7   6   5   4   3   2   1

This book is printed on New Leaf EcoBook 60, containing 60% postconsumer waste, processed chlorine free; 30% de-inked recycled fiber, elemental chlorine free; and 10% FSC-certified virgin fiber, totally chlorine free. EcoBook 60 is acid free and meets the minimum requirements of ANSI/ASTM D 5634–01 (*Permanence of Paper*). ∞

¹/07

FOR MY MOTHER, RUTH ISABEL HERB WILSON
AND IN LOVING MEMORY OF MY FATHER, COURTLAND SEYMOUR WILSON

CONTENTS

ILLUSTRATIONS

TABLES

ACKNOWLEDGMENTS

Golden Gulag is a late first book—late in my life, late to the press, and so late in the twentieth century that it appears well into the twenty-first. In some ways, the contents are old news, but alas not old enough to have become mere bad memories or the stuff of history to learn from. Over the years, as I've wrestled with the questions and evidence that shape the book, I've had so much help from so many people that this section of the volume should, by rights, be longer than any chapter and contain far more entries than the bibliography. However, well into my second half-century on this troubled planet, I'm as forgetful as I am in-debted—and hopeful that if you don't find your name here, you'll forgive the oversight. And may all, named or not, excuse the errors.

Poor Neil Smith. As Geography Department chair at Rutgers, he generously accepted a cranky middle-aged activist packing a couple of drama degrees and a headful of social theory to be his Ph.D. student and got plenty of drama in return. He also made me think systematically about society and space, accepted my formulation for what happened, why, and to what end—and then made me prove it to him, revision after revision, in my dissertation. We fought a lot. We also celebrated often, and I'm grateful to Neil and to Cindi Katz for embracing both Gilmores the moment we arrived at New Brunswick, for wining and dining and throwing parties for us for four years, and making me a *scholar-activist*.

At Rutgers, Professors Leela Fernandes, Dorothy Sue Cobble, Bob Lake, Ann Markusen, Susan Fainstein, John Gillis, and Caridad Souza taught me to work across disciplines; Leela, in particular, models the analytical courage interdisciplinarity demands. I hope Susan will accept this book in lieu of the paper I owe her.

When I headed off to Rutgers, my Los Angeles *compañeras*—especially Theresa Allison, Geri Silva, Pauline Milner, and Donna Warren—in Mothers Reclaiming Our Children wished me well, and they always welcomed me back to the fold—expecting me always to bring useful knowledge *and* help make their knowledge useful.

A coalition sparked by Mothers ROC and Families to Amend California's Three Strikes (FACTS) expanded statewide thanks to the relentless energy of Geri Silva, Gail Blackwell, Barbara Brooks, Sue Rheams, Claudia Marriott, Julia Gonzales, Mary Avanti, Doug Kieso, Dennis Duncan, Carmen Ewell, and Christy Johnson, among many other tireless people.

My capacity to think theoretically, but speak practically, I owe to the stern sisterly tutelage of my Wages for Housework mentors, Margaret Prescod and Selma James.

Without Mike Davis there would be no *Golden Gulag*. He shared ideas, research, and resources, pointed me toward Mothers ROC and Corcoran, asked plenty of great questions, read the manuscript thoroughly, and also showed me the practical connections between analytical, political, and pedagogical creativity. Years ago, when neither of us had a proper job, we shook our graying heads in dismay at a future of endless adjuncting. Now we both have steady jobs; who knew?

George Lipsitz, Dave Roediger, Robin D. G. Kelley, Don Mitchell, Beth Richie, Ed Soja, Audrey Kobayashi, Andrea Smith, Lauren Berlant, Lakshman Yapa, Cindi Katz, Greg Hooks, Amy Kaplan, George Sánchez, Chris Newfield, Fred Moten, Devra Weber, Barbara Christian, Bruce Franklin, Angela Y. Davis, Wendy Brown, Cathy Cohen, Judith Butler, Wahneema Lubiano, Steve Martinot, Joy James, Linda Evans, Cheryl Harris, Joan Dayan, Mike Merrill, Paul Gilroy, Vron Ware, Peter Linebaugh, Bobby Wilson, Cedric Robinson, Elizabeth Robinson, Agnes Moreland Jackson, Sue E. Houchins, Deborah Santana (who set me straight on my working title "Sunshine Gulag" and suggested "Golden," lest anyone think the book was about Florida), and, more than anyone, A. Sivanandan *and* Stuart Hall indelibly influenced how I think: each fiercely demonstrates how learning well is a generous art.

During graduate school, we students—Laura Liu, Rachel Herzing, John Antranig Kasbarian, Curtis Frietag, Melina Patterson, Lisa Lynch, Alex Weheliye (who made me think about land!), Yong-Sook Lee, Marlen Llanes, Nicole Cousino, and Ralph Saunders—formed communities of purpose that still bind us in our commitment to live the change.

I'd never have spent a minute, much less six years, at Berkeley were it not for the interventions, encouragement, friendship, and mentoring of Dick Walker, Gill Hart, and Carol Stack. I also had the fortune to share work-in-progress with amazing colleagues—Jean Lave, Pedro Noguera, Dan Perlstein, Barrie Thorne, Harley Shaiken, Allan Pred, Evelyn Nakano Glenn, Elaine Kim, Michael Omi, Pat Hilden, José David Saldívar, Jeff Romm, John Hurst, Caren Kaplan, and my dearest Cal pal Kurt Cuffey. Delores Dillard, Jahleezah Eskew, Nat Vonnegut, Carol Page, and Dan Plumlee made life easy for the bureaucratically challenged and, along with Don Bain and Darin Jensen, prove that staff are the backbone and conscience of academia.

The students of Carceral Geographies at Berkeley dutifully studied the manuscript and, integrating their readings with ambitious fieldwork, concluded every fall semester with group research projects full of excellent evidence and surprising insights.

The embarrassment of riches of wonderful Berkeley graduate students who inspired and challenged me around many a seminar table include Clem Lai, Dylan Rodriguez, Frank Wilderson, Micia Mosely, Judith Kafka, Sora Han, Sara Clarke Kaplan, Mark Hunter, Priya Kandaswamy, Nari Rhee, Jenna Loyd, Ethan Johnson, Chris Neidt, Wendy Cheng, Kysa Nygreen, Juan DeLara, Judy Han, Trevor Paglen, Jen Casolo, Brinda Sarathy, Joe Bryan, Sylvia Chan, Amanda LaShaw, Kiko Casique, and Kirstie Dorr.

With patience, brilliance, and skill, four research assistants—Nari Rhee, Dana Kaplan, Ari Wohlfeiler, Pete Spannagle—moved the work forward.

Many exemplary people made research possible, especially the research librarians at Alexander Library at Rutgers and the University Research Library at UCLA. Two print journalists, Dan Morain of the *Los Angeles Times,* and Jeannette Todd of the *Corcoran Journal,* gave me time and insights; Morain's exemplary work on California prisons is a starting point for any serious student of the subject, as is the investigative reporting by Mark Arax and Mark Gladstone. Public servants Don Pauley of Corcoran, Melissa Harriman of Avenal, Ed Tewes of Modesto, and Bernie Orozco of the now defunct Joint Legislative Committee on Prison Construction and Operation provided crucial guidance without hesitation. Paula Burbach at the California Department of Corrections cheerfully responded to inquiries.

Some of the research for this book received support from a Center for the Critical Analysis of Contemporary Culture graduate fellowship; a Ford dissertation fellowship; a University of California at Berkeley chancellor's postdoctoral fellowship; and fellowships from the University of California Humanities Research Institute and the Open Society Institute.

At the University of California Humanities Research Institute, Angela Y. Davis, Gina Dent, David Theo Goldberg, Sandra Baringer, Nancy Scheper-Hughes, and Avery Gordon engaged in spirited collaborative study and fieldwork; we have a book to make from that experience.

American Studies and Ethnicity at the University of Southern California is a dream job. I am especially grateful to George Sánchez, Laura Pulido, and Fred Moten for friendship and mentoring, to all my colleagues for their trust, and to Sonia Rodriguez, Kitty Lai, and Sandra Jones—along with Billie Shotlow and Onita Morgan-Edwards in Geography—for their skillful and good-humored staffing.

I've shared parts of this work with many scholars whose sharp insights rapidly improved my thinking, thanks to the support of sponsoring institutions: the National University of Singapore, University of Washington, University of Chicago, the University of Texas at Austin, Johns Hopkins, the Claremont Colleges, Scripps College, Queens University (CAN), UC Irvine, the Society for Cultural Anthropology, University of Wisconsin, the Harry Frank Guggenheim Foundation, the Social Science Research Council, New York University, City University of New York, UCLA, the Brecht Forum, Brown, and Yale.

And then there's the generosity of activists—a constant caring regard for doing things both right and well. The principal organizations I work in and depend on are the California Prison Moratorium Project, Critical Resistance, and the Central California Environmental Justice Network. In these and other groups, many thanks to Tom Quinn, Catherine Campbell, the late Holbrook Teter, Michelle Foy, Sarah Jarmon, Ellen Barry, Bo Brown, Karen Shain, Peter Wagner, Brigette Sarabi, Tracy Huling, Kevin Pranis, Dorsey Nunn, Eddie Ellis, Naomi Swinton, Joe Kaye, Ajulo Othow, Naneen Karraker, Laura Magnani, Jason Ziedenberg, Deborah Peterson Small, Jonathan Wilson, Lois Ahrens, John Mataka, Rosenda Mataka, Sandra Meraz, Yedithza Vianey Nuñez, Joe Morales, Luke Cole, Bradley Angel, Jason Glick, Amy Vanderwarker, Lani Riccobuono, Debbie Reyes, Leonel Flores, Dana Kaplan, Ari Wohlfeiler, Rachel Herzing, and the activist's activist Rose Braz.

At the University of California Press, Linda Norton and Monica McCormick did everything possible to move this book into print ... and Niels Hooper did the impossible. Suzanne Knott and Peter Dreyer are patient and thorough editors who taught me a lot about writing to be read.

My brothers, Courtland, Peter, and Jon, and their families, have waited impatiently, as have my friends who are so close as to be fictive kin: Howard Singerman, Janet Ray, Brackette

Williams, Allen Feldman, Barbara Harlow, Sid Lemelle, Salima Lemelle, Salim Lemelle, the late and always missed Glen Thompson, Rachel Herzing, Avery Gordon, Chris Newfield, Laura Liu, Clyde Woods, Mike Murashige, Laura Pulido, Julia Gonzales, Annie Blum, and Rose Braz helped me develop my capacities, while demanding, singly and in chorus: "Write it down! Send it in!"

My great regret is that my late father, Courtland Seymour Wilson, tireless activist, self-educated working-class intellectual, honest man, won't have this book on his towering stack of things to read next; he and my beautiful mother, Ruth Isabel Herb Wilson, sent me out young to do antiracist work, let me be a reader and dreamer, and always welcomed their prodigal daughter home. Finally, my husband and best friend, Craig Gilmore, should be listed as co-author of this book; so much of the thinking, and more than half the suffering of it, was his.

ABBREVIATIONS

AICCU	Association of Independent California Colleges and Universities
BJS	Federal Bureau of Justice Statistics
BPP	Black Panther Party
BRC	California Blue Ribbon Commission on Inmate Population and Management
CCPOA	California Correctional Peace Officers Association
CDC	California Department of Corrections
CDF	California Department of Finance
CDF-CEI	California Department of Finance, *California Economic Indicators*
CEZ	California enterprise zone
CO	corrections officer; prison guard
DOD	Department of Defense
EDD	California Employment Development Department
ERC	Equal Rights Congress

FACTS	Families to Amend California's Three Strikes
FIRE	finance, insurance, and real estate sector
GOB	general obligation bond
GSP	gross state product
JfJ	Justice for Janitors
JLCPCO	Joint Legislative Committee on Prison Construction and Operations
LAO	California Legislative Analyst's Office
LAPD	Los Angeles Police Department
LRB	lease revenue bond
LULUs	locally unwanted land uses
MAPA	Mexican American Political Alliance
Mothers ROC	Mothers Reclaiming Our Children
NAIRU	non-accelerating-inflation rate of unemployment
NIMBY	not in my back yard
PIA	[California] Prison Industry Authority
PRCC	[California] Prison Reform Conference Committee
ROC	Mothers Reclaiming Our Children
SPWB	California State Public Works Board
UFW	United Farm Workers

THE BUS

One midnight in the middle of April, late in the twentieth century, a bus pulled out of the Holman Methodist Church parking lot. Traveling a short way along the northern boundary of South Central Los Angeles, it geared up a ramp into the web of state and federal highways that connect California's diverse industrial, agricultural, and recreational landscapes into the fifth-largest economy in the world. On the bus, forty women, men, and children settled in for the seven-hour journey north to Sacramento and the state capitol.

A dream crowd rode for freedom: red, black, brown, yellow, and white; mothers, fathers, grandparents, sisters, brothers, children, lovers, and friends; gay men and lesbians; interracial families; English, Spanish, Tagalog, Arabic, Polish, and Hebrew speakers; Catholic, Protestant, Jew, Muslim, Eastern Orthodox, and Quaker. Their diversity embodied some 150 years of California history and more than 300 years of national anxieties and antagonisms. But the riders didn't worry about it; they got on the bus because of their sameness: employed, disabled, or retired working people, with little or no discretionary income, whose goal was freedom for their relatives serving long sentences behind bars.

The dream riders were summoned by a nightmare, made palpable by the terrifying numbers of prisoners and prisons produced during the past generation, while we were all, presumably, awake. Just as real was the growing grassroots activism against the expanded use of criminalization and cages as catchall solutions to social problems.

In order to realize their dream of justice in individual cases, the riders decided, through struggle, debate, failure, and renewal, that they must seek general freedom for all from a system in which punishment has become as industrialized as making cars, clothes, or missiles, or growing cotton. Against the odds, they had come to activism—acting out, in the details of modest practices, the belief that "we *shall* overcome" the deep divisions so taken for granted in apartheid America. In other words, they shared more than an interest: purpose made them ride.

Some snoozed. Some played cards. Some talked about who would join them on the statehouse steps, who would sit with them in the Senate Committee on Public Safety hearing room, and what best strategy would persuade a prisoner-hostile legislative committee majority to amend California's "three strikes and you're out" law. Some watched through the window, with an intensity suggesting that the night might reveal an answer. Instead, what they saw were landscapes of labor, living, and leisure stretching out beyond the horizon. Leaving Los Angeles, the bus traveled up the broad old industrial corridor's central artery. Although the city is still the manufacturing capital of the United

States, the mix and remuneration of jobs making things has changed drastically in the past twenty years. Auto and primary steel are mostly gone, replaced by apparel and rebar.

On Interstate 5, the great road over the Tehachapi Mountains, the bus passed endless residential developments and signs touting "business friendly" regions in the northern reaches of Los Angeles County before slipping into the darkness of the Angeles National Forest. The federal interstates enabled suburbanization of both residence and industry and helped secure California's historical dominance in the military-industrial complex. Indeed, for most of the families on the bus, overt wars—World War II, Korea, and Vietnam—and covert struggles—Jim Crow Mississippi and Louisiana—were the forces that had pushed and pulled them to Southern California to remake their lives, as long-distance migrants must.

Rolling down the long grade into the Great Central Valley, some of the riders speculated about the gargantuan pumping stations that propel water gathered from the state's northern and eastern regions over the mountains to quench the Southland's thirst. And yet although the water courses up out of the valley, a lot remains to irrigate the state's agricultural immensity. Indeed, while agriculture is only 3 percent of gross state product (GSP), California ranks first in the United States in agricultural production.

They stopped in Bakersfield to pick up more people: a farmworker, an unemployed journalist, some prisoners' mothers taking an unpaid day off work and contributing from their slim wages toward the $1,000 charter cost.

Outside Bakersfield, darkness drew in again around the Thomas-built coach. A small group of riders, sitting in the back, started to count sightings of intensely golden glows that eerily poked depth into the flat blackness. These concentrations of light in farmland are many of California's new prisons: cities of men, and sometimes women, that lie next to the dim towns that host them. Some passengers whispered, their words recorded as breath on glass: "Donny's over there." "Hello Richard." "I wonder if Angel's sleeping. I told him we'd pass by." The small fogs cleared as the bus labored on.

Other buses make this journey every day from central Los Angeles, leaving not from churches but rather from courts and jails. Their destinations are the old or new prisons—those that cluster along Highway 99 and make it a prison alley and others further afield, from the sturdy perimeter of fortresses along the California-Mexico border in the south up into Indian country at Susanville and Crescent City at the Oregon line. Nine hundred miles of prisons: an archipelago of concrete and steel cages, thirty-three major prisons (see map on page 10) plus fifty-seven smaller prisons and camps, forty-three of the total built since 1984.

Arriving in Sacramento, the riders joined their allies from other parts of the state for a prayer breakfast and a rally on the capitol steps. Then the day's principal activity began: the long committee session. They would try again to persuade people eager for reelection, who review and approve new criminal laws three hours a week, every week, to undo part of one law even while a major campaign contributor, the prison guards' union, summoned its lobbyist brigades to denounce any reform. For a moment before the group moved indoors, the ordinarily gray-white state buildings yellowed to reflect the warming sunrise—a sensation welcomed by a few aching elderly passengers, always alert for signs for hope. Perhaps on this trip they might knock one block out of the Golden Gulag's miles and miles of prison walls.

ONE

INTRODUCTION

THE PROBLEM

This book is about the phenomenal growth of California's
state prison system since 1982 and grassroots opposition to
the expanding use of prisons as catchall solutions to social
problems. It asks how, why, where, and to what effect one
of the planet's richest and most diverse political economies
has organized and executed a prison-building and -filling plan
that government analysts have called "the biggest . . . in the history of the world" (Rudman and Berthelsen 1991: i). By providing answers to these questions, the book also charts changes in
state structure, local and regional economies, and social identities. *Golden Gulag* is a tale of fractured collectivities—economies,
governments, cities, communities, and households—and their
fitful attempts to reconstruct themselves.

The book began as two modest research projects undertaken
in Los Angeles in 1992 and 1994 on behalf of a group of mostly
African American mothers, many of whom later rode the bus de-
picted in the Prologue. All wished to understand both the letter

and intent of two California laws—the Street Terrorism Enforcement and Prevention (STEP) Act (1988) and Proposition 184, the "three strikes and you're out" law (1994). They asked me, a nonlawyer activist with research skills, access to university libraries, and a big vocabulary, to help them. The oral reports and written summaries I presented at Saturday workshops failed to produce what we hoped for: clues as to how individual defendants might achieve better outcomes in their cases. Rather, what we learned twice over was this: the laws had written into the penal code breathtakingly cruel twists in the meaning and practice of justice.

Why should such discoveries surprise people for whom racism and economic struggle are persistent, life-shortening aspects of everyday experience? Perhaps because, for an increasing number of people, by the early 1990s, everyday experience had come to include familiarity with the routines of police, arrests, lawyers, plea bargains, and trials. The repertoire of the criminal courts seemed to be consistent if consistently unfair, with everyone playing rather predictable roles and the devil (or acquittal) in the details. But instead of showing how to become more detail-savvy about a couple of laws, our group study shifted our perspective by forcing us to ask general—and therefore, to our general frustration, more abstract—questions: Why prisons? Why now? Why for so many people—especially people of color? And why were they located so far from prisoners' homes?

The complex inquiry we inadvertently set for ourselves eventually defined the scope of this book, whose tale unfolds four times: statewide; at the capitol; in rural Corcoran; and in South Central Los Angeles. Working through California's prison development from these various "cuts" will uncover the dynamics of the social and spatial intersections where expansion emerged. There's a political reason for doing things this way. It is not only a good theory in theory but also a good theory in practice for people engaged in the spectrum of social justice struggles to figure out unexpected sites where their agendas align with those of others. We can do this by seeing how general changes connect with concrete experiences—as the mothers did in our study groups.

The California state prisoner population grew nearly 500 percent between 1982 and 2000, even though the crime rate peaked in 1980 and declined, unevenly but decisively, thereafter (see figs. 1 and 2). African Americans and Latinos comprise two-thirds of the state's 160,000 prisoners; almost 7 percent are women of all races; 25 percent are noncitizens. Most prisoners come from the state's urban cores—particularly Los Angeles and the surrounding southern counties. More than half the prisoners had steady employment before arrest, while upwards of 80 percent were, at some time in their case, represented by state-appointed lawyers for the indigent. In short, as a class, convicts are deindustrialized cities' working or workless poor.

Since 1984, California has completed twenty-three major new prisons (see map), at a cost of $280–$350 million dollars apiece. The state had previously built only twelve prisons between 1852 and 1964. The gargantuan new poured-concrete structures loom at the edge of small, economically struggling, ethnically diverse towns in rural areas. California has *also* added, in similar locations, thirteen small (500-bed) community corrections facilities, five prison camps, and five mother-prisoner centers to its pre-1984 inventory. By 2005, a hotly contested twenty-fourth new prison, designed to cage 5,160 men will, if opened, bring the total num-

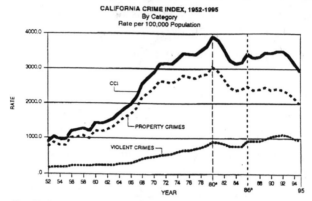

California Department of Justice ● Criminal Justice Information Services Division
Daniel E. Lungren, Attorney General

CRIME AND DELINQUENCY IN CALIFORNIA, 1995
ADVANCE RELEASE

CALIFORNIA CRIME INDEX, 1952-1995
By Category
Rate per 100,000 Population

*Since 1980 marked a high point for the California Crime Index, it has been compared to 1995 in this publication.
*Violent crime has increased 7.2 percent in rate since 1980. Part of the increase is due to a 1986 law change which required reporting domestic violence as criminal conduct. This resulted in an increase in the aggravated assault offense category.

From 1994 to 1995:

■ The California Crime Index rate decreased 7.0 percent.

■ The violent crime rate decreased 4.2 percent.

■ The property crime rate decreased 8.3 percent.

FIGURE 1. California crime index by category, 1952–1995. Source: California Department of Justice, Criminal Justice Information Services Division.

ber of state lockups for adult men and women to ninety.[1] With the exception of a few privately managed 500-bed facilities, these prisons are wholly public: owned by the state of California, financed by Public Works Board debt, and operated by the California Department of Corrections. The state's general fund provides 100 percent of the entire prison system's annual costs. Expenses spiked from 2 percent of the general fund in 1982 to nearly 8 percent

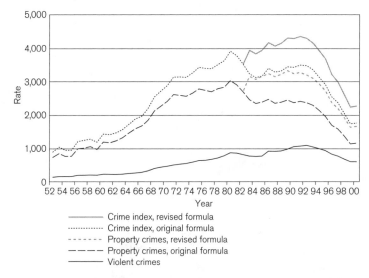

FIGURE 2. Revised California crime index, 1952–2000. Source: California Department of Justice, Criminal Justice Information Services Division. *Note:* Throughout its development, this book used the nationally accepted method for measuring crime, as illustrated by figure 1, which shows the state attorney general's 1995 California crime index. In 2003, "to give a more representative depiction of crime in California," a different California attorney general added "larceny-theft over $400" to the California crime index, retroactive to 1983. Whatever the latter's motivations, the effect as shown above has been to muddy the waters concerning when the crime rate began to decline in California and, as a consequence, what role increasing the numbers of prisons and people locked up in them has played. Subsequent to this revision, the "California Crime Index has been temporarily suspended as efforts continue to redefine this measurement." Data and quotations from Crimes, 1952–2003, table 1, Criminal Justice Statistics Center, Office of the Attorney General, http://caag.state.ca.us/cjsc/publications/candd/cd03/tabs/ (January 23, 2005).

California state adult prisons. Adapted from a map by Craig Gilmore.

today. The Department of Corrections has become the largest
state agency, employing a heterogeneous workforce of 54,000.

These alarming facts raise many urgent issues involving
money, income, jobs, race and ethnicity, gender, lawmaking, state
agencies and the policies that propel them to act, rural communities, urban neighborhoods, uneven development, migration and
globalization, hope, and despair. Such breadth belies the common

view that prisons sit on the edge—at the margins of social spaces, economic regions, political territories, and fights for rights. This apparent marginality is a trick of perspective, because, as every geographer knows, edges are also interfaces. For example, even while borders highlight the distinction between places, they also connect places into relationships with each other and with noncontiguous places. So too with prisons: the government-organized and -funded dispersal of marginalized people from urban to rural locations suggests both that problems stretch across space in a connected way and that arenas for activism are less segregated than they seem. Viewed in this way, we can see how "prison" is actually in the middle of the muddle that confronts all modestly educated working people and their extended communities—the global supermajority—at the dawn of the twenty-first century.

WHAT IS PRISON SUPPOSED TO DO AND WHY?

The practice of putting people in cages for part or all of their lives is a central feature in the development of secular states, participatory democracy, individual rights, and contemporary notions of freedom. These institutions of modernity, shaped by the rapid growth of cities and industrial production, faced a challenge—most acutely where capitalism flourished unfettered—to produce stability from "the accumulation and useful administration" of people on the move in a "society of strangers" (Foucault 1977: 303). Prisons both depersonalized social control, so that it could be bureaucratically managed across time and space, and satisfied the demands of reformers who largely prevailed against bodily punishment, which nevertheless endures in the death penalty and many torturous conditions of confinement. Oddly enough, then, the rise of prisons is coupled with two major upheavals—the rise of the word *freedom* to stand in for what's desirable and the rise of civic activists to stand up for who's dispossessed.

The relationship of prison to dispossession has been well studied. Wedged between ethics and the law, the justification for putting people behind bars rests on the premise that as a consequence of certain actions, some people should lose all freedom (which we can define in this instance as control over one's bodily habits, pastimes, relationships, and mobility). It takes muscular political capacity to realize widescale dispossession of people who have formal rights, and historically those who fill prisons have collectively lacked political clout commensurate with the theoretical power that rights suggest (see, e.g., Dayan 1999). In contrast, during most of the modern history of prisons, those officially devoid of rights—indigenous and enslaved women and men, for example, or new immigrants, or married white women—rarely saw the inside of a cage, because their unfreedom was guaranteed by other means (Christianson 1998; E. B. Freedman 1996).

But what about crime? Doesn't prison exist because there are criminals? Yes and no. While common sense suggests a natural connection between "crime" and "prison," what counts as crime in fact changes, and what happens to people convicted of crimes does not, in all times and places, result in prison sentences. Defined in the simple terms of the secular state, crime means a violation of the law. Laws change, depending on what, in a social order, counts as stability, and who, in a social order, needs to be controlled. Let's look at a range of examples. After the Civil War, an onslaught of legal maneuvers designed to guarantee the cheap availability of southern Black people's labor outlawed both "moving around" and "standing still" (Franklin 1998), and convicts worked without choice or compensation to build the region's infrastructure and industrial system (A. Lichtenstein 1996; B. M. Wilson 2000a). From the 1890s onward, a rush of Jim Crow laws both fed on earlier labor-focused statutes and sparked the nationwide apartheid craze. The Eighteenth Amendment to the Constitution (1919) prohibited the manufacture, import, export, or sale of intoxicating liquors, at a time when most drugs that are now illegal were not (Lusane 1991). In Texas, driving while drinking alcohol is legal, whereas a marijuana seed can put a person in prison for life. Prostitution is legal in some places. In others, the remedy for theft is restitution, not a cage. Murder is the result of opportunity, motive, and means, and the fact of a killing begins rather than ends an inquiry into the shifting legal nature of such a loss. Numerous histories and criminological treatises show shifts over time in what crime is and why it matters (see, e.g., Linebaugh 1992; Christianson 1998). Contemporary comparative studies demonstrate how societies that are relatively similar—industrialized, diverse, largely immigrant—differ widely in their assessments and experience of disorderly behavior and the remedies for what's generally accepted as wrong (Archer and Gartner 1984). As we can see that crime is not fixed, it follows that crime's relationship to prisons is the outcome of social theory and practice, rather than the only possible source of stability through control.

How are prisons supposed to produce stability through controlling what counts as crime? Four theories condense two and a quarter centuries of experience into conflicting and generally overlapping explanations for why societies decide they should lock people out by locking them in. Each theory, which has its intellectuals, practitioners, and critics, turns on one of four key concepts: retribution, deterrence, rehabilitation, or incapacitation. Let's take them in turn. The shock of retribution—loss of liberty—supposedly keeps convicted persons from doing again, upon release, what sent them to prison. Retribution's specter, deterrence, allegedly dissuades people who can project themselves into a convicted person's jumpsuit from doing what might result in lost liberty. Rehabilitation proposes that the unfreedom of prisons provides an occasion for the acquisition of sobriety and skills, so that, on release, formerly incarcerated people can live lives away from the criminal dragnet. And, finally, incapacitation, the least ambitious of all these theories, simply calculates that those locked up cannot make trouble outside of prison. These theories relate to each other as reforms—not as steps away from brutality or inconsistency, but as attempts to make prisons produce social stability through applying some mix of care, indifference, compulsory training, and cruelty to people in cages.

If the fourth concept, incapacitation, is not ambitious in a behavioral or psychological sense, it is, ironically, the theory that undergirds the most ambitious prison-building project in the history of the world. Incapacitation doesn't pretend to change anything about people except where they are. It is in a simple-minded way, then, a geographical solution that purports to solve social problems by extensively and repeatedly removing people from disordered, deindustrialized milieus and depositing them somewhere else.

But does the absence of freedom for many ensure stability in the form of lower-crime communities, and idled courts and police officers, for others? We can hazard a quick guess by asking a different question: would the prevailing theories shift and mingle over time, persistently reforming reformed reforms, if the outcome were stability? Probably not. And now there's more to be said on the subject, since we can count and compare outcomes. State by state, those jurisdictions that have not built a lot of prisons and thrown more people into them have enjoyed greater decreases in crime than states where incapacitation became a central governmental activity. For the latter, there are similar patterns of contrariness: within California, counties that aggressively use mandatory sentencing, such as the notoriously harsh "three strikes" law, have experienced feebler decreases in crime than counties that use the law sparingly.

Here we must briefly digress and reflect further on prison demographics, in particular, their exclusive domination of working or workless poor, most of whom are not white. Since it has never before been so easy for people of color to get into prison (jail is another matter [Irwin 1985]), we have to ask how racism works to lock in both them and more poor white people as well. To what degree has the regular observer, of any race, learned both willfully and unconsciously to conclude that the actual people who go to prison are the same as those the abolitionist Ruth Morris called the "terrible few." The "terrible few" are a statistically insignificant and socially unpredictable handful of the planet's humans whose psychopathic actions are the stuff of folktales, tabloids (including the evening news and reality television), and emergency legislation. When it comes to crime and prisons, the few whose difference might horribly erupt stand in for the many whose difference is emblazoned on surfaces of skin, documents, and maps—color, credo, citizenship, communities, convictions. The paroxysmal thinking required to make such a substitution is the outcome of many prods and barbs, in which aggression, violence, order, and duty conflate into an alleged force of American "human nature" (Lutz 2001). This thinking reveals the imaginary relationships people have with neighbors recast as strangers in a thoroughly racialized and income-stratified political economy that regularly redefines possibilities while never setting absolute positive or negative limits.

With the vexing question of difference in mind, let's return to the problem of spatial unevenness. If places that spare the cage are calmer than places that use imprisonment more aggressively, why is this so? Why wouldn't higher rates of incapacitation produce more stability? As it turns out, if we ratchet our perspective down to an extremely intimate view and compare, we see that identical locations—in terms of the social, cultural, and economic characteristics of inhabitants—diverge over time into different qualities of place when one of them experiences high rates of imprisonment of residents. And, more, the "tipping point," when things start to get really bad, is not very deep. Only two or three need be removed from N to produce greater *instability* in a community of people who, when employed, make, move, or care for things (Clear et al. 2001; Rose and Clear 2002). Why? For one thing, households stretch from neighborhood to visiting room to courtroom, with a consequent thinning of financial and emotional resources (Comfort 2002). Looking around the block at all the homes, research shows that increased use of policing and state intervention in everyday problems hasten the demise of the informal customary relationships that social calm depends on (Clear et al. 2001). People stop looking out for each other and stop talking about anything that matters in terms of neighborly wellbeing. Cages induce or worsen mental illness in prisoners (Haney 2001; Kupers 1999), most of whom eventually come out to service-starved streets. Laws (such as lifetime bans from financial

aid) and fiscal constraints displacing dollars from social investment to social expense (O'Connor [1973] 2000) lock former prisoners out of education, employment, housing, and many other
stabilizing institutions of everyday life. In such inhospitable
places, everybody isolates. And when something disruptive, con-
fusing, or undesirable happens, people dial 911. As a result, crime
goes up, along with unhappiness, and those who are able to do so
move away in search of a better environment, concentrating unhappiness in their wake. In other words, prisons wear out places
by wearing out people, irrespective of whether they have done
time (Mauer and Chesney-Lind 2002).

This book asks how prison came to be such a widescale solution in late twentieth-century California, in part by looking at the
problem through two extraordinary lenses. It asks what the relationship is between urban and rural political and economic restructuring, and how urban social expense fits into the rural
landscape. It also asks what happens in the urban neighborhoods
prisoners come from when people start talking to each other
again.

THE DOMINANT AND COUNTEREXPLANATIONS
FOR PRISON GROWTH

In its briefest form, the dominant explanation for prison growth
goes like this: crime went up; we cracked down; crime came
down.

Is this true?

The media, government officials, and policy advisers end-
lessly refer to "the public's concern" over crime and connect
prison growth to public desire for social order. In this explanation, what is pivotal is not the state's definition of crime per se but

rather society's condemnation of rampant deviant behavior—
thus a moral, not (necessarily) legal, panic. The catapulting of
crime to public anxiety number one, even when unemployment
and inflation might have garnered greater worry in the recessions of the early 1980s and the early 1990s, suggests that concerns
about social deviance overshadowed other, possibly more immediate, issues.

However, by the time the great prison roundups began, crime
had started to go down. Mainstream media widely reported the
results of statistics annually gathered and published by the FBI,
the Bureau of Justice Statistics (BJS), and state attorneys general.
In other words, if the public had indeed demanded crime reduction, the public was already getting what it wanted. California
officials could have taken credit for decreasing crime rates without producing more than 140,000 new prison beds (more than a
million nationally).

Another explanation for the burgeoning prison population is
the drug epidemic and the presumed threat to public safety
posed by the unrestrained use and trade of illegal substances. Information about the controlling (or most serious) offense of prisoners seems to support the drug explanation: drug commitments
to federal and state prison systems surged 975 percent between
1982 and 1999. Therefore, it is reasonable to conclude that the
widening use of drugs in the late 1970s and early 1980s provoked
prison expansion. According to this scenario—as news stories,
sensational television programs, popular music and movies, and
politicians' anecdotes made abundantly clear—communities, especially poor communities of color, would be more deeply deci-
mated by addiction, drug dealing, and gang violence were it not
for the restraining force of prisons. The explanation rests on two

assumptions: first, that drug use exploded in the 1980s; and second, that the sometimes violent organization of city neighborhoods into gang enclaves was accomplished in order to secure drug markets.

In fact, according to the BJS, illegal drug use among all kinds of people throughout the United States declined drastically starting in the mid 1970s (Tonry 1995). Second, although large-scale traffic in legal or illegal goods requires highly organized distribution systems—whether corporations or gangs (Winslow 1999)—not all gangs are in drug trafficking. For example, according to Mike Davis (1990), in late 1980s Los Angeles, despite the availability of stiffer sentences for gang members, prosecutors charged only one in four dealers with gang membership, and that pattern continued through the 1990s, despite media reports to the contrary.

A third explanation blames structural changes in employment opportunities; these changes have left large numbers of people challenged to find new income sources, and many have turned to what one pundit called illegal entitlements. In this view, those who commit property crimes—along with those who trade in illegal substances—reasonably account for a substantial portion of the vast increase in prison populations. Controlling offense data for new prisoners support the income-supplementing explanation: the percentage of people in prison for property offenses has more than doubled since 1982. But at the same time, incidents of property crime peaked in 1980; indeed, the drop in property crime pushed down the overall crime rate.

Throughout the economic boom of the 1990s, both print and electronic media again headlined annual federal reports about long-term drops in crime (falling since 1980), and elected and appointed officials took credit for the trends. In this context, the explanation for bulging prisons centers on the remarkable array of stiffer mandatory sentences now doled out for a wide range of behavior that used to be differently punished, if at all. This explanation, tied to but different from the moral panic explanation, proposes that while social deviance might not have exploded after all, aggressive intolerance pays handsome political dividends. The explanation that new kinds of sentences—which is to say the concerted action of lawmakers—rather than crises in the streets produced the growth in prison is after the fact and begs the question: Why prisons now?

Indeed, the preceding series of explanations and their underlying weaknesses suggest that the simple relationship between "crime" and "crackdown" introducing this section should be tweaked in the interest of historical accuracy. The string of declarative statements more properly reads: "crime went up; crime came down; we cracked down." If the order is different, then so are the causes. Here, of course, is where the prevailing alternative explanations come in. These views, like the official stories, are not mutually exclusive.

A key set of arguments charges racial cleansing: prisons grow in order to get rid of people of color, especially young Black men, accomplishing the goal through new lawmaking, patterns of policing, and selective prosecution (see, for examples, Miller 1996; Mauer 1999; Goldberg 2002). These analysts prove their claims using two decades of numbers showing the "racial disparities" in flesh-and-blood facts of prison expansion, substantial for white people and off the charts for nearly everybody else. There's no doubt what the accumulated experience is. But why now? Among many who charge racism, folk wisdom, a product of mixing the Thirteenth Amendment with thin evidence, is that prison constitutes the new slavery and that the millions in cages are there to provide cheap labor for corporations looking to lower stateside production costs. The problem with the "new slavery" argument is that very few prisoners work for anybody while they're locked up. Recall, the generally accepted goal for prisons has been *incapacitation:* a do-nothing theory if ever there was one. There has certainly been enough time for public and private entities to have worked out the logistics of exploiting unfree labor, and virtually every state, including California, has a law requiring prisoners to work. But the fact that most prisoners are idle, and that those who work do so for a public agency, undermines the view that today's prison expansion is the story of nineteenth-century Alabama writ large (A. Lichtenstein 1996; B. M. Wilson 2000a). The principal reason private interests fail to exploit prisoner labor seems to be this: big firms can afford to set up satellite work areas (what a prison-based production facility would be), while small firms cannot. Small firms then fight against big firms over unfair access to cheap labor and fight as well against publicly owned and operated prison industries (such as the federal system called UNICOR) that, due to low wages (not the same as low labor costs), unfairly compete in markets selling things modestly educated people can make and do.

Two other counterexplanations focus on the pursuit of profits. The first places emphasis on the privatization of public functions. Although the absolute number of private prisons has indeed grown, the fact is that 95 percent of all prisons and jails are publicly owned and operated. So the argument that more people are in prison due to the lobbying efforts of private prison firms doesn't stand up to scrutiny. The firms are not insignificant, especially in some jurisdictions, but they're not the driving force, either. Despite boosterish claims by stock analysts, private prison firms consistently hover on the brink of disaster (Greene 2001; Matera and Khan 2001), while public sector unions fight against losing jobs with good pay and benefits. The final profit-centered explanation focuses more generally on the potential for pulling surplus cash out of prisons (Dyer 1999). The question remains as to how these changes came into effect, given the welter of laws and rules directing the uses of capital for public investments. In other words, what does the fact that the world has gone capitalist in the past decade and a half (see, e.g., Parenti 1999) mean; and what are the conditions under which other possibilities might unfold? In particular, how has the role of the state—at various levels, from urban growth machine to federal devolution machine—changed in the attempt to produce stability and growth in the general political economy, especially if equity is no longer on the agenda?

The preceding discussion leads us to the third view, which holds that there are more people in prison in order for "the state" to help rural areas hungry for jobs; in this explanation of prison expansion, prisoners of color presumably provide employment opportunities for white guards. There's no question that rural America has been in the throes of a depression that began decades ago. In the 1980s and early 1990s, a welter of scholarly and trade articles (e.g., Carlson 1988, 1992; Sechrest 1992; Shichor 1992) promoted the local development discourse and advised prison agencies and civic boosters how to dispel fears and thereby disarm the NIMBY (not in my back yard) attitude. Such work reinforced the suspicion that prison expansion is a concrete manifestation of urban-rural competition and conflict. How-

ever, we now know the fiscal benefits to prison towns are difficult if impossible to locate (Hooks et al. 2003; Farrigan and Glasmeier 2002; R. W. Gilmore 1998; Huling 2002; King et al. 2003).
But where are the new prisons? Are the host communities and
the places prisoners come from so different? What about the demographic continuities between employees and the prisoners
themselves? Indeed, what already existing relationships make a
town eligible for, or vulnerable to, prison siting in the first place?
And why doesn't investment stick there?

A fourth counterexplanation is one we might call the reform
school. Analysts from a variety of political perspectives examine
more than two centuries of interlocking prison and legal reforms
and ask what role activists of many kinds—such as benevolent
liberals or women fighting domestic and sexual violence—play,
first in normalizing prison and then enabling its perpetually expanding use as an all-purpose remedy for the thwarted rights of
both prisoners and harmed free persons (see, for examples,
Gottschalk 2002; A. Davis 2003; Critical Resistance–INCITE
2002). This view demands consideration of how political identities defined by injury (Brown 1994) and order derived from punishment (Garland 1990, 2002) shape state norms and practices.
Through formal interaction with the state (as girl, student, citizen, immigrant, retiree, worker, owner, so forth), people develop
and modulate their expectations about what the state should do,
and these understandings, promoted or abhorred by media, intellectuals, and others, guide how, and under what conditions,
social fixes come into being. The state makes things, but it is also
a product of what's made and destroyed—of the constant creation and destruction of things such as schools, hospitals, art museums, nuclear weapons, and prisons. These issues return us to

the question of why the state changes. How do we understand such change through the development or revision of governmental institutions? Before concluding this introduction to the problem, let's look quickly at a key historical moment of the twentieth century: 1968.

LOOKING BACKWARD TO LOOK FORWARD

The preceding brief review of counterexplanations for prison growth does not account for the order of things: crime went up; crime came down; we cracked down. But of course, as every explanation suggests, something big, which proponents of "crime is the problem; prison is the solution" could be part of, directed the action. A conspiracy? Not likely. Systemic? Without a doubt. All the elements are here. Let's look back for a moment to 1968, symbolically *the* year of revolution and counterrevolution, to get one more take on the picture.

Nineteen sixty-eight was a disorderly year, when revolutionaries around the world made as much trouble as possible in as many places as possible. Overlapping communities of resistance self-consciously connected their struggles. Growing opposition to the U.S. war in Vietnam and Southeast Asia linked up with anticolonialism and antiapartheid forces on a world scale; and many found in Black Power a compelling invigoration of historical linkages between "First" and "Third" world liberation, not unlike the way people today trying to make sense of antiglobalization look to the Zapatistas in Chiapas (see, e.g., Katzenberger 1995). Students and workers built and defended barricades from Mexico City to Paris, sat down in factories, and walked out of fields. The more militant anticapitalism and international solidarity became everyday features of U.S. antiracist activism, the more vehemently the state responded by, as Allen Feldman (1991) puts it, "individualizing disorder" into singular instances of criminality.

The years 1967–68 also marked the end of a long run-up in annual increases in profit, signaling the close of the golden age of U.S. capitalism. The golden age had started thirty years earlier, when Washington began the massive buildup for World War II. The organizational structures and fiscal authority that had been designed for New Deal social welfare agencies provided the template for the Pentagon's painstaking transformation (Gregory. Hooks 1991). It changed from a periodically expanded and contracted Department of War to the largest and most costly bureaucracy of the federal government. The United States has since committed enormous resources to the first permanent warfare apparatus in the country's pugnacious history.

The wealth produced from warfare spending did two things: it helped knit the nation's vast marginal hinterland (the South and the West) into the national economy by moving vast quantities of publicly funded construction and development projects, and people to do the work, to those regions (with California gaining the most) (Schulman 1994). The wealth also underwrote the motley welfare agencies that took form during the Great Depression but did not become truly operational until the end of World War II (Gregory Hooks 1991). Indeed, the U.S. welfare state has been dubbed "military Keynesianism"— an unpronounceable name but a good thing to know—to denote the centrality of war-making to socioeconomic security. On the domestic front, while labor achieved moderate protections against calamity and opportunities for advancement, worker militancy was crushed and U.S. hierarchies achieved renewed structural salience. The hierarchies mapped both the organization of labor markets and the sociospatial control of wealth. Thus, white people fared well compared with people of color, most of whom were deliberately, if craftily, excluded from the original legislation; men received automatically what women had to apply for individually; and urban industrial workers secured limited wage and bargaining rights denied household and agricultural fieldworkers.

This quick look at the crumbling foundations of the old order, which gave way to the possibility of astonishing prison growth, raises the urgent topics that this book addresses: money, income, jobs, race and ethnicity, gender, lawmaking, state agencies and the policies that propel them to act, rural communities, urban neighborhoods, uneven development, migration and globalization, hope, and despair. Today's political-economic superstructure is grounded in the radical failures and counterrevolutionary successes of an earlier era, as exemplified by the antagonism between insurgents and counterinsurgents in 1968.

HOW TO USE THIS BOOK

How and why, then, did California go about the biggest prison-building project in the history of the world? In my view, prisons are partial geographical solutions to political economic crises, organized by the state, which is itself in crisis. Crisis means instability that can be fixed only through radical measures, which include developing new relationships and new or renovated institutions out of what already exists. The instability that characterized the end of the golden age of American capitalism provides a key, as we shall see. In the following pages, we shall investigate how certain kinds of people, land, capital, and state capacity became idle—what surplus is—what happened, and why the outcomes are logically explicable but were by no means inevitable.

A few words about scholar activism, and then our tale begins. Happily, the Social Science Research Council has taken an interest in what scholar activism is and does, and a group of us are writing a book about it. For readers of the present book, the key point is this: the questions and analyses driving this book came from the work encountered in everyday activism "on the ground." However, the direction of research does not necessarily follow every lead proposed from the grassroots, nor do the findings necessarily reinforce community activists' closely held hunches about how the world works. On the contrary, in scholarly research, answers are only as good as the further questions they provoke, while for activists, answers are as good as the tactics they make possible. Where scholarship and activism overlap is in the area of how to make decisions about what comes next. As this project grew from a modest research inquiry into a decade's lifework, so too did the need to figure out a guide for action.

We simultaneously make places, things, and selves, although not under conditions of our own choosing. Problems, then, are also opportunities. The world does not operate according to an analytically indefensible opposition that presumes that "agency" is an exclusive, if underused, attribute of the oppressed in their endless confrontation with the forces of "structure." Rather, if agency is the human ability to craft opportunity from the wherewithal of everyday life, then agency and structure are products of each other. Without their mutual interaction, there would be no drama, no dynamic, no story to tell. Actors in all kinds of situations (farms, neighborhoods, government agencies, collapsing economies, tough elections) are fighting to create stability out of instability. In a crisis, the old order does not simply blow away, and every struggle is carried out within, and against, already existing institutions: electoral politics, the international capitalist system, families, uneven development, racism.

As the example of racism suggests, institutions are sets of hierarchical relationships (structures) that persist across time (Martinot 2003) undergoing, as we have seen in the case of prisons, periodic reform. Racism, specifically, is the state-sanctioned or extralegal production and exploitation of group-differentiated vulnerability to premature death. States are institutions made up of subinstitutions that often work at cross-purposes, but that get direction from the prevailing platforms and priorities of the current government. Capital, the wealth of the profit system's development ability, is also a relation, since it could not exist if workers did not produce goods for less than they're sold for and buy goods in order to go back to work and make, move, or grow more stuff. As private property, land is also a relationship—to nonowners, to other pieces of land, to mortgagers, and to land that is not privately owned. And the state's power to organize these various factors of production, or enable them to be disorganized or abandoned outright, is not a thing but rather a capacity—which is to say, based in relationships that also change over time and sometimes become so persistently challenged, from above and below, by those whose opinions and actions matter, that the entire character of the state eventually changes as well.

This book is about enormous changes and alternative outcomes. It pauses at many different points both to show how resolutions of surplus land, capital, labor, and state capacity congealed into prisons, and also to suggest—and in the last chapters to argue—how alternative uses of the resources of everyday life might otherwise have been organized. It is thus a book for everybody who is fighting against racism, old or new, for fair wages, and especially for the social wage (in sum, for human rights). The conclusion proposes ten theses for activists who seek to craft policies to build the capacity—the *power*—that propels social change organizations, which are the backbone of social movements (Horton and Freire 1990).

TWO

THE CALIFORNIA POLITICAL ECONOMY

Fifth- or sixth-largest among the world's economies, California passed the trillion dollar gross state product mark in 1997, a level nominally equal to U.S. domestic product in 1970. However, the wealthy and productive state's poverty rate rose in the national rankings, from thirtieth in 1980 to fourteenth in 2001. Relative poverty, which compares incomes within states, also snared more households, pushing California into the company of historically poor states such as Louisiana, New Mexico, Mississippi, West Virginia, and Kentucky; with populous New York and Texas, where prisons have also expanded significantly; and with the classically bifurcated District of Columbia, which has both the highest per capita income and highest poverty in the country (Reed 2002). What happened?

GROWTH

California's diversity has always been its strength and challenge. Those who fashioned the Golden State's dominant political, economic, and cultural institutions exploited resources and methods acquired locally, nationally, and internationally. The region's development into metropolitan and agricultural empires required extensive labor power, huge infusions of public and private capital, lengthy networks of human, water, and product transport systems, and a state sufficiently powerful to maintain order and promote expansion amid complexity.

Nineteenth-century California experienced rapid changes in both population and land control. The transition following U.S. victory in the Mexican War featured the implementation of state tax and currency laws that enabled Anglo power brokers to obtain Mexican haciendas cheaply. At the same time, federal and state financial and land subventions underwrote California's railroad incorporation into the U.S. empire, ensuring that local products would have access to national markets and beyond (Bean 1973; Pisani 1984). These two movements of landownership concentrated into relatively few hands both the incentive and the power to shape regional development trajectories. Their power was not absolute; federal and state programs facilitated rapid Anglo settlement of the vast state by the inducements of cheap or even free land, and homesteaders confronted big capital in political and gun battles alike (Caughey 1940; Bean 1973), with big capital winning when it was not divided against itself (McWilliams 1946; Pisani 1984).

Not everyone who immigrated was a homesteader, and neither were all workers—immigrant or native born—of European origin. California's labor force has always been diverse (Saxton 1971; Bean 1973; Almaguer 1994). Asian, Mexicano, African, and Anglo men and women came on their own or were recruited or coerced to mine gold, build railroads, and perform

industrial, artisanal, agricultural, and service work (Bean 1973).
As is generally the case in the United States, differences among
workers, cast as race, ethnicity, citizenship, gender, and locale,
have both structured and been structured by labor markets
(Caughey 1940; Saxton 1971; Barrera 1979; Almaguer 1994).
California conferred particular form on these structures. As
simultaneously U.S. colonizers in what had formerly been part of
Mexico and controllers of a new state in the U.S. Union, the dominant Anglos organized labor and propertied classes according to
Black-white, European–non-European, and Protestant-Catholic
hierarchies (Saxton 1971; Almaguer 1994). Through legislative
edicts and institutional practices, state, capital, and labor power
blocs manipulated the unique characteristics of the population to
designate a "changing same" (Jones 1967) of those who counted
as members, servants, and enemies (Saxton 1971) of the emerging "Herrenvolk republic" (Saxton 1990). California's extension
and specification of the normative U.S. racial state (Omi and
Winant 1986) also served to sanction genocide as the final solution to the problem of how to acquire indigenous people's cov-
eted lands (Caughey 1940; Stannard 1992).

Nineteenth-century California developed an industrial and
agricultural proletariat rather swiftly. In addition to the gradual
dispossession of Mexicanos and of Anglo homesteaders whose
farming failed to pay, many workers idled by depletion of gold-
mines or completion of railroads had no recourse but to seek wage
employment in factories and fields (Daniel 1981; Jacqueline Jones
1992). Organized labor had different rates of success around the
state. Victories for white workers in the San Francisco Bay
Area—many of whom were veterans of radical struggles elsewhere—were offset by across-the-board defeats for all workers in

Los Angeles and the inland agricultural counties. Capital triumphed in courtrooms (McWilliams 1946; Bean 1973; cf. Forbath 1991) and through state-sanctioned vigilante terror (Bean 1973; McWilliams [1939] 1969). California's white supremacist, anticapital Workingmen's Party (1877–80), which emerged briefly from the economic strife of the 1870s, left as its principal legacy the 1882 federal law excluding Chinese immigration (Caughey 1940; Saxton 1971; Bean 1973). Ample but generally disorganized and segregated labor formed the nucleus of the state's rapid growth into the next century.

In addition to labor, both metropolitan and agricultural development required ample water, and, starting at the turn of the twentieth century, projects funded from federal and state coffers transformed relatively arid land into parcels suitable for farm or residential development (El-Ashry and Gibbons 1988; Pisani 1984; Gottlieb 1988; Hundley 1992). While state-developed water was sold cheaply to nearly all agricultural buyers, those with large holdings could exploit economies of scale to obtain capital for improvements, pay the high cost of transport charged by the railroad monopolies (Preston 1981; Reisner 1986; Howitt and Moore 1994), and hire cheap labor in large numbers to work the fields (Daniel 1981).

Urban-made goods, such as autos, tires, steel, aircraft, and ships, joined petroleum and rural commodities—cotton, fruit, vegetables, dairy products, lumber, cement—in California's annually expanding basket of goods. The state continued to promote development by providing both direct industry subventions (e.g., aircraft in Los Angeles [Lotchin 1992; Oden et al. 1996]) and key infrastructural amenities, such as harbors and highways, that both stimulated demand and enabled transport (Bean 1973).

Power blocs also designed municipal and intergovernmental mandates, residential restrictive covenants, and other tools to keep the state's burgeoning wealth in the reach of some and out of the reach of others (Mike Davis 1990; Weber 1994; Oden et al. 1996). The system was not static, but it was, for most of the state's history, fairly reliable. By organizing themselves politically and economically into spatial and social enclosures, U.S.-born white Californians guaranteed the conditions through which they could reproduce their collective, if not individual, supremacy (Almaguer 1994; Walker 1995).

The Great Depression threatened the racial capitalist state's progress. The period's enormous dislocations of capital and labor hit California with political as well as economic severity (Bean 1973), heightening the natural antagonisms between capital and labor and occasioning both urban and rural struggles to advance labor's cause (Bulosan 1943; McWilliams 1946; Bean 1973; Mike Davis 1990; Weber 1994; Walker 1995; Don Mitchell 1996). In the cities, radical and Congress of Industrial Organizations (CIO) activists brought together great mobilizations, capped by the San Francisco / West Coast General Strike of May–July 1934 (Caughey 1940; Dowd 1997). In the countryside, Filipino, Mexicano, and other migrant farmworkers worked with communists and the CIO to organize some of the biggest, and bloodiest, agricultural labor battles in U.S. history (Bulosan 1943; Daniel 1981; Weber 1994; Don Mitchell 1996). If capitalists engaged in urban struggles invoked the specter of "communism" (Dowd 1997), race was the bogeyman of rural class war (Weber 1994; Don Mitchell 1996; Woods 1998).[1] Dense relations among Filipino, Mexicano/Chicano, African, Chinese, and Japanese workers and labor contractors and their mostly Anglo employers took on new complexity when waves of Anglo Okies poured into the state in the later part of the depression, prompting inter-Anglo class and status strife (Bulosan 1943; Morgan 1992; Weber 1994). Upton Sinclair's 1934 gubernatorial campaign, with its call to End Poverty in California (EPIC), won 38 percent of the vote, but Sinclair lost to Republican Governor Frank Merriam, a political cipher who had inherited the office. Overall, in concert with federal programs, the reformist strategies of New Dealers and Progressives defused urban struggles (Linda Gordon 1994; Faue 1990) and undermined rural ones (Weber 1994; Don Mitchell 1996). But it was international, rather than class, war that made the biggest difference to California's future fortunes.

The "creative destruction" of World War II boosted the California and national economies out of depression. The state's military industry was large, consisting of both converted capacities and assembly lines developed specifically for production of war matériel (Lotchin 1992); by 1940, the federal government was investing 10 percent of its spending in California, a state that comprised 7 percent of the nation (Bean 1973). Millions, including several hundred thousand African Americans, moved to California to build war machines, and while wartime wages were indexed to race and gender, workers across the board made more money than they had ever dreamed possible. This prosperous period (1938–45) changed the state's demographics, and particularly the racial structure of cities, as Black homeowners established communities in San Francisco, Oakland, Berkeley, Richmond, and Los Angeles (Bean 1973; Scott and Soja 1996).

Although the war occasioned wartime domestic antiracist militancy (C. L. R. James 1980), the social organization of warmaking—especially racial segregation of the armed forces, and the dispossession and internment of West Coast, primarily Californian, Japanese Americans—preserved white supremacy. In the postwar period, the repeal of de jure school segregation (1946) and the declaration that restrictive covenants on real property were unconstitutional (1948) provoked long-lasting pro-apartheid activism on the part of white Californians. Their political labors culminated in a state constitutional amendment, organized by the realtors' association and passed by two-thirds of the electorate, that guaranteed the right of home and other property owners to refuse to sell to anybody for any reason (Bean 1973).[2] Thus, while some domestic changes wrought by warfare had lasting effects on the state's political and social economy, other changes proved illusory, in the near term at least.

Along with phantom social gains, the period's profits seemed in danger of evaporating after the hot war's end; however, public and private sector power blocs wagered the state's economic future on the burgeoning military-industrial complex and became major players in the Pentagon-centered movement to maintain expansive military preparedness in the postwar era (Markusen et al. 1991; Gregory Hooks 1991). "Industrial heartland" manufacturers generally reconverted war industry capacity to production of consumer or producer goods (Markusen and Yudken 1992). But in California, as throughout "the gunbelt" (Markusen et al. 1991), the political-economic strategy was to seek increased federal investment in the form of prime Department of Defense (DOD) contracts. California coupled aerospace (Markusen and Yudken 1992) with electronics research and development (Saxenian 1995) to achieve the highest dollar volume of prime DOD contracts of any state from 1958 on (Markusen et al. 1991). Rising with the South during the Cold War (Schulman 1994), California developed major military-industrial districts, heavily concentrated in Los Angeles and Santa Clara ("Silicon Valley") Counties (Markusen et al. 1991; Oden et al. 1996; Saxenian 1995). With its dependence on defense secured, California became the exemplary "military Keynesian" (Turgeon 1996; Mike Davis 1986) or "welfare-warfare" (O'Connor [1973] 2000; cf. F. J. Cook 1962) state.

The massive infusion of wealth designated for aeronautical and electronic warfare innovations required a new and specialized labor force (Markusen and Yudken 1992; R. W. Gilmore 1991; Geiger 1993), prompting the state to make enormous investment in educational infrastructure. Historically, California had followed the national postsecondary trajectory. Land-grant agricultural and mechanical colleges were established in the wake of the 1862 federal Morrill Act. Public and private senior research universities, such as Stanford and the University of California, developed in the late nineteenth century in tandem with the diversification and consolidation of the modern business corporation (Chandler 1990; Geiger 1985) and the expansion of U.S. imperialism. To produce, under the sign of Sputnik (1958), sufficient professional, managerial, and technical strata for the theoretical and applied challenges to come, the state crafted an unprecedented "master plan" for higher education, which pledged an appropriate postsecondary education at public expense to every high school graduate (R. W. Gilmore 1991; Walker 1995).[3]

Through the 1960s, California's relative stability depended on interlacing the military complex with consumer and producer-goods manufacturing, agriculture, resource-extraction industries, and high levels of consumption (Mike Davis 1986; Walker 1995). The state's population grew with the economy, doubling between 1950 and 1970 to over 20 million people (Teitz 1984). The federal interstate highway system and the State Water Project (SWP) allowed for extensive and intensive residential and commercial development. People and firms could be spread further and further afield thanks to excellent roadways. The guarantee of water well into the next century facilitated increasingly dense development in the relatively arid Southland and served also to subsidize Central Valley agriculture via low-cost sale of the project's surplus water to growers (Reisner 1986).

Politically and numerically, Anglos continued to control the state. However, opportunities for advancement, opened to all Californians by federal mandates that were the outcome of antiracist struggle, led to the making of new political formations. Groups opposed to inequality used campuses and desegregated armed forces units as places to promote causes and forge alliances that differed from, but often complemented, neighborhood- and work-based mobilizations; by these means, activists renovated possibilities for broad-based radical coalitions that had not been evidenced since the urban and rural strikes of the 1930s (R. W. Gilmore 1991, 1993b).

The reasons for activism centered on the period's uneven achievement of "domestic reform and . . . productivity sustained by mass purchasing power" (Mike Davis 1986: 181). In other words, a key feature of military Keynsianism only partially reorganized the structures of the racial state. Economic inequality is a political problem. African Americans who had migrated from the South and East to fight their way into wartime industries (C. L. R. James 1980) and their California-born children were poorer in real terms in 1969 than they had been in 1945, because after the hot war was over, most were pushed out of war matériel jobs, whose pay levels could not be duplicated in other sectors (Soja and Scott 1996; Ong and Blumenberg 1996). Thus, extreme poverty concentrated in Alameda County, Los Angeles, and other regions where Black people had settled (Himes [1945] 1986; Sonenshein 1993; Walker 1995; cf. Massey and Denton 1993).

The 1965 Watts Rebellion was a conscious enactment of opposition (even if "spontaneous" in a Leninist sense) to inequality in Los Angeles, where everyday apartheid was forcibly renewed by police under the direction of the unabashedly white supremacist Chief William Parker (Sonenshein 1993).[4] In Oakland, the Black Panther Party was conceived as a dramatic, highly disciplined, and easy-to-emulate challenge to local police brutality. Militant Black urban antiracist organizing that focused on attacking the concrete ways in which "race ... is the modality through which class is lived" (Stuart Hall 1980: 341) emerged from many decades of struggle in the bloody crucible of revolution against *both* southern apartheid *and* its doppelgänger in northern cities (Dittmer 1994; Kelley 1990; Newton 1996).[5] As Richard Walker (1995) notes, the Black Power movement inspired complementary Brown Power (Chicano: both urban [Acuña 1988] and rural [United Farm Workers (Pulido 1995a)] variants) and Yellow Power (Asian American) movements (Pulido 2005).

In 1967 the system began to come apart symbolically and materially. During the Summer of Love, as thousands of flower children flocked to San Francisco to repudiate the establishment, California lined up its *anti*-antiracist coercive forces behind the vanguard Panther Gun Bill (Bean 1973; Donner 1990; Newton 1996)[6]—all of this at the same time that the rate of profit began its spectacular decline (David Gordon 1996). The 1969–70 recession hit California harder than the rest of the United States because of deep cuts in military spending (Teitz 1984). Unemployment in the state nearly doubled, even though total personal income hardly wavered from its steady upward climb (CDF-CEI December 1975). Notably, the layoffs of thousands of aerospace engineers, although in the end temporary (Teitz 1984), provided an important foundation for invigorating active consciousness of a normative racial state—regardless of reports on civil disorders that concluded "institutional racism" to be a structural problem in the nation and the state (California, Governor's Commission 1965; United States, Kerner Commission 1968).[7] Thus, at the historical turn that set the stage for California's restructuring, power blocs rising from the Sunbelt (Kevin Phillips 1969; Schulman 1994), including California's Governor Ronald Reagan and U.S. President Richard Nixon, began to propose "law and order" as the appropriate response to domestic insecurity, whatever its root causes (Kevin Phillips 1990; Newton 1996).

CRISES

After several years of relative relief underwritten by new rounds of military investment, California entered another slide in the world recession of 1973–75. For the United States, the recession was a deliberate structural adjustment, effected through monetary policy—the 1971 abandonment of the gold standard in August and devaluation of the dollar the next winter (Mike Davis 1986; Shaikh 1996). Workers responded in 1974 with major strikes around the country, including a number of stoppages—especially in transport and communication—in California (CDF-CEI October 1975).[8] They also swept Democrats into office in state and congressional elections, with California no exception. However, high unemployment and high interest rates undermined the power of traditional big organized labor in California and elsewhere: workers in government sectors and in dominant industries, such as transport and steel, were disciplined by the Federal Reserve's strategic manipulation of the cost of money to divest labor of its already circumscribed midcentury gains (Dickens 1996; N. Lichtenstein 1982). The state's chronic urban unemployment (Oliver et al. 1993; Grant et al. 1996) deepened in concert with rural displacements—with unemployment running highest in inner cities and in rural counties most reliant on resource extraction and agriculture (Bradshaw 1993; CDF-CEI 1977). Mining and lumber significantly reduced operations throughout the state during the 1970s (CDF-CEI 1977). In agriculture, the devastating drought of 1975–77 drove smaller farmers into bankruptcy; many who stayed in business borrowed heavily to finance irrigation improvements and changed crops to exploit the growing international market in specialty produce (Howitt and Moore 1994; Watts 1994b). Labor-replacing innovations in major agribusiness commodities such as cotton pushed thousands of farmworkers into the production of labor-intensive, minimally organized crops such as berries and nuts (Bradshaw 1993; cf. Wells 1996). Wages have never recovered from the freeze during this key period of urban and rural labor disciplining, either in the United States as a whole or in the Golden State (David Gordon 1996; Arnold and Levy 1994; Greenhouse 1997).

During the 1970s, immigration swelled the state's labor force, particularly in the Southland (Waldinger and Bozorgmehr 1996), the San Francisco Bay Area (Walker 1995), and around inland valley farms (Bradshaw 1993; Walker 1995). The newcomers came from all over the world, but most were from Mexico, followed by other Central American countries, especially El Salvador and Guatemala (Sabagh and Bozorgmehr 1996; Walker 1995). Complementing natural population increase, immigration after 1973 inaugurated the epochal shift of the state's majority from Anglo in 1970 to not Anglo, with no single group filling the majority void, by about the year 2000. Thus, at the same time that low-wage urban and rural industries could profitably exploit substantial pools of workers who lacked both union and citizenship protections, the social structure as a whole began to come apart because of the raw, numerical threat to white supremacy represented by unorganized, but densely concentrated, new and old Californians of color.

After a brief infusion of federal job funds in 1977, the interscalar federal-state consolidation of the postwar era started to come apart in such key areas as education funding and employment opportunities for "individuals without strong marketable skills" (CDF-CEI December 1977: 6). The federal retreat required subnational polities and institutions to take responsibility for social problems whether they wanted to or not, forcing them to deal with the newly dispossessed, who ranged from unemployed youth to financially needy students to homeless families. The contemporary rise of the local state, celebrated by so many geographers, represents in part a generally reactionary move to reexternalize, or keep external, such social burdens and fiscal costs (see, e.g., Lake 1992, 1994).

When voters initiated the taxpayers' revolt with 1978's Proposition 13, California municipal and state treasuries had substantial surpluses (as was the case throughout the United States as a whole), with annual revenues comfortably exceeding expenditures (CDF-CEI November–December 1977; Gramlich 1991). Proposition 13 shielded real property from periodic reassessment and set a maximum tax rate, thus depriving municipal governments of a prime source of revenue; as a result, whereas in 1977–78, K–12 school districts received 51.7 percent of their budgets from property taxes, the percentage was only 18.1 percent in 1988–89 (Chapman 1991: 19). The compensatory implementation of regressive taxes such as sales tax and user fees helped ensure that as local governments drew down their reserves and then tightened their belts, the poor would have higher relative costs and fewer services than their richer neighbors.

California's reliance on military-industrial outlays increased steadily from 1976–77 forward, when the value of DOD prime contracts hit one of many high marks (fig. 3; CDF-CEI December 1977, December 1985). Highly paid DOD-funded positions were concentrated in research and development (Markusen et al. 1991); this, combined with a decline in military assembly-line work (Oden et al. 1996), constituted another wedge in the long bifurcation splitting apart the state's industrial, racial, and political structures (fig. 3). The location of defense and other high-technology jobs (Soja 1989; Oliver et al. 1993) exacerbated the state's residential and income segregation (Walters 1992; Mike Davis 1990; Bullard et al. 1994). Between 1980 and 1984, DOD prime contracts achieved new highs and California continued to command a disproportionate share of income from the trillion dollar arms buildup under the Carter and Reagan administrations, most of which went to higher-wage workers (Oden et al. 1966).

Thus, in advance of the 1980–82 recession, the ensuing boom, and the great recession of 1990–94, the path bifurcating Califor-

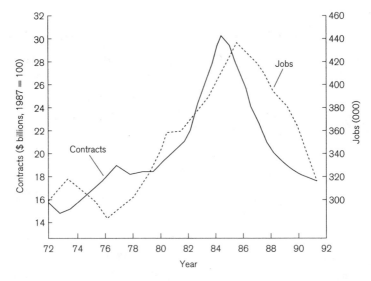

FIGURE 3. Defense prime contracts and manufacturing jobs, 1972–1992.
Source: Kroll and Corley 1994.

nia into richer and poorer had already deeply grooved the
political-economic landscape. Between 1969 and 1979, while voters schemed to make tax revenues stick in smaller and smaller
territories to ensure minimal income redistribution, poverty
among California's children rose 25 percent (Teitz 1984). The rising cost of shelter undermined the buying power of flat wages,
and the sum of these effects carried forward into the 1980s
(CDF-CEI 1975–82).

In 1980, the prime rate hit 21 percent; in 1982, unemployment
surged to 10.5 percent. These stunningly high figures repeated,
with a difference, the state's experience of the mid 1970s, when the
prime reached 12 percent (1974) and unemployment 10.5 percent
(1975). Economists competed to explain the high interest–high

unemployment coupling once thought to be mutually exclusive (Krugman 1994). The importance of the explanatory transition lies not in whether a new theory would serve as a reliable guide for action, but rather in how the public, high-profile scramble for a new theory served popularly to delegitimate the Keynesian approach to mitigating crisis, and set the stage for more deliberately undoing the welfare state (Krugman 1994; Grant et al. 1996).[9] The safety net came under attack at two levels: technically, it was condemned as a device that distorted markets by providing an employment disincentive for low-wage workers, who, in the aggregate, keep wages—and therefore prices—under control. Colloquially, the safety net was characterized as a hammock in which the undeserving poor (like Ronald Reagan's much-publicized welfare queen) lounged while industrious Anglos labored or looked for work.

The structure of manufacturing employment started to change dramatically during the 1980–82 recession. There are two general explanations for job losses in high-wage sectors. Either, as in the case of automobiles, plants had reached full amortization and management decided not to reinvest in place (Bluestone and Harrison 1982); or, as in the case of some primary metals, management either made the wrong investments or invested in labor-replacing technologies (Walters 1992; Arnold and Levy 1994). High-growth sectors, such as apparel, command wages of only about 60 percent of the average wages paid to employees in all industries (Arnold and Levy 1994).

California continued to be a manufacturing state, but it produced a different mix of goods, which meant that manufacturers drew from different labor market segments (David Gordon et al. 1982; Storper and Walker 1984). The disorganizing effect of structural change further undermined union power that had been disintegrating since the previous decade; of the few 1980s strikes around the country that capital and state took note of as possible precedent-setters, California's sole entry was the Kaiser Permanente strike of October–December 1986 (CDF-CEI 1989).[10] It was not until 1988, for example, that labor advocates could muster sufficient political authority to increase the state's minimum wage from $3.35 to $4.25 per hour; while for the typical household in 1984 and 1985, the average annual cost of rent and utilities ranged from $5,386 in Los Angeles to $6,983 in the Bay Area (CDF-CEI 1989).

Areas outside the major urban cores also experienced the intensified division between richer and poorer. Statewide, in 1982, the median house price exceeded $100,000 (CDF-CEI 1982)—62 percent higher than the national average—while per capita income, at $13,410, was only 15 percent over the national measure (California State Public Works Board 1993a–d). High housing prices, tied to and exacerbated by the high cost of money, pushed many middle-income earners seeking homeownership to move to counties where farmlands were rapidly converting to suburbs (Walters 1992; Sokolow and Spezia 1994). The desert counties east and southeast of Los Angeles and Stanislaus County in the Great Central Valley east of the Bay Area appealed to priced-out metropolitan housing markets. Developers built bedroom communities for commuters willing to drive two hours or more each way (Walters 1992; fig. 4).

Beset by unemployment and poverty rates running 67–200 percent above metropolitan levels (CDF-CEI 1982; Walters 1992), rural counties and towns not located on the commuter path tried to diversify their economies by recruiting small man-

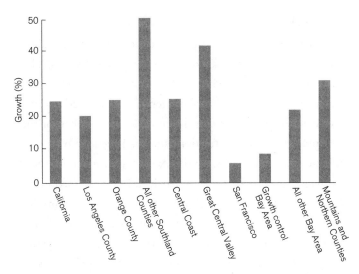

FIGURE 4. Population growth by region, 1980–1990. Source: Walters (1986) 1992.

ufacturing or back-office work (Bradshaw 1993). At the same time, California's food exports, which had been competing in the burgeoning "global food regime" (Watts 1994b), lost market share as a strong dollar forced up prices, increasing farmer bankruptcies and farm consolidations (Sokolow and Spezia 1992; Walters 1992). At the end of the day, places passed over for development fell even further behind, while development projects in high-unemployment localities summoned new entrants to the disorganized, low-wage segment of the labor market, diluting the chances for residents most in need of jobs (Bradshaw 1993; cf. Bartik 1990, 1991; Storper and Walker 1984; Chinitz 1960).

Money capital played a major role in restructuring California's built environment. Astronomical interest rates encouraged savings and loans directors to lend well beyond their capacity and falsify the value of collateral in order to look solvent for auditors and shareholders, as well as to pay themselves hefty fees (Henwood 1997). The building boom of the 1980s included both residential and nonresidential development; and the latter's overvaluation, combined with a sluggish rental or sales market for such spaces, plunged major institutions such as Lincoln Savings into bankruptcy. In rural areas, the Bank of America, a major agricultural lender from the 1920s onward, had a rash of foreclosures on farms in the Great Central Valley (Gottlieb 1988). Meanwhile, federal Farm Credit System loans aggressively marketed in the 1970s came due in the 1980s, when farmers could not pay, forcing debtors to sell collateral or default. The farm debt crisis was so severe that the Farm Credit System Board asked Congress for a $74 billion bailout (for nationwide defaults) in 1985—at the same time that failed savings and loans were tapping *their* federal insurance fund. But if unruly capital had recourse to governmental guarantees, both unruly and docile labor had a harder row to hoe.

California's safety net unraveled rapidly in the hands of Reagan's ideological successor in Sacramento, George Deukmejian. During the run-up to the 1982 gubernatorial election, it had appeared that the Democratic candidate, Tom Bradley, a retired policeman and African American in his fourth term as Los Angeles mayor, would prevail against the Republican candidate, a Sunbelt lawyer with deep roots in the Central Valley. Running against taxes, spending, and crime, however, Deukmejian won, although by a margin of less than 1 percent; in the rematch four years later, he won by a landslide. In his first term, Deukmejian achieved one of the nation's first workfare programs: whereas in

1977, 20 percent of the state's job growth was funded by cooperative federal and state programs guaranteeing employment for youth who wanted work but could not find it (CDF-CEI 1978), by 1985, California started to require paid jobs of women who were already full-time mothers, and often full-time students as well (Paddock and Wolinsky 1985). Indeed, although education seemed to be a protected arena during the campaign, the Deukmejian administration's actual spending undermined the Master Plan for Postsecondary Education. Education fees rose dramatically at nominally tuition-free institutions, and the continuity and coordination between the educational segments—community colleges through research universities—while not altogether abandoned, were displaced in favor of product specialization, efficiency, and competition (R. W. Gilmore 1991).

Planning for state and regional growth foundered in the Republican administrations of Governors George Deukmejian (1982–90) and Pete Wilson (1990–98). Indeed, the Democratic administration of Governor Jerry Brown had produced the last general plan in its first term (1974–78), and thereafter Sacramento produced no unified vision for, or coordination among, the many planning agencies in the government (Bradshaw 1992; Arnold and Levy 1994). As they had done with Proposition 13, voters stepped into the breach, and used initiatives to try to control change; but their reach grasped symptoms rather than causes of the state's disorder. In essence, California's voters—dominated by Anglos with jobs—were trying to reconcile the disjuncture between the state's 1984–89 boom and the insecurity more and more people experienced in their everyday lives. Ironically, though unsurprisingly, they looked to state power to resolve contradictions even while telling themselves, and elected officials, that government was the problem (Mike Davis 1993b, 1993c; Walker 1995).

When the California economy crashed in 1990–91, the crisis overlapped and interlocked with the previous periods of deep restructuring that reached back into the early 1970s. Premonitions of the state's crash cropped up as early as the October 1987 stock market bust, and the recession proper lasted for three years. California lost 730,000 jobs—548,000 of which were in the Southland (CDF-CEI 1996). The Los Angeles basin job-loss concentration reflected the dual dilemmas of defense industry downsizing and a stagnant market for commercial airplanes (Oden et al. 1996). Fifty years of defense dependency is hard to undo. The shift in available employments from high-wage to low-wage manufacturing (especially apparel) and service-sector jobs (Oden et al. 1996) brought into potential competition workers whose traditional labor market niches had been destroyed in twenty years of restructuring (table 1). The 1992 Los Angeles uprising shared some elements of spontaneity with the 1965 Watts riots, but what made it politically powerful was its "multicultural" nature (Mike Davis in Katz and Smith 1992); while the 1992 uprising against police brutality resulted in more police control of the streets, it also lowered segregation among grassroots activists (Gooding-Williams 1993; R. W. Gilmore 1993b; Madhubuti 1993). Activist voters responded as well and tried to enclose the effects of restructuring—and poor people's responses to it—by implementing extreme measures. They voted to exclude immigrants from social services with Proposition 187 (1994); to imprison more people for life with Proposition 184 ("three strikes" [1994]); and to monopolize opportunities in public sector education, employment, and contracts with Proposition 209 (anti–affirmative action [1996]).

TABLE 1 EMPLOYEES IN PRINCIPAL CALIFORNIA
MANUFACTURING INDUSTRIES, 1980–1995

(thousands)

Sector	1980	1995	Percentage Change
Instruments	102.4	166.5	61.5
Textiles	12.4	19.1	54.0
Apparel	102.4	146.9	43.5
Print and publishing	124.5	149.8	20.3
Rubber, misc.	61.2	70.9	15.8
Lumber and wood	46.3	52.2	12.7
Chemicals	65.7	69.1	5.2
Paper and allied products	37.3	38.8	4.0
Food and related items	182.5	179.5	−1.7
Furniture and fixtures	49.0	44.5	−9.1
Stone/clay/glass	50.4	44.2	−12.3
Industrial machinery	227.6	191.9	−15.7
Fabric. metal prod.	138.8	118.1	−14.9
Transport. equip.	266.3	163.2	−38.7
Primary metal	47.6	32.2	−32.4
Petroleum and coal	31.7	20.7	−34.7
Leather products	10.5	6.6	−37.1
Electric and electronic	358.0	219.6	−38.7
Miscellaneous	43.2	38.5	−10.9
Totals	1,957.8	1,770.5	−9.6

SOURCE: California State Controller, *Annual Report,* 1995.

TRANSITION

California functioned as "the principal engine of U.S. economic growth" (Walker 1995: 43) during the postwar "golden age" (Glyn et al. 1990) and used resources from defense-dependent prosperity to provide state residents with broadening protections from calamity and opportunities for advancement. While the legitimacy and use of welfare-state strategies to soften the effects of crises declined rapidly starting in the 1980s, the downhill path was blazed by the depression of the mid 1970s, the diminution of the Anglo majority, and the efforts by taxpayers to govern more directly through voter-made law that focused on fiscal control. An indicator of changes to come was the 25 percent increase in children's poverty between 1969 and 1979. The abandonment of the weakest members of society bespoke a fundamental change in the state's future responsibility for the alleviation of adversity and inequality. And, in fact, the poverty rate jumped again, rising 67 percent between 1979 and 1995, to afflict one in four of the state's children (Walker 1995).

The loss of high-wage, well-organized blue-collar jobs, and their replacement by high- or low-wage disorganized work, meant that an important platform from which to struggle in the realm of workplace and electoral politics had disappeared as well (Storper and Walker 1984; Katznelson 1985). Radical opposition had been crushed in the early part of the 1970s, and the disciplining power of underemployment and inflation, combined with discouraging memories of lost battles, may well have conspired to produce general quiescence, even when the state's economy boomed from 1984 to 1989, and again from 1993 to 2000. Thus, while workers did not agitate for activist state intervention in the form of Keynesian guarantees, activist voters demanded that the state become leaner and meaner, except when directed to do otherwise.

Although they claimed to pay strict attention to the will of the voters, the state's power blocs followed only half the instructions, becoming meaner but not leaner. Relocations of capital and labor meant that successful electoral candidates would have to build new political relationships across sector and space; for example, the suburbanizing inland counties were not the same places, politically, socially, or economically, that they had been when ruled by citrus or other grower elites. Tom Bradley's twin defeats suggested that most voters at the gubernatorial level rejected the urban welfare state.

The postwar pragmatic care once unevenly bestowed on labor was transferred, with an icing of solicitude, to capital. The state focused on capital's needs—particularly on how to minimize impediments, and maximize opportunities, for capital recruitment and retention.[11] However, having abandoned even the shadow of a Keynesian full employment / aggregate guarantee approach to downturns, the power bloc that emerged from the 1980s on faced the political problem of how to carry out *its* agenda—how, in other words, to go about its post-Keynesian state-building project—in order to retain and reproduce its victories (Hobsbawm 1982; Gregory Hooks 1991). Capital might be the object of desire, but voters mattered. The upheavals of the prior twenty-five years had idled many productive capacities, including labor, land, and finance capital. Having been elected under crisis conditions, Governors Deukmejian and Wilson consolidated their administrations around the anticrime theme they had popularized. The state built itself by building prisons fashioned from surpluses that the newly developing political economy had not absorbed in other ways.

CRISIS AND SURPLUS

In "Questions of Theory" (1988) Stuart Hall and Bill Schwarz provide a useful definition of crisis. "Crises occur when the social formation can no longer be reproduced on the basis of the pre-existing system of social relations" (96). The pivotal verb "to reproduce" signifies the broad array of political, economic, cultural, and biological capacities a society uses to renew itself daily, seasonally, generationally. Crisis is not objectively bad or good; rather, it signals systemic change whose outcome is determined through struggle. Struggle, which is a politically neutral word, occurs at all levels of a society as people try to figure out, through trial and error, what to make of idled capacities.

For example, when a major employer leaves a place, the individuals and households dependent on it for wages face a crisis, as does the state—at all levels—dependent on tax revenues paid by capital and workers. What are possible outcomes of crisis? Households can reorganize internal relations of authority and dependence according to who can find work or receive income assistance, creating both tensions and opportunities that significantly alter "traditional" household hierarchies. Community institutions, such as churches, unions, or street gangs, can gain or lose adherents and experience new pressures because of excessive or vanished reliance on the services and security they provide. Indeed, the expansion of community-based institutions can be a direct result of the state's reduction of social services—such as school programs. The state can also step up policing, under its mandate to maintain internal order, due to actual or imagined antisocial behaviors among idled workers or disenchanted youth. New power blocs can form around the remaining legitimate areas in which the state's power can be exercised, such as law and order, local development, or moral directives for civilian behavior. Indeed, the weakening of old social, political, and cultural forms opens the way to a wide variety of new alliances, institutions, movements, all of which are coaxed, but not directed, by already existing practices. Nothing is guaranteed, but tendencies are hard to buck.

Crises are spatially and sectorally uneven, leading to different outcomes for different kinds of people in different kinds of places (cf. Smith 1984; Walker 1995). The devaluation of the Golden Gulag's four key components created the conditions of possibility explored in "The Prison Fix" (chapter 3), "Crime, Croplands, and Capitalism" (chapter 4), and "Mothers Reclaiming Our Children" (chapter 5).

What is surplus, and how is it related to crisis? In political economy, surplus and crisis derive from a single, extremely complicated, relationship. The purpose of capitalist business activity is to make a profit, and profitability is dependent on both keeping wages as low as possible, while selling all goods produced. In fancy terms, this means that implicit in capital's imperative to accumulate is an equal necessity to disaccumulate (Wolff 1984). Systemic failure to disaccumulate constitutes crisis.

In an economy that is driven by individual consumers whose capacity to buy is tied to the fortunes of regional industrial sectors, ups and downs are likely to occur with some regularity—what's known as the business cycle. The problem is that the "down" part of the cycle does not have a guaranteed bottom; and when the bottom falls out, what's left is a mess of surpluses—in short, a crisis. The worker-consumer, who has to work to buy and buy to work, is central to this drama—and hence to this book.[12] The actual effects of crisis in a particular society are not necessarily paralyzing; rather, they invite remedies that take many forms, and therefore produce varying outcomes that are as likely further to shake up, as to settle, the original political-economic upheaval. Such remedies include moving capital out of a region altogether, or moving it out of production (research, development, or manufacture) into other investment venues such as land or financial markets, where short-term returns seem predictable (Harvey [1982] 1989). Since such investment decisions are not centrally coordinated, they might provide relief for individual investors or firms but not do much to resolve the crisis for the broad mass of people who are vulnerable to its effects. By contrast, the government can step in, as a "collective capital" (Negri [1980] 1988; Harvey [1982] 1989; cf. Foglesong 1986) to remedy crises by borrowing surplus money capital and using the proceeds to guarantee aggregate demand by way of income supports or similar programs—thereby restoring to capital its expansive momentum (Keynes [1936] 1973). The limits to the power of such collective action are found in (but not necessarily produced by) the complexities of political boundaries (borders, tariffs, and racial, gendered, and international divisions of territories and labor markets).

Surplus and crisis, then, are two sides of the same coin. The problems arising from overaccumulation—what makes surplus *crisis*—are not only economic, but also political, and therefore social. The idling of workers, the development of far-flung (labor or commodity) markets, and the immobilization of capital in devalued land are problems that require political organization—such as state building (Gregory Hooks 1991) or subaltern activism (Pulido 1996)—to solve. Political organizing produces new social relations that can, if reproducible, form the basis for a new social order (Hall and Schwarz 1988).

So far we have reviewed how capitalism as a mode of production produces the conditions for its own undoing; the production of surplus is necessary, or else there's no profit, while the overaccumulation of surplus is crisis. The system does not, however, mechanically function irrespective of time and place; crises are historically specific and their generalities play out in particular ways in particular places. Next I review the theoretical and empirical evidence for the existence of four surpluses that were key to the size and strength of the California prison expansion project.

The deepening division of California into richer and poorer is a function of what Richard Walker (among others) identifies as three "central contradictions" (Walker 1995): (1) the changing mix of jobs and industrial and residential location; (2) Anglos' fear of their demotion to minority status, coupled with capital's differential exploitation of labor market segments defined by race, gender, locality, sector, and citizenship; and (3) the state's failure to put idled capacities back to work through infrastructural, educational, employment, and other projects. As the multigenerational abandonment of California's children to poverty shows, wealth does not circulate the way it used to. "Some power resources appear to be increasing within the system, while others appear to be declining" (Mike Davis 1986: 181). It is to this summary contradiction, expressed as four surpluses—of finance capital, land, labor, and state capacity—that we now turn.

THE FOUR SURPLUSES

Surplus Finance Capital   This section looks at the political economy of surplus finance capital as it emerged in California in the form of municipal finance capital. Municipal financiers design and sell bonds to raise money for public, and certain private nonprofit, projects that contribute to the public good. We have seen that as the golden age of U.S. capitalism drew to a close, the major changes in the forces, relations, and geography of accumulation that rocked the capitalist world in general had specific regional effects in California. Between 1973 and 1989, according to David Gordon (1996: 80–81), the share of gross domestic product (GDP) paid out as property income increased (dividends by 25 percent and interest by 67 percent), and the share of GDP invested in plant and machinery halved (from 4.4 to 2.2 percent). Gordon's evidence substantiates the general theory, outlined in the previous section, that when the rate of profit falls, capital works differently than when the rate is on the rise. The shift is not immediate, because there is a lag between the profit peak and the peak of productive investment (Sherman 1997). However, value that is not in motion is not capital; thus, when productive investment opportunities wane, owners of surplus move their wealth into nonproductive income-generating investments in order to be assured of constant returns (Harvey 1989a; cf. Arrighi 1994). The credit system, the province of finance capital, is such a venue. Whereas in times of expansion, credit complements reserves, in periods of overaccumulation, "speculative fever . . . in paper assets of all kinds" emerges as a means to activate idled capital (Harvey [1982] 1989: 325).

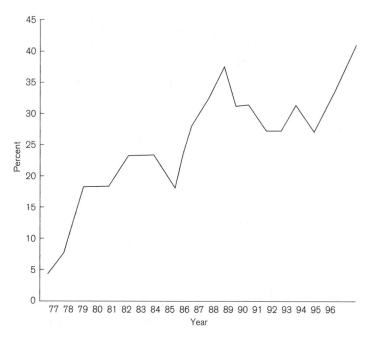

FIGURE 5. Growth in the ratio of property/proprietors' (profit) income to total income, 1977–1996. Source: CDF-CEI 1977–97.

The ratio of property and proprietors' income (interest, dividends, rent, and profits) to total income grew by 40 percent in California between 1977 and 1996, as illustrated in figure 5. Although there have been peaks and valleys along the route, what is striking is the surge in the late 1970s, the pivotal plateau of the early 1980s, the subsequent surge in the mid 1980s, and the overall steadiness of the upward trend. For those in command of the growing property surplus in the late 1970s and early 1980s, California's productive investment opportunities were limited by the fact that the state's corporations, along with U.S. corporations as a whole, were financing declining plant and equipment expansion from retained earnings (CDF-CEI 1977; Flanigan 1996; Brenner 2002). And, in the case of major industries such as aerospace and electronics, the Carter-Reagan boom in federal defense outlays generously supplemented cash on hand (Oden et al. 1996). As a result, the burgeoning surplus required other investment outlets if it was to keep expanding. Between 1980 and 1989, interest as a share of total property income expanded from 73 percent to 85 percent, even as the prime rate declined from 21 percent in 1980 to 10.5 percent in 1989 (fig. 6). During the speculative fevers of the 1980s, municipal bonds were attractive sources of tax-exempt, mid- and long-term income, serving to balance portfolios weighted by short-term, or high-risk, investments such as junk bonds.

While as a category of capital, finance capital is highly mobile, individual firms that match surplus with borrowers are often, if not always, "embedded" (Granovetter 1985) in particular political-economic geographies (cf. Chinitz 1960). Such limitation is particularly true of firms that specialize in municipal finance. Federal law requires state governments to regulate municipal finance; thus firms in the municipal sector must organize their work on a state-by-state basis (Sbragia 1996). Because public finance capital is raised by, or with the direct approval and control of, the state, the key issue for finance capital is public policy as it establishes and maintains legitimate areas for the accumulation of public debt (Sbragia 1996; see also Gramlich 1994). More than 80 percent of public infrastructure in the United States is owned by state and local governments, and its "net value per person" increased steadily for twenty-five years in the

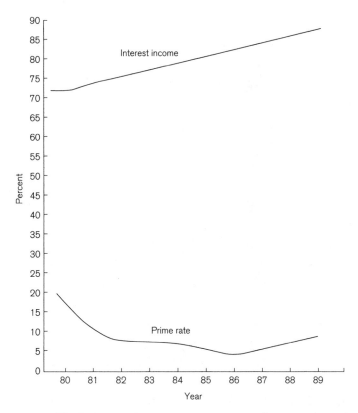

FIGURE 6. Rise in interest income as a percentage of property/proprietors' income and decline in the prime rate, 1980–1989. Source: CDF-CEI 1980–89.

post–World War II period (Gramlich 1994).[13] From 1949 to 1973, the principal components of the stock owned by state and local governments were highways, streets, and educational buildings. The total value of this stock doubled in real terms, with the per capita value of the principal components double that of all other facilities and equipment—respectively, $4,000 and $2,000. As in so many other categories of political-economic analysis, 1973 represents a turn: the share of public wealth located in highways, streets, and educational building began to diminish, while other capital investment rose at a modest rate. Twenty years later, their values converged at about $3,000 per category per capita—indicating both that the type of spending changed and the volume of spending flattened, suggesting a possible investment opportunity for private capital.

California's infrastructure did not escape the general trend of neglect starting in the late 1970s (Kirlin and Winkler 1984; Walker 1995). Stunned by the successes of the Jarvis-Gann "taxpayer revolt" launched in 1978, the Brown administration defaulted on its constitutional duty to formulate general plans for development—a political omission that extended throughout the Deukmejian administration and well into that of Governor Pete Wilson (Bradshaw 1992; Trombley 1990; CDF-CEI 1997). At the same time, the California constitution requires that voters approve any debt that encumbers their full faith and credit (California State Public Works Board 1985).[14] In the "revolutionary" times of the late 1970s and early 1980s, elected officials at both the state and local government levels became increasingly unwilling to ask, much less able to persuade, voters to commit to long-term debt, even for previously popular improvements such as parks (Trombley 1990).

In this context, the crisis for finance capital specializing in public debt centered on remedying the new political difficulty of directing surplus, via municipal bonds, into the nation's largest state economy (Sbragia 1996; see, for examples, Hurtado 1995;

Gilpin 1995; Flanigan 1996; Truell 1995). In addition to California's sheer creditworthy size, Sacramento's attractiveness to finance capital lies in the fact that historically most of the state's
bond deals have been negotiated rather than competitive. Until
the stock market crash of 1987, the profit municipal financiers
made on negotiated deals was considerably higher—as much as
double—than on competitive issues (Simonsen and Robbins
1996).[15] In a competitive deal, the state designs and documents
the issue using its own staff and then puts out an invitation to all
eligible underwriters to bid for the opportunity to sell it. In a negotiated deal, the state brings in expert firms who shape the issue,
negotiate a price with the state, and take the deal to market—
pocketing their profits. Therefore, not only do successful firms
make more money in negotiated deals, but they also become
deeply embedded as political players in state institutions (legislature, Department of Finance, Treasurer, Public Works Board)
where the issuance of debt is an unevenly legitimated exercise of
social and political power.

  Like all capital, finance capital is amoral yet politically active;
growth rather than purpose leads. The expansion of privately
held surplus value in California occurred on the heels of long-
term public disinvestment and reduced opportunities for private
investment. California-based municipal financiers could solve
the economic problem by developing public markets for private
capital. Given the state's long neglect of infrastructure, and its
overall wealth in spite of crises, California's potential capacity for
public debt was quite large. The emergence of Keynesianism in
the 1930s was designed to mitigate this mismatch. However, in
the post-Keynesian 1980s and 1990s, the situation was different,

with severe political limitations constraining the state's ability to exercise its capacity and keep private capital in motion—a topic further examined below. But first we shall take a different view of the problems inherent in the spatial control of capital by looking at surplus land.

Surplus Land   Uneven development is both a process and a product of capitalism's creative destruction (Smith 1984, 1996). As capital migrates spatially or sectorally in order to enhance its capacity to expand, whatever capital abandons—buildings, machinery, labor power, land—is devalued and its price consequently goes down. Neil Smith details the structural determinants of the flow of capital through urban land in order to illuminate how the movement of "capital rather than people" is a leading indicator whose sociopolitical symptoms include both gentrification and official racial class war carried out through criminalization and policing (Smith 1996: 70). The movement of capital across and through rural land follows similar rhythms of disinvestment and revaluation (Harvey [1982] 1989; Bradshaw 1993). Rural economies, no less than urban manufacturing and service centers, are integrated into broader economic flows, via transnational social divisions of labor (Robin Cohen 1987; Sayer and Walker 1992; Meiskin-Wood 1995) and global consumption regimes (Watts 1994a and b). Resource depletion, mechanization of agricultural labor processes, and closure of manufacturing and other employment establishments can devastate rural economies that lack flexibility due to their tendency to be dominated by monopolies or oligopolies (Markusen 1985, 1987; Storper and Walker 1989; cf. Chinitz 1960).

Politics, demographics, previous rounds of investment, and other factors affect where capital goes and when and why it accumulates (Smith 1984, 1996; Massey 1984). As Smith argues, capital's movement is contradictory, tending simultaneously toward equalization and differentiation. *Equalization,* a function of the necessary expansion of capital, is the process through which the "earth is transformed into a universal means of production" (Smith 1996: 78; Harvey [1982] 1989). The transformation is not even across all space at all times, and *differentiation* results from the "spatial centralization of capital in some places at the expense of others" (Smith 1996: 79). The phenomenon of surplus land lies in the nexus of these contradictory tendencies. In California, while the population of nonmetropolitan areas has been growing faster than the urban centers of Los Angeles and San Francisco (see fig. 4), not all rural land taken out of production has been converted to suburbs (Walters 1992; Bradshaw 1992; Kuminoff et al. 2001; cf. Smith 1996).

Changes in the extent of California farmland provide evidence for the existence of surplus land and its relation to disinvestment. Figure 7 shows the change in California farmland in the postwar period. Some 80 percent of California's annual developed water output goes to croplands (Howitt and Moore 1994), which account for 92 percent of all irrigated acreage, with the balance of farm acres being grazing land (Sokolow and Spezia 1992). While total farmland declined after 1954, the number of irrigated acres increased until 1978. Since the peak, approximately 100,000 acres of irrigated land have been taken out of production each year. The literally "sunk" capital in irrigated lands includes the technologies by which water is carried to crops: wells, ditches, pipes, pumps, rainbirds, and so forth. When

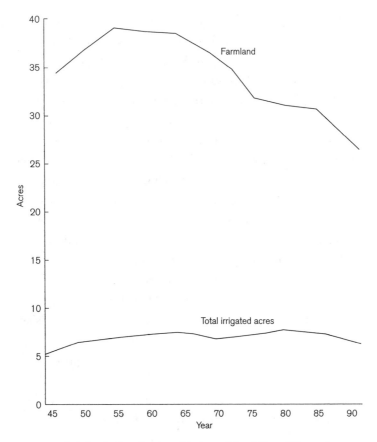

FIGURE 7. California farmland and irrigated land, in millions of acres, 1945–1987. Source: Sokolow and Spezia 1992.

farmers take irrigated land out of production, they abandon, or disinvest in, water-bearing infrastructure as well as other improvements—such as soil enhancement, or tiling to prevent subsidence—that made the land productive.

But why take irrigated land out of production? The interrelated forces of drought, debt, and development serve as explanatory factors. The severe drought of 1976–77, preceded by several dry years, raised the specter of a permanent water shortage. Farmers responded to the crisis in different ways. Some took part in federal programs that pay farmers who agree to idle lands on which they would otherwise have grown federally designated "surplus crops" (Howitt and Moore 1994; Gottlieb 1988). Other growers used land as collateral to borrow money so that they could invest in the latest irrigation technologies or drill deep wells to supplement aqueduct-provided Sierra snowmelt with fossil water from ancient aquifers. Investor-farmers included both those who planned to keep growing the same commodity, such as cotton, and those wishing to change crops (Reisner 1986; CDF-CEI 1978). And finally, some farmers got out of the business altogether, discouraged by the prospect of expensive water.

The efforts employed in the late 1970s did not stabilize the situation as hoped. By the early 1980s, both state water planners and independent analysts proposed that some acres temporarily idled during the drought should be taken permanently out of production (El-Ashry and Gibbons 1988). In 1982, voters defeated a measure to build a new water system, the Peripheral Canal, whose rejection undermined any expectations that the state would soon provide a subsidized solution to water scarcity as it had in the past (Gottlieb 1988).[16] At the same time, a string of sodden El Niño winters (1981–83) destroyed many crops, forcing heavily indebted farmers into bankruptcy (Reisner 1986), while debt drove others out of business when a surging dollar priced their products out of the export food market (Gottlieb 1988; Hundley 1992). Some bankrupt farmers were bought out by larger solvent ones, resulting in even greater centralization of agribusiness (Walters 1992; see also chapter 4). In other cases, lending institutions took title to land through foreclosure, without necessarily having a market in which to sell the seized collateral (Gottlieb 1988). And finally, some farmers sold to developers, consigning the land to suburban conversion (Sokolow and Spezia 1992).

While more than 80 percent of irrigated farmlands are in the Great Central Valley and the Inland Empire desert counties, where suburbanization has been most intensive, not all of the 100,000 acres taken out of production each year have been automatically converted to suburban development. As a corollary, not all growers who have left agriculture have been forced to do so by debt or drought. Some, such as those in the Fresno-Clovis area, found it counterintuitive to continue investing in farmland, however productive, when residential developers were paying up to five times the price that land traded for farming could command (Walters 1992; see also Carey Goldberg 1996).[17] And yet not all lands taken out of production lay in development's immediate path. Why did farmers who could invest stop? Perhaps the intensification of Fresno-Clovis area suburbanization, and Fresno County farmlands' 50 percent decline in price (in real dollars) between 1978 and 1982, is partly explained by the phenomenon of anticipatory disinvestment, with owners figuring that further improvements to farmland destined for development would be wasteful (Walters 1992; Smith 1996). The combination of these forces—drought, debt, and development—was a central means by which land surpluses emerged in the 1980s amid massive suburbanization.

The removal of irrigated lands from production far exceeded the rate of land use for suburbanization. Some 76 percent of the irrigated land in California is in the Great Central Valley. The surge in the gross population in the valley over ten years added 1.1 million people to the area. The average California household in that area is 2.8 people (CDF-CEI 1989). If all new households represented new houses built on suburbanized farmland, at the average of three houses per acre (Sokolow and Spezia 1994), residential development over ten years would absorb about 122,000 acres, or about 16 percent of the idled acres in the Great Central Valley. Thus we can see that the idling of land, and the coming of suburbanization, did not produce a transfer of land uses, but rather stiff competition between places trying to attract developers' capital to absorb the surplus land.

The second source of surplus, related to but not identical to the first, is the land in and about depressed towns throughout rural California; this is the counterpart to the surplus land produced in central cities upon which gentrification capitalizes (Smith 1996). Surplus land is not empty land. Devalued residential, retail, manufacturing, and other built improvements are symptoms of stagnant or shrinking local economies (Bradshaw 1993). High unemployment can serve as a guide for locating surplus land, because it is an indication that capital has reorganized in, or withdrawn from, the area. An example of reorganization is investment in labor-saving technology: capital is still there, value is still produced, but less value circulates as wages. In other words, the local production of surplus land—or labor—can go hand in hand with a rise *or* a fall in the local production of surplus value, as we shall see in chapter 4.

The 1980s ushered in a period of intense suburban/exurban development of rural land at the same time that an unprecedented surplus of land also emerged. For some, the surplus converted into capital, because developers bought the farm. For others, the surplus constituted crisis, in the form of both "fictitious" costs (declining income produced from land use) and real costs (taxes, insurance, maintenance) necessary to maintain a nonproductive asset. The relative (and in some cases absolute) abandonment of this land, as capital concentrated and centralized elsewhere, also constituted for rural areas—as for urban—the simultaneous abandonment of labor, to which we shall now turn.

Relative Surplus Population   California's restructuring since the early 1970s included the reorganization, or the termination, of many capital-labor relationships that had been secured through struggle during the golden age. All kinds of workers experienced profound insecurity, as millions were displaced from jobs and entire sectors. Poverty more than doubled. Racist and nationalist confrontations heightened, driven by the widely held—if incorrect—perception that the state's public and private resources were too scarce to support the growing population, and that some people therefore had to go. But as has always been the case, more people *came,* with immigrants reconfiguring the state's demographic composition. The ferment produced a growing relative surplus population—workers at the extreme edges, or completely outside, of restructured labor markets, stranded in urban and rural communities. In this section, we shall review the theoretical basis for why this surplus developed. Then we shall look at the raw dimensions of California's surplus population: its size and how it has grown. And finally we shall zero in on some more detailed characteristics of the relative surplus population in the five counties of the Los Angeles region, where 60 percent of state prisoners are produced.

Capital must be able to get rid of workers whose labor power is no longer desirable—whether permanently, by mechanical or human replacement, or temporarily by layoffs—and have access to new or previously idled labor as the need arises. These necessities, as Marx's ([1867] 1967) science of capital accumulation demonstrates, are not due to the personalities or preferences of heads of firms: CEOs who resist such "adjustments" to the labor force jeopardize profits. The progressive nature of capitalism requires *the* essential commodity—working people's labor power—in varying quantities and qualities over space, sector, and time.

As systemic expansions and contractions produce and throw off workers, those idled must wait, migrate, or languish until— if ever—new opportunities to sell their labor power emerge. While Marx formulated the category "abstract labor" in order to theorize the origin of value, his writings acknowledge that workers have specific social characteristics drawing them into, or locking them out of, specific labor markets. Marx's analysis concerning capitalism's long-term tendency to bifurcate, with increasing wealth for the few and immiseration for the many, centers on the production of what he called the "pivot" of labor power supply and demand—the "relative surplus population" or "reserve army of labor" (Marx [1867] 1967: 640–48).[18]

One indicator of the "relative surplus population" in the U.S. political economy is the hegemonic principle of a non-accelerating inflation rate of unemployment (NAIRU). According to the theoretical framework that guides the Federal Reserve Bank—the nation's gatekeeper against inflation—unemployment should "naturally" hover above 6 percent of the labor force that wants to work (Corbridge 1994; Krugman 1994). Mainstream economists no longer assume that an interventionist state can determine the acceptable mix of unemployment and inflation, as was argued by A. W. Phillips in 1958. At the same time, again, in mainstream economics, tight labor markets indicate possible price rises, due to labor's power to raise up wages under conditions of labor shortages (Sherman 1997; Hunt and Sherman 1972; Krugman 1994).

Table 2 is a macro snapshot of California's growth from 1973 to 2000 in five categories: total state population, labor force, employment, unemployment, and prisoners. The relative surplus population is represented in the latter two categories.[19] Two striking trends have developed over time. In the 1970s, the rate of increase in the labor force and employment was about equal, even though unemployment hit extremely high levels during the period. In the period 1980–94, with two additional recessions, employment failed to keep up with the labor force, and the number of prisoners goes off the chart. The overall trend is for labor force growth to exceed employment growth by about 4 percent. The sum of the state's average annual number of unemployed persons, plus the average annual number of prisoners, is about 1 million. These million constitute the empirical minimum of California's relative surplus population, because the number does not include anybody who wants to work but is not registered with either the California Employment Development Department (EDD) or the CDC.

If NAIRU explains the systemic existence of the relative surplus population in the most abstract neoclassical macroeconomic terms, its sociological presence is bounded by the fatal coupling of power and difference, which resolves relationally according to internally dynamic but structurally static racial hierarchies.[20] In

TABLE 2 CALIFORNIA POPULATION, LABOR FORCE,
JOBS, UNEMPLOYMENT, AND PRISONERS, 1973–2000

(thousands)

Year	Total Population	Labor Force	Jobs	Unemployed People	Prisoners
1973	21,250	8,910	8,286	624	22.5
1974	21,646	9,317	8,638	679	24.7
1975	22,042	9,539	8,598	941	20.0
1976	22,438	9,896	8,990	906	21.0
1977	22,834	10,367	9,513	853	19.6
1978	23,235	10,911	10,137	775	21.3
1979	23,700	11,268	10,566	702	22.6
1980	24,006	11,584	10,794	790	24.5
1981	24,278	11,812	10,938	875	29.2
1982	24,805	12,178	10,967	1,210	34.6
1983	25,337	12,269	11,095	1,187	39.3
1984	25,816	12,503	11,631	980	43.3
1985	26,403	12,981	12,048	934	50.1
1986	27,052	13,332	12,442	890	59.5
1987	27,717	13,737	12,946	791	66.9
1988	28,393	14,133	13,385	748	76.1
1989	29,142	14,518	13,780	737	87.3
1990	29,976	14,750	13,747	1,003	97.3
1991	30,575	14,833	13,714	1,119	102.0
1992	31,187	15,187	13,805	1,382	104.3
1993	31,810	15,700	14,130	1,570	115.5
1994	32,155	15,450	14,122	1,328	124.8
1995	32,291	15,412	14,203	1,209	131.3
1996	32,501	15,512	14,392	1,120	141.0

(continued)

TABLE 2 (continued)

(thousands)

Year	Total Population	Labor Force	Jobs	Unemployed People	Prisoners
1997	32,985	15,947	14,943	1,004	152.5
1998	33,387	16,337	15,368	969	158.2
1999	33,934	16,597	15,732	865	162.1
2000	34,480	17,091	16,246	845	161.5

SOURCES: SPWB 1986, 1993, 2001; CDC 1994b; CDC, 2002.

the rubble of extensive restructuring, individuals and families have developed alternative modes of social reproduction, given their utter abandonment by capital. These modes include informal economic structures for the exchange of illegal and legal goods and services (W. J. Wilson 1987); social parenting, especially by women, in extended families of biological and fictive kin (Collins 1990; Stack 1996); and the redivision of urban space into units controlled by street organizations (Bing 1991; cf. Fanon 1961). The "concentration effects" (W. J. Wilson 1987) of sociospatial apartheid (cf. Massey and Denton 1993) also include high rates of intentional and accidental violence, leading to premature death from a wide range of causes (Greenberg and Schneider 1994; Bing 1991), and persistent but hostile interaction with state agencies, especially welfare, family services, courts, and the police (W. J. Wilson 1987; R. W. Gilmore 1993).

At the most abstract level, about a million people in California have been locked into isolated enclaves by being locked out elsewhere. Changes in labor-market structures have had particularly harsh effects on African American men in the prime of life (Miller 1996), while displacing other workers as well (Grant et al. 1996; Leiman 1993). Underemployment and worklessness are higher among men than among women of similar demographic profile. The lower-echelon jobs produced by more recent rounds of investment in regions where jobs making and moving things have disappeared are either native-born women's (low-paid, nonbrawny) work, or secondary market jobs targeting recent male or female immigrants (Sassen 1988; Grant et al. 1996). The lower a man's income, the more likely he is to have been unemployed, and a disjuncture of skills and expectations exacerbates the difficulty of marginalized workers finding new jobs. Finally, Black men are 30 percent more likely than their white counterparts to have lost permanent jobs between 1979 and 1989, with the long-term effect that only 51 percent of Black men have *steady* employment, compared with 73 percent twenty-five years ago—although 90 percent of all Black men work at least part of the time (Nasar 1994).

The five-county Los Angeles region is the origin of 60 percent of state prisoners.[21] A comparison of census data for 1970, 1980, and 1990 reveals that while the region's Black men who work have closed the racial wage gap, all but the most highly educated have experienced steady declines in employment. The lower the educational attainment, the more precipitous the drop (Grant et al. 1996). Black women who have moved out of traditional labor market niches (such as domestic service) have gained higher-paying clerical and technical employment in the finance, insurance, and real estate (FIRE) and governmental sectors. However, the correlation between education and employment still holds, with steadily declining workforce participation among Black women with less than high school diplomas. The organization discussed in chapter 5 constitutes a gradually and self-consciously politicized consequence of these bifurcations.

Increased underemployment and joblessness is not an exclusively African American domain, however, although Black people are disproportionately represented in it. Between 1970 and 1980, the earnings of Chicanos[22] aged 25–34 in the Los Angeles region declined from those of the previous decade, and although earnings improved in the 1980s, they did not regain the old highs. At the same time, Chicanas did not experience a compensatory gain serving to maintain household income levels (Ortiz 1996). During the same period, overall joblessness for young adult Black men increased 25 percent, while that of white males in the cohort decreased. However, when education is factored in along with age, a different picture emerges: among the less-educated, joblessness increased for both groups—by 84 percent among Black men and 30 percent among white men (Ong and Valenzuela 1996).

The spatial configurations of Los Angeles's secondary school dropout rates, heavy industry closures, and technopole development show how rates of underemployment and joblessness, while meeting a need for capital, are not apolitically visited upon workers (Oliver et al. 1993; see also Massey and Denton 1994): the "market" did not do it. Rather, the post-Keynesian state participated in the production of the relative surplus population through specific actions and inactions. Twenty years of laissez-faire economic policy have politically and ideologically freed capital to move (Oliver et al. 1993; cf. Bluestone and Harrison 1982). Defunded community-based organizations no longer provide services and training to youth, and abandoned educational programs no longer provide opportunity for advancement (Oliver et al. 1993). The state registers its indifference in the growing dropout rate—as high as 63–79 percent in some Black and Latino high schools (Oliver et al. 1993; cf. Horton and Freire 1990). Changes in public policy with respect to the working poor have contributed to the abandonment of entire segments of labor, with the result that the "social safety net has been replaced by a criminal dragnet" (Oliver et al. 1993: 126). Examining California by region, Dan Walters ([1986] 1992) arrived at similar findings for all of the state's metropolitan areas.

These selected examples indicate who is in the relative surplus population. The numbers do not include the unemployed fraction of California's half-million agricultural workers—mostly immigrant and native-born Latinos—who migrate through the state's annual harvests (Walker 1995; Landis 1992).

Capital's requirement for a relative surplus population, in one of the world's richest political-geographic formations, provokes crisis on a number of levels. For each jobless individual and household, the crisis centers on daily and intergenerational re- production. For voters, the crisis centers on how to ensure that the surplus population, who rebelled in 1965 and 1992, is con- tained, if not deported. In tightening labor markets through de- portation of reserve labor force cadres to prison or abroad, fear- driven voter-made laws may seem contradictory for capitalism (cf. Foglesong 1986); but the contradiction may only be an illu- sion when employers are able to exploit actual and implied un- documented workers' political powerlessness. Voter-made laws—which imply an identifiable stratum of electorally ex- pressed "common sense"—can also provoke new struggles in a rapidly restructuring state, where newly dominant blocs seek to exercise power in an era characterized by a crisis of state legitimation. This brings us to our fourth and final surplus, that of state capacity.

Surplus State Capacity   Insofar as the capitalist state must both help capital be profitable, and keep the formal inequality of capitalism acceptable to the polity (Habermas 1972; Hirsch 1983; Negri [1980] 1988), it develops fiscal, institutional, and ideological means to carry out these tasks. These means—or capacities—are made up of laws and lawmakers, offices and other built environments, bureaucrats, budgets, rules and regulations, rank-and-file staff, the ability to tax or borrow, and direct access to mass communication and education to produce "primary" definitions of social reality (Skocpol 1985; Stuart Hall et al. 1978; Gramsci 1971). The historically specific arrangements of these capacities— how they are combined, and to what end—indicate the "balance of power relations" in the social formation as a whole (Negri [1980] 1988; Mike Davis 1986).

The balance of power, in turn, is explained—or legitimated—through politically fought-out interpretations of seemingly neutral overarching principles (the Constitution, individual freedom, equality) that, in common sense and law, ideologically bind state and society (MacKinnon 1989; O'Connor [1973] 2000; Stuart Hall et al. 1978; Stuart Hall 1986).[23] When a new bloc attains state power, it must "renovate and make critical already existing activity" by using the ideological and material means at hand to transform its intervention from an ad hoc to a durable presence in society (Gramsci 1971; Hobsbawm 1982).

The short-lived Keynesian state had secured a general balance of power by developing agencies that promised to guarantee uses for surplus when markets failed. Keynesian institutions congealed legitimacy and revenues into highly differentiated, but reproducible, units of state power (Piven 1992). Income and employment programs for workers, infrastructural programs for capital, and subsidy programs for farmlands were designed to keep surpluses from again accumulating into the broad and deep crisis that had characterized the Great Depression.

The uneven development of the New Deal's "creative government" (Baldwin 1968) resulted not only from the uneven capitulations of capital to a massive social wage but also—and perhaps more so—from the desperately dense relationships between southern (and western) and northern Democrats. The racial, industrial, gender, and regional divisions reflected in eligibility for and the scope of New Deal agencies and programs institutionalized Jim Crow without speaking his name (see, e.g., Mink 1995; R. W. Gilmore 2002b). In other words, the anomaly that emerged in the 1930s was not only the welfare-warfare state, but also the extension of regional norms to national relationships (e.g., county-determined eligibility for federal aid to dependent children). The political remains of those agencies form the armature of the workfare-warfare state.

The peculiar welfare-warfare, or military Keynesian, state form began to lose its legitimate ability to manage crisis, and thus to reproduce itself and endure, at about the time the profit rate started to flatten and then fall in the mid to late 1960s. As we saw in chapter 2, we can witness the delegitimation of redistribution of income via the welfare function in any number of positions espoused from 1965 on, from revisionist liberal to New Right. Another way to look at the problem is to investigate shifts in the

structure of taxation, which both reveal profound reconfigura-
tions of power (understood here as responsibility, which is also
authority and autonomy) between levels of the state, and newly
emerging relationships between all kinds of capitalists and all
kinds of workers. These dynamics exhibit no less unevenness
than what characterized the interlocking and overlapping periods of the Great Depression, World War II, and the Cold War
through the mid 1960s. The point here is a simple one: now
things are different, but the difference is grounded in history, not
conspiracy or mechanical certainty.

Marx observed that "tax struggle is the oldest form of class
struggle" (1867; cited in O'Connor [1973] 2000: 10). When examined abstractly, tax struggle appears to be a *general* indicator
of state illegitimacy. However, the historical specificity of actual
tax revolts is evidence of opposition to the *particular* means by
which the balance in power relations is realized as a *particular*
state form.[24] The way the New Deal bureaucracy and agency formation happened indicates the complexity of "class struggle" and
also points to how inter- and intraclass antagonisms are waged
through, in, and as the state. In other words, the rejigging of
power, dynamically played out in tax struggle, is not achieved
along pure lines of capital and labor. For example, businesses
stuck in particular political geographies (e.g., tourism or agriculture) might support different tax schemes from firms that are
more mobile, while multinational corporations can promote
hikes or cuts inimical to small business interests (O'Connor
[1973] 2000; Foglesong 1986). High-wage labor might try to
shield its relative prosperity from low-wage and unemployed
workers. In the aggregate, however, tax struggle is a struggle
over who gets to keep the value that produces profit. The strug-

gle is decoupled from the economic point of production (the factory or firm) and often explosively recoupled in the political milieu of the state.

In the California case, the rhythms of tax reduction are strong indicators of structural change and, as table 3 demonstrates, show how the Keynesian state's delegitimation accumulated in waves, culminating, rather than originating, in Tom Bradley's 1982 and 1986 gubernatorial defeats. The first wave, or capital's wave, is indicated by the 50 percent decline in the ratio of bank and corporation taxes to personal income taxes between 1967 and 1986 (California State Public Works Board 1987). Starting as early as 1968, voters had agitated for tax relief commensurate with the relief capital had won after putting Ronald Reagan in the governor's mansion (Mike Davis 1990). But Sacramento's efforts were continually disappointing under both Republican and Democratic administrations (Kirlin and Chapman 1994). This set in motion the second, or labor's, wave, in which actual (and aspiring) homeowner-voters reduced their own taxes via Proposition 13 (1978).[25] The third, or federal wave, indicates the devolution of responsibility from the federal government onto the state and local levels, as evidenced by declines of 12.5 percent (state) to 60 percent (local) in revenues derived from federal aid. The third wave can be traced to several deep tax cuts the Reagan presidential administration conferred on capital and the wealthiest of workers in 1982 and again in 1986 (David Gordon 1996; Krugman 1994).

The sum of these waves produced state and local fiscal crises following in the path of federal crisis that James O'Connor ([1973] 2000) had analyzed early in the period under review when he advanced the "welfare-warfare" concept. As late as

TABLE 3 THREE WAVES OF STRUCTURAL CHANGE IN
SOURCES OF CALIFORNIA TAX REVENUES, 1967–1989

First Wave: Bank and Corporate Taxes per Dollar of Personal Income Tax[a]

1967	72 cents
1986	36 cents

Second Wave: California State and Local Government Revenue Sources[b]

Source and Year	Percentage
Personal income	
1977–78	12.5
1988–89	16.8
Sales and use	
1977–78	16.1
1988–89	16.5
Property	
1977–78	25.1
1988–89	12.7
Fees and charges	
1977–78	6.8
1988–89	15.8
Enterprises	
1977–78	19.6
1988–89	22.3
Other taxes	
1977–78	15.4
1988–89	15.8

TABLE 3 (continued)

Third Wave: Federal Aid to California State and Local
Governments (% of general revenues)[c]

Year	State	Local
1981	25.8	6.7
1988	22.6	2.7

SOURCES: [a]SPWB 1987; [b]Chapman 1991: 19; [c]Chapman 1991: 16.

1977–78, California state and local coffers were full (CDF-CEI 1978; Gramlich 1991). By 1983, Sacramento was borrowing to meet its budgetary goals, while county and city governments reached crisis at different times, depending on how replete their reserves had been prior to Proposition 13. Voters wanted services and infrastructure at lowered costs; and when they paid, they tried not to share. Indeed, voters were quite willing to pay for amenities that would stick in place, and between 1977–78 and 1988–89, they actually increased property-based taxes going to special assessment districts by 45 percent (Chapman 1991: 19).

In this historical context, old markets for certain fractions of finance capital, land, and labor were dying, while new ones had not yet been born that might absorb the surpluses. The central contradiction for the waning welfare-warfare, or military Keynesian, state was this: the outcomes of tax struggle translated into delegitimation of programs the state could use to put surpluses back to work, while at the same time, the state retained bureaucratic and fiscal apparatuses from the golden age. The massive restructuring of the state's tax base in effect made surplus the Keynesian state's capacities. However, the state did not disappear—just as surplus workers, or land, or other idled factors of production do not disappear. Rather, what withered was the state's legitimacy to act *as* the Keynesian state. The state's crisis, then, was also a crisis for people whose protections against calamity, or opportunities for advancement, would be made surplus by the state, into which their hard-fought incorporation was only ever partial and therefore contingent. A related crisis, for the entire surplus population, rested on how absolutely they would be abandoned and whether their regulation would take new forms.

It is possible, of course, that the post-Keynesian state could shrink. Figure 8 shows the trends for the state's general fund and the numbers who voted for governor in elections from 1978 to 1994. Legitimacy diminished, and the state budget grew. The best explanation for the budget expansion is that the underlying conditions that led to the waves of tax revolts on the part of capital, labor, and the federal government continued to be in flux, and therefore the challenge for maintaining a general balance of power required an excess of resources at the California level. This would suggest that the new power bloc's intervention has not achieved hegemony. But a corollary to such an explanation might be that the new power bloc cannot rejig power in the figure of the state with any greater cost-efficiency than it has already exhibited. The "big stick" approach used by U.S. capital to discipline labor requires an enormous, expensive industrial bureaucracy (David Gordon 1996); the same thing may be true of the capitalist state in crisis.

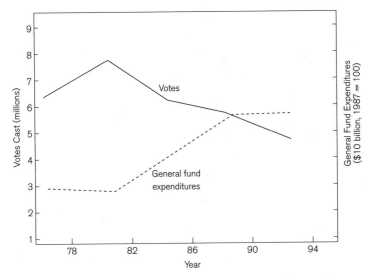

FIGURE 8. Votes cast for governor and general fund expenditures, 1978–1994. Sources: *Los Angeles Times,* November 9, 1978, November 3, 1982, November 6, 1986, November 8, 1990; Martin 1994; California State Controller, *Annual Report,* 1982, 1995.

CONCLUSION

As we shall see in the detailed analysis that follows, the new state built itself in part by building prisons. It used the ideological and material means at hand to do so, renovating its welfare-warfare capacities into something different by molding surplus finance capital, land, and labor into the workfare-warfare state. The result was an emerging apparatus that, in an echo of the Cold War Pentagon's stance on communism, presented its social necessity in terms of an impossible goal—containment of crime, understood as an elastic category spanning a dynamic alleged continuum of dependency and depravation. The crisis of state capacity then became, peculiarly, its own solution, as the welfare-warfare state began the transformation, bit by bit, to the permanent crisis workfare-warfare state, whose domestic militarism is concretely recapitulated in the landscapes of depopulated urban communities and rural prison towns. We shall now turn to the history of this "prison fix."

THREE

THE PRISON FIX

The rhetoric of imprisonment and the reality of the cage are often in stark contrast.

NORVAL MORRIS AND DAVID J. ROTHMAN, *THE OXFORD HISTORY OF THE PRISON* (1995)

You know, in my life I've rarely been amazed. Rarely been amazed. But I'll tell you what amazed me is the last time I was in [prison, in 1992]. I thought, you know, look at all these guys in here. I thought, all these guys were in there for something, you know, that they had done SOMETHING. But then people started telling me what they were in for. More than half the guys, they were in for drugs, for possession. I mean, for NOTHING. That was truly amazing, you know, to me.

40-YEAR-OLD EX-GANGSTER, PERSONAL COMMUNICATION (1994)

How did California go about "the largest prison building program in the history of the world" (Rudman and Berthelsen 1991: i)? We have already seen that California's political economy changed significantly in the 1970s, due both to changes in the location of industrial investment—capital movement—and to "natural" disasters. Those changes, and responses to them, provided the foundation upon which new rounds of capital movement and new natural disasters were played out. These shifts produced surpluses of finance capital, land, labor, and state capacity, not all of which were politically, economically, socially, or regionally absorbed. The new California prison system of the 1980s and 1990s was constructed deliberately—but not conspiratorially—of surpluses that were not put back to work in other ways. Make no mistake: prison building was and is not the inevitable outcome of these surpluses. It did, however, put certain state capacities into motion, make use of a lot of idle land, get capital invested via public debt, and take more than 160,000 low-wage workers off the streets.

FROM REFORM TO PUNISHMENT

Just as the rounds of disinvestment and calamity that occurred in the 1970s political economy set the stage for how the 1980s crises proceeded, so changes in California's prisons in the 1970s formed the basis for the system's expansion. Not once, but twice, the rising power bloc of "tough on crime" and antiurban strategists seized hard-won reforms designed to make the prisoner's lot less desperate and transformed them into their inverse mirror images. Efforts to make the California Department of Corrections (CDC) take rehabilitation seriously wiped rehabilitation from the books. Efforts to free prisoners from crumbling prisons led to the construction program that has never ended.

In 1977, California ended its sixty-year commitment to use the state prison system as the sociospatial means to rehabilitate all but the most intransigent prisoners (Rudman and Berthelsen 1991; Cummins 1994). The 1977 Uniform Determinate Sentencing Act was the legislature's response to a series of executive branch courtroom losses during a twenty-five year struggle with state prisoners. Prisoners had successfully used the federal bench, under the 1867 Habeas Corpus Act, to demand that California treat prisoners equitably, relieve overcrowding, and respect constitutional rights (Cummins 1994).[1] Prisons have never been pleasant places, and overcrowding was not a new phenomenon.[2] Prisoners have always fought both legally and extralegally to secure decent conditions (Cummins 1994; Wicker 1975). However, the post–World War II civil rights movement's courtroom successes encouraged prisoners to use the system against itself; and the growing fraction of Black people in the prison population was cause for identification with struggles in the streets (Jackson 1970; Angela Davis 1971; Wicker 1975; Cummins 1994). The movement also influenced prisoners from behind bars, because the criminalization of political activists brought them into the prison population (Cummins 1994; Angela Davis 1971).

The key issue was sentence length. California's 1917 Progressive rehabilitation scheme had been coupled with indeterminate sentences, on the theory that technically qualified "corrections" professionals would help prisoners become useful and reliable and that the "corrected" prisoners would then persuade local parole boards of their readiness to rejoin society (Norval Morris

1995; E. B. Freedman 1996). In practice, parole boards were capricious and racist, representing local elites; prisoners sentenced to one year to life languished in the penitentiary for decades, petitioning at prescribed intervals for a chance to talk their way out of cages (Jackson 1970).[3] California's Progressives had argued that they were devising a new system vastly different from both the exploitative plantation models of Mississippi and Louisiana (Oshinsky 1996; Lichtenstein 1996) and the Golden State's older, punitive system (Bookspan 1991; Rudman and Berthelsen 1991). However, the Progressive movement was generally committed to preserving racial and property hierarchies, while creating institutions that would turn out people who respected authority and knew their own limits (Thelan 1969; Allen 1994; Linda Gordon 1994; see also Don Mitchell 1996). In practice, California's indeterminate sentences extended to life sentences for Black, Latino, and white prisoners whose failures to be rehabilitated translated as their refusal to learn their proper places in the social order (Irwin 1985; Jackson 1970; cf. Himes [1945] 1986, 1971).

A second class of issues that prisoners litigated centered on conditions of confinement. State, media, and intellectuals of the late 1960s and early 1970s participated in the ideological production of "moral panics" (Stuart Hall et al. 1978) to explain the social and political disorder sweeping the United States. At all levels, states worked hard to characterize people agitating for justice as morally wrong rather than politically dissident. The ensuing criminalization of such activists swept what were then record numbers of men and women off the streets and into custody, with California in the vanguard (Miller 1996; Donner 1990; cf. Stuart Hall et al. 1978; Bean 1973). The state's prison population grew from about 16,500 to just under 23,000 between 1967 and 1971; the number rose and fell within a fairly narrow band over the next few years, peaking at 24,700 in 1974 and bottoming out at 19,600 in 1977 (CDC 1992; Rudman and Berthelsen 1991; Cummins 1994). In addition to, or as a result of, problems of sheer physical incapacity, the CDC could not or would not respect the rights of inmates to "adequate life safety, health care and recreation, food, decent eating . . . and sanitation standards, . . . visitation privileges, and access to legal services" (Silver 1983: 118; cf. Cummins 1994). Thus, the hostility, density, and confusion that characterized state prison environments at the time undermined any rehabilitative capacity prisons might have had (Rudman and Berthelsen 1991; Cummins 1994).

Federal courts throughout the United States in the 1970s favorably evaluated many prisoners' writs of habeas corpus and put state corrections departments under federal order to remedy constitutional wrongs (Benton 1983). Courts directed California to relieve overcrowding and also to group prisoners according to a transparent system of classifications in order to enhance the potential for every individual's reform (SPWB 1985; Cummins 1994; Rudman and Berthelsen 1991; see also Bookspan 1991 for earlier attempts at prisoner classification). If the purpose of these federally demanded social and spatial remedies was to carry out the mandates of Progressive-era lawmaking, the legislature responded by voiding the 1917 statute. The 1977 Uniform Determinate Sentencing Act was California's formal abdication of any responsibility to rehabilitate, stating neatly: "[T]he purpose of imprisonment for crime is punishment."

In the 1977 Uniform Determinate Sentencing Act, and again in that year's Budget Act, the legislature directed the CDC to

forecast prison bed need (LAO 1986).[4] The CDC's initial attempts to predict shortfall were quite modest and focused on renovating aging facilities and replacing the two oldest prisons—
San Quentin (built in 1852) and Folsom (opened in 1880). The
department's 1978 Facilities Planning Report proposed renovating 3,000 prison beds around the state. In 1980, the Facilities Requirement Plan expanded the number of new and replacement
beds to 5,000, and forecast an increase in the capital needed to
carry out the project (LAO 1986).

In the turbulent years of his second and final term (1978–82),
Governor Jerry Brown took up the initial CDC analysis and
started work on designs for new facilities to replace the tier-and-
catwalk-style gothic structures at San Quentin and Folsom
(Morain 1994c; LAO 1986). Brown's new prisons were supposed
to be used for rehabilitation, in spite of the legislature's 1977 declaration. The 1977 statute did not *forbid* rehabilitation; rather, it
excised its central importance (Rudman and Berthelsen 1991). By
his own testimony, Brown could have used his power as the
state's chief executive to relieve overcrowding by ordering parole
for indeterminate-sentence prisoners who had served time equal
to the new sentencing requirements and by commuting sentences for others who had been in the system a long time.[5] Instead, he began to investigate the best way to improve plant and
modestly expand capacity, intending—or so he claimed—to use
state-of-the-art prisons for the benefit of prisoners and society
(Morain 1994c).

By 1980, the legislature had already approved replacing San
Quentin with two 500-bed, maximum-security units. In the
summer of 1982, Brown brought in a premier prison architect-
engineer, Paul Rosser, to design small, program- and common-

space-oriented prisons that would focus on education and other rehabilitative activities (Morain 1994c; LAO 1986). Brown's planning combined vestiges of the early twentieth-century Progressive sensibility—seeking to produce social peace through old and new institutions and techniques of control—with a late twentieth-century political shrewdness—seeking to convert the moral panic over crime into an opportunity by having a skeptical electorate support the exercise, rather than the restraint, of state expansion (cf. L. M. Friedman 1993).

There were so many contradictory processes at work in the 1982 transition year from the lapsed welfare-state Democratic to the supply-side Republican gubernatorial regime that it is sometimes difficult to grasp how they all coincided. The split widened between Brown's commitment to what had become, in law, secondary (rehabilitation), and the primary purpose enshrined in the new penal code. Without opposition from the lame-duck chief executive, the legislature gave the CDC permission to build on a larger scale than Brown had envisioned (Morain 1994d). Brown had financed prison design studies out of reserve funds appropriated by the legislature and initiated the era of new facilities construction by approving a $25,000,000 expansion at the California Correctional Institution in southern Kern County. But in 1982, new commitments to the CDC started to rise steeply, and the department revised its forecast—for the first time proposing several major *capacity-expanding* facilities instead of concentrating on renovation and replacement (LAO 1986). To meet needs forecast by the CDC, the 1982 legislature approved siting new facilities in Riverside, Los Angeles, and San Diego Counties. That same year, the legislature successfully petitioned voters to approve $495,000,000 in general obligation bonds

(GOBs) to build new prisons—based on the argument that more prison cells would enhance public safety and punish wrongdoers (Morain 1994d).

Also in 1982, the legislature reorganized the statutory relationship between itself, the CDC, and the prison expansion project by forming a new entity, the Joint Legislative Committee on Prison Construction and Operations (JLCPCO).[6] Thereafter, the CDC stood apart from all other state agencies in two ways. First, its capital outlays would not be managed by the Office of General Services, which meant that its bidding and budgeting practices varied from long-standing procedures for construction of state physical plant. Indeed, the CDC was explicitly exempted from a competitive bidding process and instead allowed to assign work to outside consultants (BRC 1990; LAO 1986).[7] The explanation for this extreme deviation from normal procedure focused on the CDC's unique new charge to build an unspecified number of similar, expensive, highly specialized facilities in rapid succession (R. Bernard Orozco, interview, 1995; Rudman and Berthelsen 1991; BRC 1990; LAO 1986). Second, the establishment of the JLCPCO kept the CDC's ordinary and extraordinary activities under close scrutiny and direction by elected officials (Rudman and Berthelsen 1991; LAO 1986). The latter appeared to keep the expansion of the prison system in the public eye, insofar as the JLCPCO was required to hold hearings *before* either Department of Finance disbursement of appropriated funds or Public Works Board implementation of CDC plans (BRC 1990).

George Deukmejian's gubernatorial victory in 1982 completed the turn to the right California had begun under Ronald Reagan in the 1960s. Deukmejian used the accumulating illegitimacy exemplified by tax revolts to attack the status quo—starting with the weakest targets, such as persons receiving welfare (cf. Piven 1992). He followed, rather than led, the tax struggle, and at the end of California's second straight year of well-reported declining crime rates, he proposed budget increases to fight crime, appealing to voters' insecurity. It is more than ironic that he campaigned against big government by arguing how the government should grow. Deukmejian's gubernatorial opponent, Tom Bradley, had as mayor of Los Angeles successfully controlled the rising share of the city budget that the LAPD and the police and fire pension fund had commanded for more than a decade.[8] The police fought back by campaigning—statewide, in uniform—for Deukmejian (Sonenshein 1993). Deukmejian seized the issue and used the Los Angeles dispute to project race, crime, and the need for state-building as a single issue, claiming that the African American mayor's tightening of the LAPD budget could only be the work of a man who was soft on crime.

Once Deukmejian took office in 1983, the administration broadened Jerry Brown's new prison plan but dropped rehabilitation as the reason for new buildings. With punishment, in the form of "incapacitation," now the rationale for prison, the administration, the legislature, and the CDC (all three partially consolidated via the JLCPCO) joined forces to expand the state's built capacity for incarceration. But the state still had two immediate problems: first, how better to guarantee potential prisoners, and second, how to finance the facilities to cage them. Toward solution of the former problem, the legislature changed the classification of certain offenses—such as residential burglary (Rudman and Berthelsen 1991) and domestic assault (E. G. Hill 1994)—to felonies requiring prison terms upon conviction. Similarly, new drug laws—to some degree modeled on New York's Rockefeller minimum mandatory sentence laws enacted in the early 1970s (Flateau 1996; Miller 1996)—also enhanced the likelihood of prison time for people not formerly on the prison track (Rudman and Berthelsen 1991). The legislature further authorized a State Task Force on Youth Gang Violence to study what it called "street terrorism"—a topic to which we shall return. The Board of Prison Terms, overseeing parole officers, made common cause with the legislature, and instructed its field staff to be liberal in revoking parole—an option used sparingly before the new prison era; as a result, since 1983 people on parole have had great difficulty remaining out of custody through their supervisory period, with about 70 percent being returned to prison for some portion of that time without having been convicted of new crimes.[9]

With these legal measures in place, the CDC deepened and widened its planning. Beginning with the 1983 Facilities Master Plan, it projected shortfalls in available beds as a crisis (LAO 1986). It is surprising neither that the CDC bed shortage estimates varied considerably nor that they tended to climb. The estimates ranged from 16,100 to 55,000 throughout the 1980s to a 1994 all-time high of 151,641 for 1998, generated by the "three strikes" law (SPWB 1985, 1986a, 1987, 1991; LAO 1986; CDC 1993, 1994, 1996). Under Deputy Director James Gomez, who moved to the CDC from the Department of Social Services Adult and Family Division in 1983, the department expanded its planning staff (from 3 to 118), honed its forecasting, and from 1984 on began to produce five-year master plans that combined technical number-crunching skills with a flair for emphasizing the drama inherent in the "crisis" (LAO 1986).[10] Projected need moved in tandem with the judiciary's legislature-produced capacity to remand persons to CDC custody. With the problem of identifying wrongdoers partially solved, the question was how to pay for all the new beds; and it was the new beds, rather than court commitments, that led the system's growth.

CAPITAL FOR CONSTRUCTION

Although Sacramento had successfully persuaded taxpayers to vote for the 1982 Prison Construction Bond Act, most elected officials were susceptible to an ongoing fear, inspired by Proposition 13, of asking voters to approve too many general obligation bonds. GOBs pledge the full faith and credit of the state of California, and the state constitution requires that any such debt be approved by the legislature *and* ratified by the electorate (SPWB 1985). GOBs also provide a way to circumvent the constitutional requirement of a balanced budget, because debt service for voter-approved bonds is exempt from the rule (SPWB 1985). The problem became how to expand a politically popular program (prisons) without running up against the politically contradictory limit to taxpayers' willingness to use their own money to defend against their own fears.

Frederic Prager of L. F. Rothschild, Unterberg, Towbin (LFRUT),[11] one of the most creative and well-connected underwriters in the California world of municipal finance, and his new associate Tom Dumphy, came up with a plan approved by a bipartisan power bloc, including Democrats Jess Unruh (treasurer) and Willie Brown (Speaker of the Assembly), the Republican governor, George Deukmejian, and prison-expansion activists in the legislature, led by State Senator Robert Presley (R–Riverside) and Assemblyman Dick Robinson (R–Orange

County). The capitalists and the statesmen crafted a new way to borrow money for prisons from existing debt-raising capacities. The scheme involved using lease revenue bonds (LRBs) to supplement GOB debt. Prager's savvy and experience had led LFRUT to dominance in California's private college facilities market. The state's independent, not-for-profit postsecondary institutions could borrow in the tax-exempt markets to develop or renovate infrastructure; for California, these debts constitute "off-book" or "no-commitment" loans, because their repayment does not entail any taxing or other fiscal capacity of the state (SPWB 1985; Sbragia 1986). Under Prager, LFRUT put together LRBs for the state's richest and most powerful private universities—Stanford, the University of Southern California, and the California Institute of Technology. The creative firm also devised successful bond issues for schools with more modest debt capacity, such as St. Mary's, Moraga, Cal Lutheran, and the University of the Pacific, so that they, too, could improve their facilities. In 1981–82, Prager worked with the Association of Independent California Colleges and Universities (AICCU) to issue an innovative revenue bond whose proceeds would constitute a forward-funded market for student loans. Thanks to an exposé in the San Jose *Mercury News* (September 5, 1982), the voters got the incorrect idea that only rich schools (and by inference, rich students) had access to these public funds. Treasurer Unruh, looking to be reelected that fall, demanded that public institutions be included in the deal. The spike in interest rates in the early 1980s made it difficult for middle-income families to borrow for college in the private sector, while at the same time, mounting energy and other costs pushed up tuition (R. W. Gilmore 1991). The loan deal was extended to all students in the state; and Unruh used the program during his campaign to reassure the state's 1.5 million students and their parents—presumed members of the voting class—that his office was looking out for their interests.[12] A blunt politician of the old school, Unruh also knew when to reduce flows to the public trough; and in the early 1980s, a bad economy and a transitional gubernatorial regime kept the old power broker's fist tight on the spigot.

Prager brought Dumphy to LFRUT in 1983 to exploit his talents and connections in city government; he had previously been a planner in Los Angeles Mayor Tom Bradley's administration and had also served as a youth probation officer in Massachusetts early in his career (Dumphy 1996). Together, Prager and Dumphy worked hard to develop new California markets for public debt (cf. Sbragia 1986). The private college business was already starting to tighten, because of most institutions' limited capacity to increase tuition—the major source of operating revenue for all expenditures, including student aid and debt service, at all but the wealthiest schools (R. W. Gilmore 1991). They were the pivot men between surplus private capital available for investment in the not-for-profit and public sectors and decreasing state-approved outlets where the capital could be put to work. The new prison construction program, in its infancy in 1983, constituted an excellent long-term opportunity for capital investment. Sacramento's old and new guards were ready to unite behind the prison program, but they had to raise much more money than anyone was brave or foolhardy enough to request from voters.

Lease revenue bonds were the solution. LRBs are issued by the Public Works Board of the state of California, established in 1946 to help smooth crisis as California adjusted to the postwar economy (SPWB 1985). Typical LRBs issued by the Public Works Board are for real property loans for veterans and farmers, as well as loans for public college and university facilities and hospital buildings. In all cases, nongovernmental borrower payments or user fees are used to pay back the debt. While in all cases the Public Works Board is forbidden to pledge California's full faith and credit, in the case of public debt for public use, there is an implied *moral* obligation that the state will exercise due diligence to avert defaults (cf. Sbragia 1996). It was a risky but successful political suspension of disbelief to use the state's implied moral obligation to script a scenario in which the Public Works Board and the CDC were characterized as entities buying, selling, and leasing property and rights between them (SPWB 1985). For the prison LRBs, the "revenue" has consisted of general fund appropriations authorized by the legislature to the CDC annual operating budget, designated as "rental payments" to the Public Works Board, which is the actual issuer of the debt (SPWB 1985, 1986a, 1986b, 1987, 1990, 1991, 1993a, 1993b, 1993c, 1993d). Unlike with mortgage, postsecondary, or hospital issues, there is no potential or actual nontax revenue stream at all.

The economics of prison LRBs is almost identical to the economics of prison GOBs; the greatest difference between them is political—the scope of approval needed to borrow huge sums. The economic downside is that LRBs are slightly more expensive than GOBs precisely because they do not pledge the state's taxing power; for any debt, the higher the risk of nonpayment, the higher the interest. However, in order to persuade all members of the prison power bloc to exploit the LRB option, Prager and Dumphy underscored the sole positive economic difference—

one that is in large part political as well. LRBs do not have to be placed before the voters in general elections, and on approval by the legislature, they can be relatively quickly organized and issued in order to maximize favorable credit conditions, enabling the CDC to build prisons closer to the time the facilities are bid on, thus theoretically avoiding cost hikes. The capitalists and the statesmen agreed that the trade-off between slightly higher interest costs and quicker cash availability would balance the economic difference and provide an effective political shield from organized antitax activists.

In less than a decade, the amount of state debt for the prison construction project expanded from $763 million to $4.9 billion dollars, a proportional increase of from 3.8 percent to 16.6 percent of the state's total debt for all purposes (SPWB 1985, 1993). During the same period, state debt service (annual expenditure for principal plus interest) increased from 1 percent to 2.8 percent of per capita income (California State Controller 1996: 161).

The new source of capital enabled the CDC to follow the second of two approaches it had proposed. The earlier of these, in the late 1970s, had centered on keeping people convicted of nonviolent offenses in their communities and providing treatment programs for the 70 percent or so of all convicted persons who are addicted to drugs and alcohol (BRC 1990; LAO 1986; PRCC 1996). The state-of-emergency approach, which started to emerge in 1982–83 (in Gomez's first year as deputy director for CDC operations), sought simply to build as many prison cells as possible. The end run around taxpayer-voters in order to raise what turned out to be more than $2.5 billion in LRBs—in addition to nearly $2.5 billion in GOBs—was thus not only a political strategy of economic subterfuge but also one of social policy that set the Golden State in a new direction (SPWB 1985, 1986a, 1986b, 1987, 1990, 1991, 1993a, 1993b, 1993c, 1993d).

SITING THE PRISONS

In order to realize the prison expansion program, the state needed space in which to build the facilities.[13] California acquires from one to three sections of land (640–1,920 acres) for each approved site. For a typical facility built since 1982, the buildings, yards, parking lots, roads, perimeter, and fences incorporate 300–350 acres.[14] Initially, too, there was some concern that siting might prove a challenge because communities would be afraid to have prisons in their midst (BRC 1990). There was ample evidence from around the United States that prison siting could be difficult, with the facilities constituting highly contested locally unwanted land uses (LULUs), producing "not in my back yard" (NIMBY) dramas (see, for examples, Lake 1992, 1994; Krause 1992; Sechrest 1992; Carlson 1988, 1992; Travis and Sheridan 1983; cf. Lake 1992, 1994). As a result, the state was prepared to exercise its right of eminent domain and condemn lands in order to accumulate sufficient acreage for project development (LAO 1986; State of California 1990).

In anticipation of future siting struggles, the legislature at first determined that new prisons should be located south of the Tehachapi Mountains, whence, at the time, 59 percent of prisoners originated. The reasoning was that those who produced the prisoners deserved the LULUs. However, the regional edict was almost immediately revised, starting in 1982. The legislature approved new maximum security facilities adjacent to the expanded California Correctional Institution in Tehachapi (a tiny, high-altitude, sod-producing agricultural valley in southern

Kern County) to replace San Quentin (which was in any case never closed). The legislature also approved a new hospital prison to supplement the crowded and deteriorating hospital prison at Vacaville (Solano County) in the Great Central Valley, forty-five minutes' drive southwest of Sacramento. As word of these authorizations traveled back to legislators' constituencies from 1982 on, word returned by way of delegations of community boosters, "But what about us? Why not right here?"

In 1983, the CDC established a Prison Siting Office under the general direction of the department's Government and Community Relations Branch. A nasty fight in Los Angeles over the siting of the prison authorized for that county provided the backdrop for the political and marketing work of the siting office. The legislature had selected a site in East Los Angeles, the heart of the city and county's Mexicano and Chicano community. The characterization of Los Angeles as a county producing criminals but unwilling to shoulder its responsibility to house them played well across the state political map, especially in the suburbs and the inland valleys. At the same time, both the governor and legislature presumed that the promise of jobs would offset the hesitancy of a working-class community of color to have a prison located in its midst. The state was surprised by the vehement political opposition to the prison organized by neighborhood mothers ("Las Madres") in the area's public housing project and an activist Roman Catholic priest (Pardo 1998; Krier 1986; Pulido 1995b). The political danger in imposing the prison on East Los Angeles against the will of the area's residents lay in the fact that any elected official, Democrat or Republican, was increasingly vulnerable to the voting power of California's expanding Latino population (Paddock 1986). The governor thus

retreated before the potential identitarian political bloc presented by protesters, even though he had vowed that the prison
would be sited in the city. Eventually, the owner of the tract sold
the land to a nonstate entity (Paul Jacobs 1986), although it was
another year before the project was officially shelved (Wolinsky
1987).[15]

The LA prison battle gave legislators from other state regions
the chance to voice their constituents' willingness to have a prison
in their midst, and the siting office helped by sending representatives—usually women—to talk reassuringly at town meetings
about the benefits and costs associated with such a development
plan. An anti-LA righteousness, which turned on an almost patriotic notion of duty, cloaked the eagerness of small-town delegations who came to Sacramento looking for prisons to revive
isolated, flagging economies (Wolinsky 1987). Industry closures,
downsizing, and capital abandonment left large tracts of land
available for development. Contrary to contemporary folklore,
the towns where prisons were sited, while deeply divided by
class, are not all Anglo communities, and unlike in Los Angeles,
the political opposition to prison development was more easily
managed by pro-prison forces, aided by the CDC's persuasive
prospectuses promising jobs and other amenities. In largely rural
areas with few employers, opposition to the prisons did not gal-
vanize so readily. In Avenal, Corcoran, Coalinga, and Del Norte,
for example, the major opposition came from those materially, or
romantically, dependent on the traditional economy.[16] At the
same time, with few or no alternatives available to raise income
(such as rent) generated by real property, smallholders in the
towns and most workers, then and now, have clung to the gen-

erally unsubstantiated belief that the benefits of a prison out-weigh the negative effects.

The concentration of new prisons in the Central Valley, and along the state's southern and southeastern perimeter from Rock Mountain (southern San Diego County) to Blythe Valley (Riverside County), is the result of the confluence of political and economic forces embedded in, and built on, the historical power of agriculture and resource extraction in the state. Although agricultural and resource extraction activities account for only about 3 percent of total state product, these sectors, running at about $30 billion annually, have commanded great power in Sacramento, not least because they dominate the districts and counties where they are located, controlling many local legislators and county and town governments, in part through making substantial campaign contributions (Walters 1992; Don Mitchell 1996; Pisani 1984).

In the midst of the LA prison debacle, the CDC Siting Office determined that rural communities would be the most easily managed sites.[17] The 640 to 1,920 acres sought for each site would not come laden with costly political opposition in small towns. Those that were eventually successful in having prisons sited in their vicinity had well-organized delegations and very few objections to or demands on the CDC's proposals. They also had large landholders willing to sell nearby surplus acres that the towns could incorporate in order to reap the imagined harvest of state subventions, sales tax, and other incomes. We have already seen that 100,000 acres per year of irrigated agricultural land had been coming out of production starting in 1978; eighteen of the twenty-four new prisons sited between 1982 and 1998 were (or are being) built on formerly irrigated agricultural lands, and all but four of the twenty-four at the time of their siting lay outside the swathes of suburbanization moving into the Central and Inland Valleys.[18]

It seems contradictory that large, powerful landholding capitalists, accustomed to activating the state's capacity in enormous profit-enhancement projects, such as water development, would relinquish acres to the state. What was in it for them? First, they sell land—often the worst—that would otherwise be idle and more often at an inflated price (CCPOA n.d. [1996]; BRC 1990). Second, the state improves the land, and those improvements, coupled with the promise of employment, in the short run increase nearby land values. These two goals were summarized by a former head staffer of the JLCPCO concerning a dispute between the CDC and a site where the owners had surreptitiously extended the state-owned infrastructural improvements—at state cost—onto an adjacent parcel they intended to develop into a shopping mall: "They have all this land, and they are trying to bring up the values so they can develop it. That's how they hope to save their town."[19]

Surplus land connects to surplus labor; as in the past, rural capital has successfully externalized to the state costs associated with changes in production. Prison development has had the intended, although rarely realized, effect of providing jobs, and therefore supplementing household incomes for workers, who presumably would be less likely to organize for jobs, higher wages, or more radical goods, such as land reform, that can be gained only at capital's expense (Woods 1998). Rather, the actual and almost dispossessed (Jacqueline Jones 1992) have in this instance, as in so many others, been deflected to petitioning the

state for benefits within the narrowing scope of prison development and related opportunities.

PRODUCING MORE PRISONERS

The state initiated new rounds of criminalization as elected officials scrambled to sponsor new laws. The rationale for the laws
purported to be reducing violence in communities. The means
was sentence enhancement, or intensified "incapacitation"—to
prevent people from committing crimes by keeping them in cages
for as long as possible. Sentence enhancement adds fixed amounts
of extra time to standard sentences for certain offenses. The legislature relieved the judiciary of the responsibility to determine a
wide range of sentences by writing the specifics into the law. Legislators from across the political spectrum, from Robert Presley
(R–Riverside) and Bill Jones (R–Fresno) on the right to Jim Costa
(D–Fresno) in the center to Maxine Waters (D–Los Angeles) on
the left, sponsored sentence-enhancing legislation; almost everybody sponsored some law, collectively creating a plethora of new
crimes for the state's fifty-eight district attorneys to prosecute.

The legislature had commissioned a State Task Force on
Youth Gang Violence in 1984, whose findings, reported back to
the legislature in 1986, resulted in the Street Terrorism Enforcement and Prevention (STEP) Act of 1988, as subsequently
amended. With that law, California established a mandate directing all local law enforcement agencies to identify street gang
members and enroll them in a statewide database. The law en-
hances sentences imposed on those whom enforcement has identified as street gang members.[20] Upon future encounters with law
enforcement, listed persons face additional charges based on
their alleged status as gang members. Thus, while a non–gang

member arrested for a particular offense would be charged only with that offense, a gang member would be charged both with the offense and with being a gang member who had committed the offense. Upon conviction, the sentence for the original offense would be "enhanced" by from one to five years of extra time.

The decriminalization of controlled substance possession in the 1970s had caused the number of people in prison on drug-related charges to plummet (CDC 1992, *Historical Trends*). Drug recriminalization, coupled with mandatory sentences for drugs that had not been decriminalized and for new drugs such as crack cocaine, pushed controlled substance commitments back up throughout the 1980s. Whereas in 1977, drug offenses had accounted for only some 10 percent of new admissions to the CDC, by 1990, they accounted for 34.2 percent (Rudman and Berthelsen 1991; CDC 1992, *Historical Trends*), although all drug use peaked in 1978 and fell thereafter (Tonry 1995).

In addition to new laws designed to control drugs and gangs, the state launched a high-profile "three strikes" campaign. Although, as in most other jurisdictions in the United States, California had had sentence enhancement for repeat convictions for many years, the legislature passed the nation's second "three strikes" law in March 1994, and an initiative on the following November ballot solidified the statute into an expression of "the people's" will (Reynolds et al. 1996).[21] More broadly written than any law of its type in the United States (John Clark et al. 1996), the California version includes nonviolent prior convictions among eligible "strikes," sets no age, temporal, or jurisdictional limitations on priors, and allows prosecutors to use their power to "wobble" charges in order to make current misdemeanors into felonies and therefore strikable.[22]

From 1980 onward, crime was objectively and subjectively different from what it had been prior to the 1977 Uniform Determinate Sentencing Act and the subsequent authorization, funding, and siting of new prisons. Politicians of all races and ethnicities merged gang membership, drug use, and habitual criminal activity into a single social scourge, which was then used to explain everything from unruly youth to inner-city homicides to the need for more prisons to isolate wrongdoers. The media amplified the message by giving crime reporting top billing (Hadjor 1995; Males 1996; Miller 1996; Glassner 2000). Inner-city residents were, indeed, seeking relief from fearful disorders in their communities, and they, like their suburban counterparts, tended to accept the primary definitions of what crime was and what should be done about it—until direct experience of the law's unevenness raised questions about the actual intent of the legislation in the first place (chapter 5).

The legislature and initiative-passing voters handed prosecutors powers once reserved for judges—such as evaluation of mitigating factors or eligibility for diversion programs (Tonry 1995; Miller 1996; Reynolds et al. 1996; for federal precedents, see Baum 1996). While prosecutors could decide not to exercise the full extent of their new powers—and some did—such agents of law enforcement were in a contradictory position. As elected officials, prosecutors were expected to run "against" crime, and if they failed to do so, they risked being thrown out of office, and their bureaucracies risked losing ground in county-level budget competitions.[23] The largest jurisdictions in the Southland, especially Los Angeles County, eagerly embraced the legislative rulings and began vigorous enforcement campaigns, paid for by both state and federal funds (Sengupta 1992).[24] Police forces throughout the state, from tiny rural sheriffs' offices to the highly capitalized LAPD, systematically fulfilled their mandates through enhanced surveillance of neighborhoods and individuals suspected of extralegal activity (Sengupta 1992).[25] Concentrating power through the use of status determinations (gang/not gang; prior/no prior) and minimum mandatory sentences, the new laws widened and deepened the capacity of police, prosecutors, and judges to identify, arrest, charge, and convict people and remand them to CDC custody. Indeed, the legislature embarked on a criminal-law production frenzy, passing more than 100, and sometimes as many as 200, pieces of new legislation each year since 1988—up from the former output of 20–25 pieces, which included routine amendments of existing statutes (Greenwood et al. 1994). As a result, by 1994, the backlog had become so great that it was impossible to clear the legislative calendar by the end of each term, and the criminal law subcommittees of the judiciary committees in both houses of the legislature had become regular standing committees dealing exclusively with criminal legislation. The establishment of the new committees also produced powerful legislative niches for their chairs in the two houses, because legitimizing the prison expansion and operation program of the state's fastest-growing department directly depended on the path taken by criminal legislation (SPWB 1985, 1993a, 1993b, 1993c, 1993d; LAO 1986, 1996).

Working-class African Americans and Latinos—especially Chicanos—experienced the most intensive criminalization (Schiraldi and Godfrey 1994), trailed by urban and rural Anglos of modest means. As we can see in table 4, Anglos dominated the prisoner population in 1977 and did not lose their plurality until

TABLE 4 CDC PRISONER POPULATION BY RACE/ETHNICITY

Year	Total Number	Anglo (%)	African (%)	Latino (%)	Other (%)
1977	19,623	43.0	34.0	21.0	2.0
1982	34,640	36.0	36.0	26.0	2.5
1988	76,171	30.8	37.1	27.8	4.3
1995	135,133	29.5	31.3	34.1	5.0
2000	162,000	29.4	31.0	34.8	4.8

SOURCES: CDC 1992, table 4; CDC, *Characteristics of Population*, 1995, 2002.

1988. Meanwhile, absolute numbers grew across the board—with the total number of those incarcerated approximately doubling during each interval. African American prisoners surpassed all other groups in 1988, but by 1995, they had been overtaken by Latinos; however, Black people have the highest rate of incarceration of any racial/ethnic grouping in California, or, for that matter, in the United States (see also Bonczar and Beck 1997).

The structure of new laws, intersecting with the structure of the burgeoning relative surplus population, and the state's concentrated use of criminal laws in the Southland, produced a remarkable racial and ethnic shift in the prison population. Los Angeles is the primary county of commitment. Most prisoners are modestly educated men in the prime of life: 88 percent are between 19 and 44 years old. Less than 45 percent graduated from high school or read at the ninth-grade level; one in four is functionally illiterate. And, finally, the percentage of prisoners who worked six months or longer for the same employer immediately

TABLE 5 CDC COMMITMENTS BY
CONTROLLING OFFENSE
(%)

	Violent	Property	Drug
1980	63.5	24.2	7.4
1995	41.8	25.3	26.4
2000	25.3	26.0	39.0

SOURCES: CDC 1992; CDC, *Characteristics of Population,* 1995, 2000.

before being taken into custody has declined, from 54.5 percent in 1982 to 44 percent in 2000 (CDC, *Characteristics of Population,* various years).

At the bottom of the first and subsequent waves of new criminal legislation lurked a key contradiction. On the one hand, the political rhetoric, produced and reproduced in the media, concentrated on the need for laws and prisons to control violence. "Crime" and "violence" seemed to be identical. However, as table 5 shows, there was a significant shift in the controlling (or most serious) offenses for those committed to the CDC, from a preponderance of violent offenses in 1980 to nonviolent crimes in 1995. More to the point, the controlling offenses for more than half of 1995's commitments were nonviolent crimes of illness or of illegal income producing activity: drug use, drug sales, burglary, motor vehicle theft.

The outcome of the first two years of California's broadly written "three strikes" law presents a similar picture: in the period March 1994–January 1996, 15 percent of controlling offenses were violent crimes, 31 percent were drug offenses, and 41 percent were crimes against property (N = 15,839) (Christoper Davis et al. 1996). The relative surplus population comes into focus in these numbers. In 1996, 43 percent of third-strike prisoners were Black, 32.4 percent Latino, and 24.6 percent Anglo. The deliberate intensification of surveillance and arrest in certain areas, combined with novel crimes of status, drops the weight of these numbers into particular places. The chair of the State Task Force on Youth Gang Violence expressed the overlap between presumptions of violence and the exigencies of everyday reproduction when he wrote: "We are talking about well-organized, drug-dealing, dangerously armed and *profit-motivated* young hoodlums who are engaged in the vicious crimes of murder, rape, robbery, extortion and kidnapping *as a means of making a living*" (Philibosian 1986: ix; emphasis added). The correspondence between regions suffering deep economic restructuring, high rates of unemployment and underemployment among men (cf. S. L. Myers 1992), and intensive surveillance of youth by the state's criminal justice apparatus present the relative surplus population as the problem for which prison became the state's solution (see also Males 1999).

INDUSTRIALIZING PUNISHMENT

As should be clear by now, surplus state capacity is not an absolute thing, but rather a quality that can emerge over time as a result of the difference between what states can do *technically* and what they can do *politically*. Technical capacity does not disappear even when certain practices lose legitimacy in the eyes of voters, or capitalists, or other key interests. The idea here is not that there are idle bureaucrats on "pause" waiting for someone to hit "play," but rather, more modestly, that power is not a thing but rather a relationship based on actually existing activities. Thus, the renovation of surplus state capacity, the putting into motion of its potential power, is grounded in contradictory political economic conditions—conditions that are at once enabling and constraining. The successful political promotion of fear of crime as *the* key problem, and the ideological legitimacy of the U.S. state as the institution responsible for defense at all levels, allowed California to act (cf. R. W. Gilmore 2002a). The state could build prisons, but not just anywhere. The state could borrow money, but not always openly. The state could round up persons who correspond demographically to those squeezed out of restructured labor markets, but not at the same rate everywhere. After twenty years, $5 billion in capital outlays, and the accumulation of 161,394 prisoners (as of April 2004),[26] the CDC has become the state's largest department, with a budget exceeding 8 percent of the annual general fund—roughly equal to general fund appropriations for postsecondary education.

The rapid growth of the CDC in the 1980s, aided by the cooperation of police, city councils, county supervisors, district attorneys, and legislators, prompted agency critiques that focused not on justice but rather on efficiency. Was the CDC fulfilling its mandate in the most cost-effective manner? The critiques did not discuss whether crime was, indeed, the central social problem for state action, nor did they refer to the post-1980 decline in crime rates—even incorrectly to claim that prisons work. The Legislative Analyst's 1986 report "The New Prison Construction Program at Midstream" proposed streamlining features of the CDC's design, bid, and build system in order to gain cost savings and have new beds available when the projected shortfalls were expected to occur. The report also criticized the department's planning and productivity, whose weaknesses, according to the analyst, derived in part from variables associated with consulting, siting, and scheduling problems. The report revealed the dialectics of politics and economics that shaped the prison expansion program from the start. It characterized the department's productivity shortfall as the result of an insufficiently rationalized process and recommended that the legislature take charge of moving the department into greater efficiency through "milestones" (or "speedup") from concept through occupancy—in effect, by legislating efficiency (LAO 1986: see esp. 43–45).

The year 1990 saw a major turn in the political atmosphere: voters approved a prison construction GOB in April but then roundly defeated another prison GOB the following November. In 1990 and 1991, reports prompted by the Legislative Analyst's 1986 report suggested that the CDC could do a better job of forecasting the types of prisoners it would have in custody, and therefore do a better job budgeting for expanded capacity. As noted earlier, the CDC has consistently forecast high growth in highest-security (Level IV) prisoners, and, according to both the Blue Ribbon Commission on Prison Population Management (1990) and Rudman and Berthelsen (reporting to the legislature in 1991), it consolidated the tendency to classify those in custody as higher risks than they might actually be.[27] Level IV beds are the most expensive to build; and Level IV prisoners are the most expensive to maintain, because of low guard-prisoner ratios.

In 1991, California experienced what turned out to be a temporary decline in the number of arrests leading to felony convictions, but when James Gomez, who had assumed the CDC director's mantle the year before, was asked by a reporter to comment on the news, he expressed concern that a drop in actual prisoners from forecast numbers might adversely affect the department's construction program (Hurst 1991b). Growth and efficiency were the primary considerations in the view of this career bureaucrat, who had been hired by the department for his experience managing large budgets and staffs and for his planning skills (SPWB 1985). The ideological and material processes at work made Gomez's shocking response on some level an expression of common sense.

Crime topped most polls as public anxiety number one in 1991—perhaps because of the sudden rise in violence following the U.S. victory in the Persian Gulf (R. W. Gilmore 2002a; Archer and Gartner 1984)—even though California was deep into its worst recession since the Great Depression (Walker 1995). Indeed, the recession brought about a temporary decline in arrests, because urban police forces under emergency budgetary constraints decided not to pursue drug users and some other categories of arrestable people (Hurst 1991a, 1991b). The lull in arrests did not last, however, and law enforcement around the state reintensified across-the-board surveillance and arrests in 1992, prompted by the general crackdown following the Los Angeles uprising in April of that year (Mike Davis 1993b, 1993c). The CDC ratcheted up forecasts again, and the legislature approved $985 million in LRBs, which were issued in 1993 (SPWB 1993a, 1993b, 1993c, 1993d). Consistently, from 1982 to 1996, the CDC had six to ten new prisons in some stage of planning, design, or construction, at an average cost per establishment of a quarter-billion dollars.

The size, cost, and complexity of CDC construction and operations prompted a new round of critical studies, published in the spring of 1996. The California Department of Finance Performance Review cited the department for lax attention to budget lines and for outsourcing functions, such as medical care, that could more efficiently, and cost-effectively, be internalized by the department inside prison walls (CDF 1996). The CDC's enormous operating budget is also a rather flexible one, and the department has been able to move costs among line items during a fiscal year. Thus, funds designated for prisoners' medical expenses can be used to pay guards' overtime, when guards escort prisoners to outside facilities for treatment. In the CDF report, guards' overtime constituted a general cause for concern, with the department following U.S. big-firm industrial practice by requiring lots of overtime rather than expanding the size of benefit-basis staff (CDF 1996; cf. Harrison 1994; David Gordon 1996; Henwood 1997). The CDF pointed out that straight-time pay to permanent part-time guards (reserves) would be cheaper than overtime pay to the average rank-and-file benefit-basis guard (CDF 1996). The overtime issue focused both on the cost of overtime and on the CDC's failure adequately to plan for staffing needs.[28] The issue of planning was, for the CDF, a sign that the CDC, the state's agency of control, was itself out of control, and might require the kind of direct oversight by another agency—such as the CDF—that it had been exempted from for the previous fourteen years (CDF 1996; LAO 1986; cf. Gregory Hooks 1991).

The second critical study published in 1996, commissioned by the University of California, brings into sharper focus the intrastate competition that the CDC's growth had produced (Ashley and Ramey 1996). The report demonstrates how rival agencies tried, via critique, to situate themselves at the CDC's trough.

David Ashley and Melvin Ramey, professors of civil and environmental engineering from UC Berkeley and UC Davis, respectively, took on the question of capital cost reduction. As with the earlier studies, the central *problem* remained crime and its mitigation through imprisonment, and the *solution* turned on cost-effectiveness in the design-bid-build sequence for prison construction—rather than any reevaluation of, for example, the relation between crimes (old or new), education, and recidivism (Ashley and Ramey 1996; cf. Rudman and Berthelsen 1991). The unspoken power of this study lies in the way the university presents itself, via its sober, analytical engineering faculty, as an eminently efficient institution. Certainly, the university had been struggling to transform its image from that of a product of Progressive Era–through–Cold War social welfare activism to that of a competitive knowledge factory increasingly responsive to market forces (R. W. Gilmore 1991).[29] To that end, in 1995 the Regents of the University of California formally shed affirmative action over the objections of faculty, staff, students, and senior administration at the university's nine campuses, because, in the race-neutral language of racism, affirmative action is an inefficient (nonmarket) mode of resource allocation. The pitched competition between the CDC and all others dependent on the general fund seems to have prompted the university to criticize the CDC in such a way that the university itself would become a necessary player in the CDC project as a supplier of efficiency expertise, while freeing up funds for other productive state activities.

Community colleges approached cooperation more straightforwardly than did the elite University of California. The number of applicants for prison guard jobs was consistently high during the 1980s and 1990s, with as many as 200 competing for each apprentice slot. To tighten the pool, and to enhance the professional specialization associated with being a guard, the CCPOA, in conjunction with the CDC, determined that new recruits after July 1, 1995, should be minimally armed with an approved A.S. degree in correctional science before reporting for basic training at the department's Richard McGee Training Facility. Community colleges throughout the state in the immediate labor market of new prisons, such as West Hills College in Coalinga, instituted A.S. degree programs with the explicit aim of both preparing new applicants for apprentice appointments and educating current guards, who become eligible for raises and promotions after completing the program (West Hills Community College District 1996). The colleges hoped that in addition to enhancing enrollments, the program would give local residents a better chance of filling one of the state's best working-class career slots. They also provided basic orientation for all new guards and some training for reserves (permanent part-time officers); for all enrollments, they charged the state general fund according to average daily attendance (ADA), as they would do with any other academic program (West Hills Community College District 1996; LAO 1996).[30]

The new degree requirement for guards, with a prescribed curriculum, illustrates one tendency of the state's burgeoning punishment system to both specialize and centralize staff and functions (cf. Chandler 1990). Professional expertise and technical specialization in the governmental sector is not new, having evolved over several generations from the Progressives' movement to make the state at once immune to corruption and more active in people's everyday lives (see, for examples, G. E. Gilmore 1996; Linda Gordon 1994; Hooks 1991), and from capital's need to spread out the costs of developing productive infrastructure and controlling labor to as many pockets and balance sheets as possible (O'Connor 1973; Piven and Cloward 1971; Woods 1998). We have seen that the legislature established permanent committees to review the proliferating crime bills. In addition, after 1993, the legislature slowly moved toward rationalizing and unifying the state's trial court system, with the goal of making the jurisdictions more uniform, efficient, and cost-effective (LAO 1993, 1996).

In the manner of a modern industrial enterprise (Chandler 1990), the CDC further embraced the move toward centralization and functional specialization by establishing an internal finance capital department headed by Tom Dumphy, the underwriter who helped devised the LRB solution to the politics of debt issuance. Dumphy's appointment responded to allegations of inefficiency by having an expert on staff who could guide the structure and sale of either LRBs or GOBs and enable the CDC to issue competitive rather than negotiated bonds. The move came at a time when the difference between negotiated and competitive bond costs, while still measurable, had dropped (Simonsen and Robbins 1996). However, the key argument for setting up the office was the CDC's forecasting, which continued to project severe shortfalls in prison capacity a decade into the twenty-first century (CDC 1996; LAO 1996). The "midstream" in the title of the Legislative Analyst's 1986 report seems to have been a moving metaphor, with the CDC never more than halfway to completion of its project.[31]

PIGS GET FATTENED, BUT HOGS GET SLAUGHTERED

In the summer of 1996, rival power blocs staged a showdown in Sacramento. On one side were Governor Pete Wilson, James Gomez, director of the California Department of Corrections (CDC), and Don Novey, president of the California Correctional Peace Officers' Association (CCPOA), who sought to issue $1.6 billion dollars in lease-revenue bonds to build six new prisons. The other bloc, led by the powerful Democratic State Senators Bill Lockyer (Hayward) and Dan Boatwright (Contra Costa), had rejected the CDC's request, approved by the governor and promoted by the CCPOA.

On the heels of the deeply critical performance reviews by the CDF and the University of California, the *Los Angeles Times* published an exposé about the extraordinary number of prisoners shot dead by guards in Corcoran, one of the state's two new supermax facilities. Such sudden, intense, and unfavorable scrutiny puzzled the CDC director. For most of the prior fifteen years, the CDC had been California's fastest-growing department, with an operating budget that had grown to nearly 10 percent of the state's general fund. The CDC prison construction project was, according to a number of analysts, the largest in the world. Strategists envisioned packaging the design, engineering, and contracting successes that emerged from the experience of building nearly two dozen new small-city–sized complexes, and selling the Golden State prison plan to the rest of the United States and abroad.

Director Gomez asked his political boss, Senator Boatwright, then JLCPCO chair, what the department could possibly be doing wrong suddenly to attract so much negative attention— after so many years as the state's darling agency. According to an eyewitness, the senator replied in his dry, Arkansas-bred drawl, "Aw Jim! Don't you know? Pigs get fattened, but hogs get slaughtered!" (R. Bernard Orozco, interview, 1996). But was it yet a fully grown hog? Surpluses that accumulated in California, combined with the state's need to legitimate itself in the face of profound fiscally expressed voter disapproval, enabled the CDC to expand into the state government's largest department. As in the rest of the United States, crime became firmly established as a permanent problem, for which the solution is the continued proliferation of laws, courts, judges, bailiffs, law enforcement personnel, technologies of surveillance, helicopters, and other means of domestic warfare, including, of course, prisons. And yet, as Dan Boatwright pointed out to the dispirited James Gomez, something that got as big as the CDC would sooner or later come up against a limit to growth. Why? At least theoretically, because the variably assessed returns on investment—in legitimacy, in safety, in securing the Central Valley voters or local economies, or big-rancher contributions—would dwindle to a margin no longer worth the costs.

The combatants who lined up on opposing sides in Sacramento represented several perspectives on the future of the CDC hog. Some thought it should reproduce smaller versions of itself at lower levels around the state. Others thought it should be sold while the market for hogs was good. And still others thought it should just grow as big as it might. How to decide? Those who favored putting the GOB on the ballot wanted the voters to tell them what to do. The opponents of that plan insisted that the voters had spoken again and again and unequivocally empowered the state to determine the correct path.

Bill Lockyer and Dan Boatwright were determined to test the

CDC's (and their own) legitimacy by putting the first prison GOB in six years on the November 1996 ballot. Don Novey and his union, the CCPOA, aligned with Governor Pete Wilson, were afraid that if the voters said no, the prison expansion program would be hamstrung, because few legislators would be brave enough to pass an LRB immediately after a negative referendum on prison debt. Wilson decided not to fight Lockyer and Boatwright, Gomez started to look for a new job, and the CCPOA, one of the state's largest political donors, circulated a 400-page report on the most efficient way to build and staff new facilities, endorsed by testimonials from CCPOA-funded victims' associations, the National Rifle Association, and other such experts around the nation.[32]

Lockyer formed a bipartisan, bicameral Prison Reform Conference Committee to figure out how Sacramento could free itself from across-the-board primary responsibility for punishment (PRCC 1996). In the scenario that Lockyer proposed, "reform" meant both rationalizing and extending the system further, filling in the gaps between the homes and streets where prisoners come from, and the state cages where they serve time, with an assortment of community and county-based surveillance, custody, punishment, and treatment structures and programs (PRCC 1996). The vertical integration envisioned in the reform plan returned the responsibility for dealing with certain types of convictions, such as drugs, routinely committed as felons to the CDC, back to local law enforcement, promising that Sacramento would foot the bill, at least at the outset.[33] The CDC's average daily cost of keeping a prisoner in the system has hovered around $59; Lockyer intended to give that amount to local and county jurisdictions that come up with plans for dealing with people who might be supervised outside CDC facilities. There was an incentive; successful jurisdictions would not need to spend the full $59 per prisoner retained. Thus, if a prisoner were sentenced to a program of drug testing and day reporting, at a daily cost of $12 for staff, equipment, and facilities, the jurisdiction could keep the balance and use it for whatever law enforcement needs it might have (PRCC 1996).[34]

While the Lockyer plan seemed to promise an end to the endless expansion of prison cells, it still depended on forecasts of ever-growing numbers of criminals eligible for the lockup. The plan also called for construction of two more state facilities (E. G. Hill 1996, in PRCC 1996). The plan also recapitulated, at the state level, the ways and means that federal programs, from welfare to crime control, are being pushed down the political scale with near-term funds attached. In the case of crime, legal, fiscal, and programmatic linkages form an unbroken criminalization armature across every conceivable landscape of the future. In other words, surplus and crisis reemerged, at this conjuncture, in the form of too many prisoners on the one hand—products of the earlier surpluses—and on the other, a changing sense of the CDC's ongoing legitimation to expand, rather than simply refine, technologies of incarceration.

For Dan Boatwright, who "termed out" of the Senate at the end of 1996, and other fiscal conservatives in the legislature, privatization was the proper route to take. In April 1996, the Senate held hearings on SB 2156, a bill to establish a "Correctional Facilities Privatization Commission" to sell bonds to build private prisons, and to lease private space for prisoners (SB 2156, April 16, 1996). Those in attendance to support privatization included representatives from the United States' largest prison operators in the private sector: Wackenhut and Corrections Corporation of America, both of which hired former state employees to lobby Sacramento (Morain 1994c). When the bill got to the Senate floor later in the spring, it failed to pass, because, according to one observer, the "Republicans did not line up"—perhaps because the CCPOA had registered its unalterable opposition to privatization.[35] The CCPOA feared, rightly, that if the private sector were brought in, the new guards would be low-wage, nonunion workers, as is the case throughout the private security industry (Greene 2001; cf. Christie 1993).

The guards published their own plan, titled *Meeting the Challenge of Affordable Prisons: A Plan to Reduce the Cost of Building and Operating California Prisons to Ensure Incarceration of Violent and Habitual Offenders without Bankrupting Taxpayers* (CCPOA n.d. [1996]). The report's long title managed to condense, onto a bright red cover, all the key words in mainstream prison debate. The CCPOA's plan was to build "megaprisons"[36] that would each hold 20,000 people—up from the 2,500–6,000. The megaprisons would be built where there were already prisons—in places such as Delano and Corcoran—creating intensive districts (of which there are already several, although none so big as those proposed). Prisoners would do much of the building, thus saving labor costs. And, finally, the state would continue to fund prisons using LRBs, in the name of fiscal efficiency (CCPOA n.d. [1996]).

CONCLUSION

California began to come apart during the world recession of 1973–75. After a false boom in the late 1970s, fueled by federal outlays that created jobs in both the military and aerospace industries and at the community level, California entered a new phase of political and economic restructuring in the early 1980s, during which time the bifurcation between rich and poor deepened and widened. While profits rose, capital's need for new infusions of investment dollars was increasingly met out of retained earnings. Deep reductions in well-waged urban jobs that had employed modestly educated men of color—especially African Americans and Chicanos—overlapped with changes in rural industrial processes and a long drought. These forces produced surpluses of capital, labor, and land, which the state, suffering a prolonged period of delegitimation, manifested in the taxpayers' revolts, could not put back to work under its declining military Keynesian aegis (cf. Hall and Schwarz 1988). However, by renovating and making "critical already-existing activities" (Gramsci 1971: 330–31), power blocs in Sacramento and elsewhere throughout California did recombine these surpluses—and mixed them with the state's aggressive capacity to act—by embarking on the biggest prison construction program in the history of the world.

What has happened to each component, each surplus in this story? Have their crises been resolved? Finance capitalists achieved what they were after by issuing $5 billion in bonds for new prison construction, with more issues in the wings; while they did not make any more money than if they had raised the funds by precisely the same means to build schools or parks or anything else, state capacity to issue debt was circumscribed by defensible categories as (and through which) the role of government changed. Landowners concentrated in the agricultural counties have divested themselves of surplus acreage and brought in the state as local employer and local government sub-

sidizer. Labor remained divided, by race, region, and income—
while "taxpayers," who themselves are mostly working people,
used polling booth power inconsistently—sometimes but not always against "stranded communities" (Jacqueline Jones 1992) of
under- and unemployed people of color and white people who
have the highest risk of spending time in prison. Voter vagaries
suggest that even politician- and media-fueled fear embodies
contradictions, especially as prison and felony expansion touch
more and more households that once might have believed themselves immune. Did the new power blocs achieve total, unques-
tioned legitimacy?[37] The answer is embedded in the kinds of
practices this operationalization of state capacity have produced.
The JLCPCO was disbanded in November 2003. Yet there is no
end in sight for the elaborate, expensive, and constantly multi-
plied apparatuses of coercion and control developed in harmony
with, and sometimes by the makers of, the weapons of destruction produced for hot and cold warfare throughout the twentieth century (cf. Bartov 1996; Guérin 1994).[38]

FOUR

CRIME, CROPLANDS, AND CAPITALISM

O n Thursday, June 6, 1985, the *Corcoran Journal* (Kings County) ran a picture on page 4 of César Chavez and a local union organizer, César Arviszu, speaking to an attentive group of people, whose burnished faces, well-worn visored caps, and deep squint lines around the eyes indicated they worked outdoors in the sun. The caption identified "union organizers" and "Salyer employees" but did not mention Chavez by name. The United Farm Workers (UFW) was trying to organize field hands whose hourly pay had been cut from $6.35 to $4.75. The state's second-largest cotton grower with 77,000 acres in production, Salyer had recently defaulted on a loan from the Bank of America. To reduce operating costs, the family-owned firm dropped workers from direct employment, offering to rehire them immediately via contractors who would pay the lower rate.

In the same edition of the weekly newspaper, an enthusiastic front-page story reported that the Kings County Board of Supervisors had voted unanimously to ask the California Department of Corrections (CDC) to site a prison near Corcoran in order to aid the town's flagging economy. The crowd photographed at the supervisors' meeting—including, no doubt, some of the farmworkers who had met with Chavez and Arvisu—looked as attentive and grim as those considering the benefits and risks of voting to unionize. A few weeks later, Jim Hansen, scion of one of Corcoran's cotton oligarchs, drew an explicit connection between the two events during his speech at the town's annual Fourth of July picnic. "The community isn't the same as it was 15 or 20 years ago. . . . Agricultural mechanization is not going to stop; the farm economy is as bad as I've ever seen it. Corcoran needs another anchor as far as industry [is concerned]" (*Corcoran Journal,* July 4, 1985, 1).

As we have seen, the series of crises delineated in chapter 2 separated urban and rural communities from their industrial, cultural, and political moorings and produced surpluses of land, labor, finance capital, and state capacity. Chapter 3 showed in general ways how power blocs partially resolved these crises of surplus through prison expansion. Thirteen new prisons (plus five old facilities) light the night sky along the Central Valley's "prison alley"—a 375-mile stretch from Tehachapi to Folsom. The towns where the new prisons are located sought publicly capitalized development projects to "fix" the trends relentlessly surplusing significant segments of labor and land.

Corcoran, located in the depths of the alley, is typical of the new prison towns. Long dominated by a few firms in a single industrial sector, the town is majority Latino, unemployment and poverty are two to five times the statewide averages, and the land converted to prison use was formerly irrigated cropland.

Why did particular kinds of places embrace the prison fix?
How does a peculiar new outlay of state expenditure refigure the
landscape? Both questions can best be approached for any locality by looking closely at already existing political and social—as
well as economic—geographies, which I shall do by examining
Corcoran's history and transition in great detail. Then, after
looking at how unsatisfactorily prison-siting literature engages
locational conflict, I shall take up the strand of opposition—quite
slender in Corcoran—and follow it to other valley places where
different ways of thinking have emerged in the context of crime,
croplands, and capitalism.

Two prisons have been sited in Corcoran since 1985. The first
opened in February 1988, and the second received its first prisoners in the summer of 1997. Corcoran is one of four incorporated cities in Kings County (pop. 116,300). For more than forty
years, Kings has ranked with Madera, Kern, Tulare, and Fresno
among the six wealthiest agricultural counties in the United
States, as measured by capital investment and value of product
(Reisner 1986: 354). In the past quarter century, it has also consistently ranked near or at the bottom among the state's fifty-
eight counties in per capita income (CDF-CEI 1995). J. G.
Boswell Company, the world's largest cotton producer, has its
California headquarters in Corcoran (pop. 8,800), where the California Department of Correction (CDC) facilities held more
than 12,600 in April 2000.

If, in order to understand the prison fix, we must develop
complex understandings of how prisoners became so massively
available as carceral objects, we must likewise figure out how the
ground the prisons stand on becomes available for such a purpose. In both contexts, changing relations of power and belong-

ingness, mixed with uneven capacities for mobility (another way to think about political economy in an everyday way) set the stage for ordinary working people to accept extraordinary measures in hope of securing livelihoods. What is the history that produced such a mismatch in wealth in Kings County? What were the local manifestations of statewide restructurings? Why did the city seek a prison as the solution? Who benefited? What were the unforeseen consequences of the prison construction project? How has the coming of the prison affected Corcoran as a place? What else might have happened?

GROWTH

No matter how familiar one may be with "rural" California, it is always rather surprising to note the manners and appearance of the gentry who step forward to speak in the name of "the farmers" at Legislative hearings in Sacramento. The California "farm industrialist" . . . wears a neat Stetson, travels in an airplane, and has the breezy manners and the swagger of a Texas cattle king.

CAREY MCWILLIAMS, *SOUTHERN CALIFORNIA: AN ISLAND ON THE LAND* (1946)

The history of Kings County cotton features rapid centralization and concentration in an industry that began to expand throughout the southern San Joaquin Valley shortly after World War I. The boll weevil's long devastation of the traditional cotton belt across the U.S. South (Marks 1989) presented an opportunity for western growers to seize a share of an enormous transnational market, provided they could match California's capacities to the requirements of the crop (Daniel 1981; Pisani 1984; Weber 1994).

The firms that achieved dominance, and absorbed their competitors, were the first in the cotton industry to develop the attributes of the modern industrial enterprise (cf. Chandler 1990). Large firms' access to capital enabled them to install the large-scale irrigation systems necessary for mass production of the water-intensive crop; the resultant economies of scale, enhanced by labor-saving machines such as tractors (Weber 1994), lowered unit costs, while keeping competitors out with high entry costs (Pisani 1984; Reisner 1986; Gottlieb 1988; Hundley 1992). They also successfully coordinated California cotton into a highly standardized crop; the uniform use of Alcala seeds removed some of the uncertainty from agricultural production, enabling producers and dealers to promise customers the same type and quality of cotton year after year (Weber 1994). And vertical integration of functions and operating units, overseen by professional managers, allowed producers to control supplies, financing, processing, sales, marketing, and distribution of the product to national and international markets (Pisani 1984; Weber 1994).

The region's extensive agricultural workforce was key to the industry's growth: although cotton production shifted steadily toward machines, in the years the crop came to dominate Kings County, it was both capital- and labor-intensive (Daniel 1981; McWilliams 1946; Mitchell 1996).[1] In the nineteenth century, the thousands of Chinese and other workers who had mined gold and built railroads and infrastructure, Mexicans dispossessed by U.S. colonials, and Anglo homesteaders ruined by the high cost of acquiring water or moving products from farm to market by railroad, formed the nucleus of the region's agricultural proletariat. These workers were, in turn, augmented by twentieth-century long-distance migrants of all ethnicities (Daniel 1981).

Four families gained control of the Tulare Lake Basin productive landscape by the end of World War I (Preston 1981; Weber 1994; Mitchell 1996). The Boswell, Salyer, Hansen, and Guiberson clans achieved the transformation "from family farm

to agribusiness" (Pisani 1984) by mixing private capital with social and political power. State intervention was crucial to guarantee the basin's geography of accumulation. Indeed, under federal, state, and railroad land ownership schemes and public and
private irrigation projects, the geography into which they intro-
duced cotton had already been extensively reworked by rural
wage laborers into a region increasingly characterized by extensive holdings (Preston 1981; Mitchell 1996). The Jeffersonian
ideal of white family farmers tending small, general-production
farms, struggled against, but lost out to, the parallel development
of large capitalist farms producing commodity crops (Preston
1981; Daniel 1981; Pisani 1984).

Boswell emerged as the most powerful of the cotton capitalists (Arax and Wartzman 2003). The firm's founder, Colonel
J. G. Boswell, was a cotton merchant descended from a Georgia
plantation family that had become rich in the slave economy. He
worked in Arizona and Los Angeles cotton trading centers before settling in Corcoran in 1924, where he bought a 400-acre
ranch, at a time when 90 percent of San Joaquin Valley farms
were smaller than 160 acres (Weber 1994; Hundley 1992). The
company expanded, integrating backward from distribution into
ginning and financing, as well as growing (Weber 1994). Well
capitalized from the start, Boswell acquired thousands of acres
during the 1920s and 1930s through purchases, mergers, and tax
sales, as well as by taking title to lands securing defaulted loans;
by 1940, the company was the biggest business in the county.
Thenceforward, the family was the dominant political and philanthropic force in Corcoran, while the company became a powerful agribusiness on a national scale (Gottlieb 1988; Weber 1994;
Arax and Wartzman 2003).

By 1933, 45 percent of cotton crops were financed by the ginners, who themselves had direct access to bank-based capital. Financier-ginners exerted direct control over small growers: the annual loan fixed the price of the product and guaranteed business for the gins (Weber 1994). Under these debt relations, smaller growers could not compete, and many were "proletarianized" on their own land—when they did not lose it altogether—growing cotton for a preset price, not unlike a wage (Weber 1994; cf. Watts 1994b). Other small producers lost their land via tax defaults when their profits were too meager to satisfy both financiers and tax assessors (Weber 1994; Goldman 1991).[2]

In 1925, the big cotton interests were able to squeeze out smaller competitors and other crops by skillfully exploiting the state's regulatory capacities. Kings County ginners, merchants, and large growers, along with their counterparts in Kern and Fresno Counties, the utility companies, and dominant valley lender, the Bank of Italy,[3] persuaded the California legislature to pass the "one variety law" making Alcala cotton the Central Valley's only legally cultivable strain (Weber 1994). Alcala had been developed by the U.S. Department of Agriculture for use in World War I matériel—tires and airplane wings. Those who promoted the single-variety rule praised Alcala for its long, strong staple, which made ginning and milling it easy. Processors could be assured of a product that would not gum up their works, and with standardization, they would not have to rejig the machinery for each grower's load. With input costs set by the ginners' financing mechanism, and speedy processing set by the one-variety law, the larger industrialized cotton firms could as-

sure their customers of more reliable prices and delivery than
could any smaller growers (Weber 1994; Bean 1973; cf. Chandler
1990).

As California cotton became an enormous, concentrated, and
centralized commodity crop, it became more vulnerable to labor
and other market fluctuations, and also to labor militancy
(Daniel 1981; Weber 1994). Growers organized privately, as well
as through the state's coercive and infrastructural capacities, to
push the agricultural proletariat into and out of fields on sched-
ule (Mitchell 1996; Weber 1994; Bulosan 1983; McWilliams
[1939] 1969), and to take hiring and wages out of competition
(Weber 1994).[4] To supplement the material powers of state and
capital, governmental activists—such as California's Progressives (Mitchell 1996)—and agricultural industrialists employed
the ideological capacity of white supremacy to justify the degra-
dations of farmworker life and to produce or reinforce divisions
between and among Mexican, Chinese, Filipino, Anglo, African,
and Japanese workers (Bulosan 1973; Gregory 1989; Almaguer
1994; Weber 1994; Mitchell 1996; cf. Saxton 1971). Some workers, particularly dispossessed dustbowl Anglos ("Okies"), promoted these divisions to advance their own belongingness as en-
franchised white Americans (Gregory 1989; Morgan 1992). But
there were others who had participated in radical, nonagricultural industrial politics, not only in the United States
(McWilliams [1939] 1969; Weber 1994) but in U.S. colonies such
as the Philippines (Bulosan 1983) and in the ongoing struggles of
revolutionary and postrevolutionary Mexico, who formed alliances in the Central Valley fields (Weber 1994).

In Kings County, Mexican, Anglo, and African workers allied

to fight deadly battles for adequate wages, for decent temporary living conditions, and for the right to establish permanent residence in the area (Weber 1994; Mitchell 1996). Strikes shut down harvests in 1933 and again in 1938–39. In the early years of the New Deal, California agricultural labor activism and its brutal suppression by county, state, and farmer vigilante forces (McWilliams [1939] 1969) provoked some movement toward extending the Wagner Act to farmworkers, and the conditions at Corcoran provided an occasion for congressional investigation (Weber 1994; see also Mitchell 1996). However, the investigation produced no statutory changes, in part because the New Deal had already excluded agricultural labor from the right to organize. The federal failure to sanction suppression in effect strengthened the industrialists' position (Weber 1994). The outcome in cotton's favor resulted in part from how the overarching New Deal labor compromise had operationalized reformist politics by renovating structures of the racial state: the division of the rights to organize and bargain between agricultural and nonagricultural workers was also a normative (although by no means absolute) division of rights between workers of color and white workers (Jacqueline Jones 1992; Linda Gordon 1994).

World War II drew most of the Anglo farmworkers from the fields into wartime industries or uniforms (Gregory 1989; Morgan 1992). To replace them, California's farmers persuaded the federal government to institute the bracero program (1942–65) supplying contract Mexican "guest workers," which undermined the last major California organizing effort in the 1940s and kept agricultural labor on its knees for nearly two decades (Calavita 1992).

As Boswell, Salyer, and other major cotton growers expanded

production in the 1940s, they needed to secure abundant water in the relatively dry valley. Nineteenth-century California growers had tried to enter the undersupplied cotton market during the Civil War, but failed to bring more than 2,000 acres into production because of inadequate irrigation (Caughey 1940). The Tulare Lake Basin of the southern San Joaquin Valley overlies a deep fossil aquifer derived from glacial meltwater and rain, with a mean annual precipitation of about ten inches, ranging from four to nineteen inches (Preston 1981). All that means is that the water table needs surface water from rivers and canals to supplement—and perhaps in the long run replace—the subterranean supply (Reisner 1986; El-Ashry and Gibbons 1988; Howitt and Moore 1988).[5]

Prior to cotton's ascendancy, the 1902 Federal Water Reclamation Act changed the scale and cost of water production by developing "surplus" (i.e., not yet domestically or commercially exploited) water for farmers throughout the arid West (Reisner 1986; Hundley 1992). Water districts seeking cheap development dollars cropped up everywhere (Pisani 1984). Early on, the act's acreage limitation (160 per farmer, or 320 per farming couple)[6] for purchasers of subsidized developed water drove down the average farm size (Pisani 1984; Hundley 1992), but it crept back up again as politically astute capitalist growers—including Boswell and Salyer—disguised their illegal holdings within contractual blinds such as "land lease out lease back agreements" (Reisner 1986) and "farm management arrangements" (Gottlieb 1988; see also Pisani 1984; Hundley 1992).[7]

At the beginning of World War II, in order to supplement the water developed by the 1935 Bureau of Reclamation Central Valley Project (Reisner 1986), Boswell and Salyer exploited federal interagency strife between the Departments of the Interior and War to get what they wanted. While Interior, responsible for administering the Reclamation Act, continued to press for acreage limitations—whether or not they were complied with—War, responsible for the Army Corps of Engineers ("the Corps"), was looking for large-scale projects to raise its profile and legitimacy on the domestic front (Reisner 1986; Hundley 1992; Arax and Wartzman 2003).

Boswell and Salyer and their Kern County counterparts, Miller-Lux and the Kern Land Company, persuaded the Corps that the Kings and Kern Rivers (which drained, respectively, into the Tulare and Buena Vista Lakes) were flood hazards that threatened the economic well-being of southern San Joaquin Valley agriculture. According to spheres of influence established by the 1902 Federal Reclamation Act, surplus water constituted a national public good, and any federal project to dam and divert water in the western United States came under the aegis, and acreage limitations, of the Bureau of Reclamation (Hundley 1992).[8] However, the Corps agreed to handle the "problem," and without prior authorization from the Roosevelt administration or Congress, built the initial diversion gates in 1942 (Reisner 1986).

Armed with evidence showing no flood danger, and a study showing the culturally depressive effects of large capitalist farmers on small towns, the bureau was prepared to fight the Corps, believing it could activate East-West animosity in Congress in support of its position. But in wartime Washington, the bureau could not summon much interest in a domestic problem, against the War Department, or against productive capitalists (Hundley 1992; cf. Hooks 1991). The Corps, in turn, backed by Senator

Sheridan Downey (D–Calif.), accused the bureau of communism for fighting against big capital on behalf of small family farmers (Reisner 1986; Hundley 1992; see also Downey 1947). The controversy did not stall Boswell and Salyer's growth; since they already owned the lake, its drainage gifted them 80,000 fecund acres. The political struggle over the water was finally resolved when they paid $14,250,000 as a "one-time user fee" for Pine Flat Dam, built by the Corps at a cost of $48 million in 1948. The payment entitled them to all the water, because it was not surplus developed for irrigation but rather a by-product of flood control (Preston 1981; Reisner 1986; Hundley 1992).[9]

In the 1960s, the California State Water Project, conceived and built during the administration of Governor Edmund G. "Pat" Brown, was designed to guarantee adequate water for the rapidly growing Southland well into the twenty-first century (Hundley 1992; Howitt and Moore 1988; Reisner 1986). However, since the California Aqueduct carried more water than Los Angeles Metropolitan Water District (Met) customers could use in the short run, valley growers persuaded the Met to sell them the surplus for the energy cost of delivery (Reisner 1986; Gottlieb 1988). Eligible purchasers were limited to those whose lands overlaid the San Joaquin aquifer, so that, in the long run, once Met customers required all the water, farmers could revert to well water and therefore not lose the capital they had sunk in their lands (Gottlieb 1988; Reisner 1986). As part of the agreement, the Met charged Southland customers the difference between the growers' cost ($4.50–$7.00 per acre foot) and the cost of production ($35 per acre foot) via a property assessment charged on top of monthly water bills.[10] In the Westlands Water District, encompassing Kings County, corporate growers benefiting from the lower cost included agricultural establishments of the Southern Pacific Railroad, the Standard, Bellridge, Tidewater, and Richfield Oil Companies, and the J. G. Boswell Company (Preston 1981; Reisner 1986; Hundley 1992).

Boswell and other Corcoran-based cotton producers used the state's capacities at the federal, California, and regional levels to transform their family firms into modern industrial enterprises. They exploited state power and social connections to standardize product and to move surface water and workers into their fields. They used interagency rivalries and patriotic rhetoric to gain position and renovated race ideology to secure what they had created. To the greatest extent possible, they externalized substantial costs to the state, to ratepayers in other regions, and to workers in order to guarantee the geography of accumulation for their "white gold" (Weber 1994; see also Arax and Wartzman 2003).

Workers in turn fought back, but their real gains as agricultural laborers in the cotton industry were difficult to sustain. The end of the bracero program (1965) coincided with the rise of the United Farm Workers, which, in spite of agriculture's specific exclusion from New Deal legislation, began to organize in ways reserved by law for nonagricultural industrial workers (Edid 1994; Pulido 1995). In its early years, the UFW targeted labor-intensive crops such as grapes and lettuce. Cotton was a much more difficult crop to organize in the mid 1960s than it had been in the prewar period, because the level of mechanization inaugurated in 1942 by the International Harvester reaper (table 6) had undermined labor's ability to shut down cotton fields at harvest time.

Some Mexicano/Chicano and African American workers

TABLE 6 MECHANIZATION OF COTTON PRODUCTION,
1940–1980

Year	Number of Labor Hours to Produce One Bale of Cotton
1940	423
1960	26
1980	8

SOURCE: Preston 1981.

who had migrated to the Central Valley during the depression settled in Corcoran during World War II (Weber 1994). Displaced by machines, and disorganized by the Bracero program, they were increasingly dispossessed as workers. But at the same time, their local residence established potential ground for future political struggles—at least in the realm of formal representation—as Mexicanos/Chicanos became Corcoran's numerical majority by the end of the golden age.

CRISIS: DEBT, DISASTERS, AND RESTRUCTURING

Sixty months of drought, commencing in 1973, culminated in California's third driest (1976) and driest (1977) years on record. The drought forced improvements in groundwater pumping and surface irrigation systems. Growers who could afford the capital outlays both upgraded existing fields and, hoping to eke out additional return from investment dollars, extended irrigation infrastructure to previously unimproved acres (Sokolow and Spezia 1992; U.S. Department of Agriculture, Census of Agriculture 1992). Experts warned, however, that expanded irrigation would lead to excessive use of groundwater (already in evidence during the drought), and eventually require some land to be permanently removed from production (Howitt and Moore 1988, 1992; El-Ashry and Gibbons 1988).

Salyer had become financially overextended in its bid to keep up with other corporate growers, particularly Boswell, in production intensity and efficiency. The company's investment timing was wrong; it had sunk borrowed capital into equipment and irrigation improvements right before a series of devastating El Niño winters (1978–79; 1979–80; 1982–83) when torrential rains delayed plantings, reduced usable acreage, and flooded crops (Reisner 1986).[11] The combined costs of dry years, flood years, and bigger and better John Deere harvesters pushed Salyer into default.

Boswell prospered through ten years of crazy weather, but drought-idled acres caused the firm to take action against future water shortages that would undermine the productivity of its 206,000-acre empire. In 1982, Boswell and Salyer formed a strategic political alliance, spending more than $1 million to defeat the Peripheral Canal—a California ballot initiative seeking voter approval for bonds to develop more water for the Southland. They opposed the measure because it included a constitutional amendment, fought for by some environmentalists, to shield all key Northern California rivers from future damming or diversion (Reisner 1986; Gottlieb 1988; Hundley 1992).

While the Peripheral Canal's defeat squelched the plan to protect the rivers, it also bespoke voters' unwillingness to pay for new water development projects. In the short run, then, Boswell and Salyer could not use the victory to get more subsidized water to the Tulare Lake Basin. At the same time, some water economists proposed that water scarcity would best be solved by a self-regulating water market, in which unsubsidized prices would compel users to be more efficient in the selection of crops and irrigation techniques (Howitt and Moore 1988, 1994). The growers did not want that solution either. Growers voluntarily or involuntarily took acres out of production in the 1980s because of problems with water supply, high debt, and, in some cases, federal payment-in-kind subsidies for *not* growing certain surplus crops (Reisner 1986).

Table 7 shows the extent to which Kings County farming was in the process of restructuring in the 1980s. Between 1982 and 1992 nearly 150,000 irrigated county acres came out of production. Salyer did not default alone; the valley's dominant lender, Bank of America, took title to thousands of collateral acres throughout the Central Valley in the early 1980s (Gottlieb 1988). At the same time, farms—especially those planted in cotton—concentrated in ownership. The contradictory movement of market value per acre (down) and productivity per acre (up) shows the general decline in nonurban income from the use of the land lamented by every county's farm bureau (Walters [1986]1992). The movement also suggests that the improvements to the *land* made at great expense during the 1970s drought (Sokolow and Spezia 1992) were successfully exploited via cultivation and harvest technologies—the constantly evolving mechanization Jim Hansen envisioned as the future of agribusiness. The explanation is supported by the fact that while there was virtually no change in the number of regular, year-round farm jobs in the county between 1973 (5,405) and 1983 (5,371), there was a small but significant increase between 1983 and 1993 (5,617) (U.S. Bureau of the Census, County Business Patterns). These jobs in-

TABLE 7 OVERVIEW OF KINGS COUNTY AGRICULTURE, 1982–1992

	1982	1987	1992
Agricultural acres	808,084	702,173	775,829
Average farm size (acres)	681	583	710
Market value of land and improvements per farm*	2,059	1,794	1,694
Farms, by acreage			
1–9	254	246	224
10–49	344	360	297
50–179	245	236	241
180–499	189	194	139
500–999	68	85	94
+1,000	87	83	97
Cropland farms	1,033	1,037	934
Cropland acres	613,693	566,245	519,526
Harvest crop farms	942	936	844
Harvest crop acres	567,425	441,602	431,212
Irrigated farms	1,011	997	865
Irrigated acres	554,114	476,037	409,507
Market value of agricultural production ($000)*	478,412	486,912	581,846
Cotton farms	464	481	364
Cotton acres	275,310	234,104	235,509
Cotton bales	589,237	535,565	627,189

SOURCE: U.S. Department of Agriculture, *Census of Agriculture*.
*Constant dollars: 1982 = 100.

clude managers, mechanics, and other skilled or professional positions that typically accompany increased investment in machinery (Bradshaw 1993; cf. Harrison 1994; David Gordon 1996).

The reconfiguration of Kings County agriculture indicates that the 1980s were crisis years both for growers—such as Salyer—and for workers—among whom seasonal farm labor unemployment ran between 30 and 50 percent (Walker 1995).[12] Cotton's deep delaborization was not offset by opportunities in other agricultural sectors; there was no increase in demand for seasonal agricultural labor, as measured in weeks of work, between 1970 and 1985 (Goldman 1991). On top of a stagnant job market, farm wages, averaging only 55 percent of California's nonfarm wages, had been flat since 1973 (Goldman 1991; Greenhouse 1997).

Unemployment and poverty did not provoke many people to move away permanently.[13] Rents were low, and those who had managed to buy modest houses and lots could not hope to sell to their equally poor neighbors. Corcoran residents continued their annual long-distance migration through the California and Pacific Northwest harvests. Some traveled even further afield, both to other states (onions in Utah, sugar beets in South Dakota) and sectorally (house framing in San Bernardino County). And finally, some workers followed still other patterns of labor-reserve circular migration, with younger people—single men, siblings, married couples—going to the Southland to work and sending remittances home to aging parents and children (cf. Ferguson 1990). However, the fragility of these various reproductive strategies is highlighted by the fact that in 1980, nearly 18 percent of Corcoran households were receiving public assistance—as compared with 13.7 percent for Kings County as a whole (Hornor 1988).

The decline in Corcoran's retail tax revenues through the late 1970s is another indicator of the town's diminished capacity to sustain itself. Prior to 1976, the ratio of the city's per capita sales tax to that of California as a whole—the "pull factor"—had been greater than 1, demonstrating that Corcoran retailers served a wider market than the average state town (Parks et al. 1990). Downtown's post-1976 defunct furniture, apparel, and other consumer goods establishments demonstrated both the dearth of items for sale in the city, and the lack of shoppers able to pay for the range and quantities of goods local retailers had once offered.

Corcoran's empty downtown and significant poverty also translated into declining property values for homeowners. Those who worked at somewhat secure jobs—whether or not in agribusiness—were concerned that they, like their poorer neighbors, could not sell even if they wanted to. In 1982, newspaper classified ads for houses like their own asked for 35 percent to 50 percent less than in 1978. On the evening news, by contrast, they heard how home equities in the Southland and the Bay Area, and to a lesser extent in Bakersfield and Fresno, were climbing in tandem with phenomenally high inflation.

People who lived in Corcoran stayed not only because economic adversity left them stuck in space, but also because they had struggled to make Corcoran their home, building a community that, while organized in a race and class hierarchy, was also a place proud of its small-town ethic of care. Mexicano/Chicano and African American subcultures flourished in the interstices of the dominant paternalistic Anglo social structure. Some marriage between Okies and Mexicanos weakened, but did not break down, the division between the two groups, who had, uneasily, allied at the forefront of the 1938–39 labor strikes (Weber

1994; Gregory 1989).[14] A single middle school and a single high school educated all the children who did not drop out; indeed, the most academically ambitious kids rarely transferred from Corcoran High School, because of the chance to compete for one of two full-tuition (price unlimited) four-year Boswell scholarships. And finally, nearly every adult in town who was not a Boswell, Salyer, Guiberson, or Hansen had, at some time in her life, if only for a summer, chopped Alcala cotton in the southern San Joaquin sunshine.

The restructuring of Corcoran's economy produced local surpluses. Debt and drought forced growers to idle land, while drought and mechanization made workers redundant. The city's built environment reflected the economic shifts. The tax base dwindled, pushed downward by derelict retail establishments as well as declining paychecks. Proposition 13 had already shrunken the taxable basis of real property. Capital lacked local markets because growers such as Salyer had pushed borrowing to the limit in the previous decade, whereas Boswell, continuing the march toward monopoly, had money in the bank and could finance expansion without recourse to crippling debt (Reisner 1986). The local state could not act to connect California's then-abundant finance capital with local surpluses because, in spite of its legal capacity to issue debt for public works, it lacked the tax base to pay off such loans: better-off homeowners were too wary, agricultural workers were too poor, and the dominant cotton empires were too impervious. Alternative medium-run development schemes—such as residential suburbanization—were not an option, because Corcoran lay outside Central Valley growth paths, as evidenced by the lack of commercial or individual takers for low-priced homes, empty buildings, and unbuilt land. In the aggregate, Corcoran's surpluses added to the city's crisis.

THE SEARCH FOR A PRISON FIX

As Corcoran's chronic unemployment translated into child poverty rates running above 30 percent, the challenge to secure the future propelled townspeople to request state intervention in the form of a multimillion dollar prison. In 1983, Corcoran learned that Avenal (pop. 4,137), in the nonproducing Kettleman Plains oilfields of western Kings County, had had a 3,000-bed prison authorized by the state legislature. That May, the Corcoran City Council directed the city manager, George Lambert, to ask County Supervisor Joe Hammond whether Sacramento might be amenable to siting a prison in Corcoran as well.

While appointed and elected officials lobbied in pursuit of legislative authorization for a Corcoran prison, the city also entered into dialogue with CDC Siting Office staff to gain a better sense of the costs and benefits of a prison as an economic development project. In the 1980s and 1990s, the CDC marketing professionals presented every new prison establishment as an open-ended good. The spiral-bound, clear-plastic-covered proposal they sent out to inquiring townsfolk was not a slick, flashy publication; rather, the photocopied document was simply written and neatly illustrated with maps, plans, and timelines. In a consistently optimistic tone, it enumerated the kinds of benefits a locality would gain from the facility, and what made the optimism persuasive was the modesty of the promises. A struggling working-class town such as Corcoran could make direct connections between what it *is* and what it might *be* if a prison were added to the local economic mix.

When the CDC promoted the economic development features of a prison, it promised both the short-term benefits associated with facility construction—jobs—and the long-term benefits derived from inserting a multimillion dollar allegedly recession-proof industry establishment into the local economy—growth. In the metaphorically twisted, but imaginatively catchy, phrase of CDC community relations professional Theresa Rocha, the "prison doors would unlock" the town from its persistent depression, by putting labor and real property back to work (Drew 1984: 1).

The following summary of potential benefits shows what Corcoran found so appealing about the prison, and why the prison development project seemed an appropriate foundation on which to rebuild the crumbling city (source for all items, unless otherwise noted: CDC 1994a):

· Land and construction. The CDC's proposal stipulates one section (640 acres) of relatively flat land per prison, but it ordinarily buys two or more (CDC 1990). While the benefit of the land sale would go to the seller, the ensuing $250 million dollar construction would create up to 900 temporary jobs of varying skill levels, some of which could be gained by Corcoran residents. The number of permanent positions for a typical new prison ranges from 800 to 1,600—depending on the completed facility's occupancy level—with the total split in half between guards and all other positions; the corresponding annual payroll is $30 to $50 million dollars. The CDC was frank with Corcoran concerning the prospects of current townspeople finding jobs at the prison. At new prisons, management and correctional officer (CO) work is assigned to veterans who apply for transfer from other prisons around the state; the extra pay given to staff at new facilities ensures that even an out-of-the-way location such as Corcoran obtains ample experienced personnel. However, every facility has a number of well-paying jobs—from automobile mechanics to X-ray technicians—featuring a wide range of skills that do not require prison experience.[15] In addition, the CDC estimated that the local job market would also gain 400–600 multiplier, or spin-off, employments—principally in food service and retail.

· Onetime mitigation funds. Onetime mitigation funds offset the infrastructural costs associated with a town's anticipated near-term growth. These mitigation funds, each of which would have to be legislated upon the recommendation of the Joint Legislative Committee on Prison Construction and Operations (JLCPCO), would pay part or all of the cost of expanding educational, sewage, water, road, and jail and courthouse capacities.

· Local purchases. The CDC annually spends from $1 to $4 million at area vendors for small but steady quantities of a broad assortment of ordinary goods, ranging from auto supplies to medical dressings, trophies, and signs. These expenditures would both stimulate local retail business and enhance tax revenues.

· Annual subventions. Sacramento allocates vehicle license, gasoline, and other taxes to counties and cities on a per capita basis, and counties and towns count prisoners in their populations. The subventions allocated per prisoner constitute windfall revenue, because prisons—and their occupants—receive all services directly from the state. The CDC estimated the city's share at $110,000 to $210,000.

· Donated labor. The CDC donates the labor of the lowest security (Level I) prisoners to the towns and counties allied with prisons. Typical tasks include cleaning parks and other public spaces, sprucing up school buildings, and repairing public property.

With all of this information to evaluate, the city council appointed a five-person committee in June 1984 to do an in-depth study of the proposed prison. The committee quickly expanded to ten because of the workload and to ensure representation of differing points of view. They met with Sacramento officials, siting consultants, and groups from other cities seeking prisons. The committee also took field trips to see for themselves what a prison town was like.

A delegation went to Susanville in Lassen County, site of the California Correctional Center—one of the state's last "original" prisons (built in 1954). Meeting with town and county representatives, the Corcoran committee learned that their hosts attributed the area's economic security to the facility and were actively seeking a new one.[16] In the report back to the city council, the delegation emphasized that greater Susanville had three shopping malls, as compared with none in the immediate Corcoran environs (the nearest was in Hanford, twenty miles away). The delegates saw in Susanville what they envisioned for their own town. These amenities included a wide variety of jobs suited to the local skills mix, opportunity for those seeking to advance in the CDC, and a broad middle-income stratum. What they failed to see was how a wide range of public sector (federal, state, county) jobs had for decades offset declines in ranching and resource-extraction incomes.

A study commissioned by the CDC (Lofting and Linton 1985) supported the view that well-paid prison-employed newcomers would enhance the town's economic and social profile and induce retail, entertainment, and residential investment. The report concluded that in the first two years of the prison's operation, Corcoran would gain more than 950 people in 353 households. The study also projected countywide retail revenues of about $3 million per year—well within the range of the CDC's proposed expenditures—some of which Corcoran could expect to capture if it had appropriate establishments in place. In short, it appeared that the prison would jump-start growth with a major infusion of new jobs and capital outlays and provide for sustained local development by way of prison-based and growth-induced jobs for both old and new residents.

But there was opposition. About 20 percent of the town formed an antiprison coalition centered around a tiny group representing some of the few remaining small Tulare Lake basin farmers. They objected to introduction of an economic development project that would change the nature of the town. Martha Owens lived south of Corcoran on a Bureau of Reclamation–compliant 160-acre ranch her grandfather had homesteaded, which the family had consistently refused to sell to Boswell. She maintained that the prison would make people who had always gotten along and welcomed strangers fearful of one another.[17] Nobody, pro or con, doubted that the prison would change Corcoran. However, as other residents pointed out, the prevailing sense of place included "our empty downtown! Why are you trying to preserve what's already dead?"

Many were afraid that inviting presumably dangerous people to settle in their midst, even behind a death fence, barbed wire, towers, guns, and bars, was a recipe for disaster. Owens, who lived alone, imagined escaped prisoners roaming the countryside. Diana Johnson, the CDC marketing representative assigned to Corcoran, assured residents that CDC escapes were extremely rare, having peaked in 1942, and that when prisoners do break out, they usually leave the area immediately (CDC 1992).[18] A trustee of the Corcoran Unified School District raised another fear—that the prison would bring along with it extramural trouble in the form of prisoners' families. "What support can we expect from the state with these families, such as counseling?" he asked. "Are you just going to dump them on us?" (*Corcoran Journal,* May 28 1987). In that room, as in much of U.S. society, nobody objected to stigmatizing prisoners' families, even though the law convicts individuals, not kin groups. The CDC spokesperson let the stereotype stand. Her answer to the second question was yes, but with a mitigating factor: because of the CDC's policy of moving prisoners among facilities with little or no notice, very few prisoners' families relocate to where their loved ones are incarcerated (CDC 1994b).

Several farmers were particularly concerned about water. Agriculture in the mid 1980s was in a slump, and smaller growers did not relish the prospect of competing with the CDC for water should future scarcity raise prices or necessitate direct rationing. The CDC assured the farmers that it would use fresh water sparingly and buy treated wastewater for most nondietary uses.

The antiprison activists, although few in number, were tenacious in trying to persuade others of the accuracy of their analysis. They held meetings at one another's homes, attended all public forums and council meetings, and wrote letters to the newspaper at every opportunity. Their activism provoked a great deal of acrimony, and people who had ordinarily been civil with each other engaged in public shouting matches at meetings, in restaurants, and on the street. Some actual or imagined minor acts of vandalism were tied to the prison controversy, and opponents of the project who complained of logs filched from woodpiles or fences tampered with accused their foes of unfair and unlawful escalation. The prison proponents' counteraccusations turned on status and location. Townspeople suggested that ranchers whose spreads were in unincorporated Kings County did not actually care about Corcoran's future but only about their own wellbeing and position. In other words, from the point of view of the boosters, the small growers, while in the shadow of Boswell and the rest of the cotton oligarchy, enjoyed economic independence from the city and its problems. The small growers were themselves seasonal employers, generally hiring from two to twelve people for two months or less (Reisner 1986; cf. Goldschmidt 1946). As the lead people seeking the prison were Anglos like their opponents, charges of racism did not surface explicitly in these confrontations. However, quietly and informally, people began to talk about the opponents' careless or willful disregard of underemployed Chicano and Black workers who desperately needed jobs. Issues of race and power surfaced openly later.

The pro- and antiprison forces in Corcoran were emphasizing different aspects of the city in their respective evaluations of a prison's likely impact on the town. The antiprison fears combined the stereotypically anticipated dangers with nostalgia for a town that in some ways had never existed. Prison boosters saw a development project commensurate with the locality's characteristics. The confrontations between factions were structured by already existing relations, although not all of the town's hierarchies were spotlighted as a result of the controversy. While small farmers came under some critical scrutiny, the powerful cotton clans did not; while poverty and joblessness were constant subjects of discussion, race and class were not.

CORRECTIONS COMES TO CORCORAN

The CDC identified three sites outside the city boundaries that appeared suitable—two to the north and one to the south. The sites to the north had the advantage of being close to the railroad and to the major east-west artery that runs between Interstate 5 and Highway 99—the Great Central Valley's principal roads running northwest. The third site, two miles south of town, was less suitable from a cost perspective because of the added distance along which materials for the facility would have to be hauled. In addition, while the south parcel was, indeed, relatively flat, its west side was plagued by a tendency to sink; to fix the problem, the CDC would have to spend extra money to lay drainage tile.[19]

In 1985, the CDC bought the least desirable of the three parcels from the J. G. Boswell Company. The sale enabled Boswell to get rid of 1,920 relatively poor acres that had been idled during the drought and again during the flood years at an estimated ten times what the sale price as farmland would have been.[20] The only other way of achieving such a markup would have been to sell to a residential or retail developer in the private sector, and developers would not have been attracted by unstable land. In any event, there had been no developers shopping for land in and about Corcoran for any reason, because in the mid

1980s, it was too far away to be a suburb of the growing Fresno-Clovis area to the northeast or the greater Bakersfield area to the south and much too close to compete with Hanford and Lemoore in the county. Boswell's problem in making a sale was the company's size; there was no larger competitor to take the land off its hands, and no smaller farmers could make this difficult area pay any better than the dominant cotton firm. Sacramento was a noncompeting entity large enough to absorb Boswell's surplus acres.

If the CDC's problem was simply to find relatively flat open space on which to build a prison, it had ample alternatives both around Corcoran and in the Central Valley as a whole. Corcoran had the two northern parcels, and there were also thousands of forfeited collateral acres around the valley that Bank of America was trying to sell (Gottlieb 1988), including, about eighteen months after the Boswell deal was complete, 40,000 of Salyer's 77,000 to which the bank held title.[21] Therefore, it seems not immoderate to conclude that the CDC's siting dilemma was not simply a problem of finding adequate space, but rather one of politics and therefore of place. Corcoran was a struggling working-class Tulare Lake basin town, populated by current and former agricultural workers striving to maintain and renew it. But Corcoran's quality as place was shaped by agribusiness oligopolies that had worked closely with, and exploited rivalries within, the state government at different levels over the century to achieve land and labor control, resource subsidies, and other forms of economic power, and that now sought a transformation of the local geography of investment that would complement, not compete with, cotton's continued dominance (cf. Woods 1998; Preston 1981).

Boswell's parcel came with Boswell power, which extended from the Kate G. Boswell Senior Center, where meetings to debate the prison were held, to the state legislature, where the bill to approve the Corcoran prison put the project on a fast track, so that monies were appropriated, environmental review waived, studies concluded, and construction begun before prisons with earlier approval had even gotten out of the rudimentary planning stage (LAO 1986). In the legislature, Assemblyman Jim Costa climbed the punishment ladder to the California Senate by siting three prisons in his district in the 1980s (Corcoran, Avenal, and Coalinga), sponsoring three more in the 1990s (Corcoran II, Delano II, and California City), and co-authoring high-profile pieces of criminal law—most notably the 1994 "three strikes" act.

The legislature's approval of the prison propelled Corcoran into a phase of anticipatory development that lasted through the prison construction and into the first year of operation. The CDC's projections, set forth in a department-commissioned study by a planning research firm (Lofting and Linton 1985), indicated that the city should prepare for higher than normal growth in the near term. The expectation was that 20 percent of CDC employees at the new facility would make their homes in Corcoran. Developers put up new housing, and the city borrowed $1.2 million to build new civic buildings and spruce up Whitley Avenue, the main thoroughfare, in advance of the retail outlets that were expected to revive the empty storefronts there. Shiloh Inns developed a motel on Whitley, and the Chamber of Commerce started making inquiries into the possibility of getting a fast food franchise, such as MacDonald's, in the city.

As was the case in Avenal, Corcoran ground rent rose during the pre-prison period (just under two years), even as it fell in the surrounding county. In both cities, lack of demand pushed prices back down to pre-siting levels—although rents stayed about 15 percent higher than before the boom (Parks et al. 1990). Avenal's failure to attract prison employee-residents foreshadowed Corcoran's failure to gain more than a 7.5 percent increase in population that could be attributed to the prison (Parks et al. 1990). CDC employees shunned both localities because of their lack of retail, entertainment, and educational amenities. In addition, the towns' isolation added several thousand dollars to the cost of a new house—because of transportation charges—compared with similar abodes in larger cities.

Corcoran is situated close to larger small cities—Hanford (1985 pop. 24,450) and Lemoore (1985 pop. 12,000)—that have malls, movie theaters, and other desirable amenities. It is within an easy California commute (about fifty miles each way, no traffic) of major valley cities such as Fresno, Visalia, and Bakersfield. Finally, for those who want to live in more picturesque surroundings, the foothills of the Sierra Nevada to the east and the Coastal Range to the west are also within a more challenging, but still doable, California commute. Some of those who lived more than fifty miles away rented apartments in Corcoran, which they shared with other CDC employees for the typical four-day workweek, with all going home to their families for their staggered three-day weekends (Parks et al. 1990).

Paradoxically, then, Corcoran is a fine location for the prison from the employees' point of view, but only because it is an easy spot to get home from, not because it is from their perspective a good place to live. As a result, rather than the prison inducing a booming market for residential and retail real estate, as in Susanville, Corcoran's modest increase in housing stock was met by

TABLE 8   ANNUAL CHANGE IN CORCORAN HOUSING STOCK
AND VACANCY RATE, SELECTED YEARS

Year	Total	Single Unit	Multiunit	Mobile	Vacancy (%)
1977	1	1	0	0	3.31
1982	48	−22	−40	7	3.66
1984	20	13	4	3	4.85
1987	252	60	194	−2	5.47
1988	83	74	0	9	7.40
1989	40	17	2	21	7.50

SOURCES: Parks et al. 1990; U.S. Bureau of the Census, *Census*, 1990, 2000.

an increased vacancy rate (see table 8). Prison employees new to the area did not settle in Corcoran, and Corcoran residents did not get prison jobs. About a year before the facility started receiving prisoners, the CDC held several job fairs at the Kate G. Boswell Senior Center. At the largest fair, 823 people filled out preliminary applications and talked with CDC representatives, but only 178, or fewer than 10 percent of the jobs at the prison, were filled by Corcoran residents; 40 percent went to residents within a stretched local labor market—roughly, a seventy-five-mile radius—and 60 percent went to people from elsewhere (Parks et al. 1990). These are results slightly worse than the average yield from local economic development projects (cf. Bartik 1991). The labor market stretched because of easily traveled terrain, mild climate, relatively high wages, and the proliferation of amenities elsewhere.

Disappointment launched the city into an entrepreneurial role. City boosters discovered that local job seekers found the peculiarities of the state's employment application system alien to anything they had ever encountered when looking for work. Thus, operating on the assumption that the lack of how-to-apply skills was the principal barrier between Corcoran residents and CDC positions, the city organized "how to" workshops at the high school. Volunteer trainers, assisted by representatives of the state Employment Development Department, painstakingly explained to prospective applicants how to complete state employment applications properly (leave no blank spaces!), how to register for and take the required tests, and how to provide adequate proof of training, experience, creditworthiness, and licensing for specialized positions. The workshops can, perhaps, be credited with pushing Corcoran's success rate up over 20 percent by the mid 1990s; but it is not clear whether Corcoran residents who gained the increasing share of jobs had lived there before the coming of the prison or prior to getting a prison job. At any rate, the number of Corcoran residents in poverty rose (Hornor 1993), and the average Kings County public assistance caseload continued the gradual but steady climb that had started back in the late 1970s (Parks et al. 1990).

Since Corcoran is majority Mexicano/Chicano, with a significant African American population, it is tempting to explain the failure of local people to gain jobs as symptomatic of racially exclusive hiring practices. While that may be true of other state departments, the CDC had the most aggressive affirmative action hiring policies of any California state agency (PRCC 1996). There are reasons for this, embedded in changes in corrections policy on a national scale. In the early 1980s, white corrections professionals debated whether demographically diversifying corrections personnel, especially guards, might not help maintain peace and thus enhance security in prisons' increasingly caging persons of color. The alternate view was that racial and ethnic identification would have a stronger effective pull on a diverse workforce than loyalty to the state (see, e.g., the special issue of *Corrections,* October 1982). The forces for diversity won out in many jurisdictions; and in California, even while the University of California was preparing to void affirmative action, every piece of prison legislation and regulation that involved expanding the CDC workforce explicitly stipulated that "minorities" (people of color and white women) be actively sought out to join the ranks at all levels.

A better explanation for Corcoran's failure to capture jobs lies with the educational system in farmworker communities, where students "learn to labor" (Willis 1977) in specific ways. The disjuncture between the disappearance of agricultural jobs and the inconsistent use of school time results in young people educated for nothing at all: a fact as true of many urban as of rural working-class youths. Corcoran's reading scores in 1991–92 were in the 61st percentile compared with the state as a whole; Avenal's were in the 20th percentile (Hornor 1993).

Although the prison's operating budget did not produce the expected growth in income for either new or continuing Corcoran residents, it did, as promised, produce a small but steady level of annual commodity purchases. The purchases, while high enough to support a partial realignment in city political power— a subject to which we will return—were not sufficient to push the city's tax pull factor above 1 (Parks et al. 1990), which meant that retail in the city remained (proportionately) below the statewide average.[22] Indeed, while CDC expenditures in Kings County as a whole were higher than predicted, the chief beneficiaries were nonlocal electricity, gas, and water utilities (Parks et al. 1990).[23]

In the south San Joaquin Valley, water is *the* controversial utility. Even as Boswell was organizing the land sale to the CDC, smaller farmers in the Kettleman Plains on the west side of the county, hit hard by groundwater depletion during the drought, viewed the coming Avenal prison as a competitor for resources rather than as a complementary employer. They brought a lawsuit against the CDC that indirectly pitted them against the big landowners in the area—including Standard Oil, and the vegetable and grape grower Bill Mouren, who sold the three Avenal sections to the state. The lawsuit resulted in a court order forbidding the CDC to use any groundwater for the facility. That meant the prison had to use surplus water obtained under the city of Avenal's contract with the Metropolitan Water District of Southern California (Met). At the lawsuit's conclusion, the State Attorney General's office reiterated the CDC's position in the matter, indirectly acknowledging the general problem of surplus, to which the prison provided a solution: from the state's perspective, Avenal or any other new prison would benefit farmers and the water table by permanently removing land from agricultural production.[24]

At Corcoran, the CDC drilled a deep 1,000-foot well at the site to supplement drinking water bought from the city and purchased surplus and treated effluent for other uses. Corcoran invested $3 million in a treatment facility and was prepared to sell to any buyer at $5 per acre-foot, but presumed the prison would be its biggest customer. The prison contracted instead to buy surplus water from the Corcoran Irrigation District (a regional utility) at $45 per acre-foot, and continued to do so until the city managed to get word to the JLCPCO in Sacramento that the facility was wasting money (CDF 1996). The charge of wasted funds, lodged with the prison oversight committee, was the only way Corcoran could compel the CDC to direct the local prison to buy Corcoran's treated water, since there was no rule requiring the CDC to integrate with, rather than bypass, the local economy.[25]

The prison had to be territorially integrated with the city in order for Corcoran to receive its share of annual tax subventions from Sacramento, and the annexation proved more difficult than prison boosters had imagined.[26] Given that the subventions would augment city revenues by approximately $65 per prisoner per year, it seemed reasonable to expect that those who lived in Corcoran's sphere of influence in unincorporated Kings County and used city amenities, such as parks and schools, would support shifting the political boundary to lasso in the southern site. The Kings County Local Agency Formation Committee (LAFCO) had approved the annexation in principle—viewing it as a rational expansion of the city rather than a tax-hungry land-grab—but voters in the proposed annex, who included some of the staunchest antiprison forces, defeated the measure in 1986. The city succeeded in annexing the site in late 1987, by drawing the new boundary close to the prison and the connecting road, while skirting recalcitrant property owners' intervening lands. The move instantly increased the city's revenues by about 6 percent the first year, thanks to the high number of prisoners locked in the facility.

Because the prison had produced such disappointing results, apart from the subvention money, some Corcoran residents, like their counterparts in Avenal, Crescent City (R. W. Gilmore 1994; Parenti 1997), and other new prison towns (Huling 2002; Gilmore and Gilmore 2004), denounced the CDC for having made promises it did not keep. But others, in Corcoran as elsewhere, viewed the development failure as evidence of mistakes made by the city, rather than misrepresentations made by the CDC. These political entrepreneurs successfully prevailed upon the town to seek a second prison facility to be built adjacent to the first one on the unused segment of the Boswell parcel. They intended to use their experience with the first prison to avoid errors the second time around.

The city was trying to develop a new image; while it continued to be a cotton town, it needed to project a strong alternative industrial identity to diversify. Susanville, Corcoran's model for development, had several CDC offices in addition to its 1954 and future prisons. In 1990, the CDC opened a regional accounting office at Visalia, Tulare County; Corcoran fought successfully to have the establishment relocated to its territory, where it reopened at the end of 1991. Corcoran argued that it was unjust for Visalia to benefit from a "clean" office—with pink- and white-collar jobs—when it did not at the same time serve public safety by having a prison in its immediate environs. Corcoran's victory was somewhat Pyrrhic. The city borrowed $775,000 to build the new office (using subvention money to pay back the loan), while the people who got the jobs were mostly Visalians, who commuted to work and took their paychecks home.

Corcoran's capture of the prison and the accounting office was an example of how the city could use political power to form an apparently distinctive space economy; but, as the accounting office struggle especially illustrates, spatial demarcation via political boundaries does not necessarily translate into economic stickiness. The city turned to its taxing capacities in the hope that by selectively using those powers, it could get a piece of vulnerable construction expenditures and induce new, as yet unidentified, investment.

Since the payoff from the first prison was so much lower than expected, and the city had spent quite a bit of time and borrowed about $5 million in anticipation of a return that did not materialize, Corcoran decided in 1993 to assert its territorial prerogative by taxing the second prison's suppliers at the construction site. Ordinarily, such items are taxed where they are bought, but under California law, the city could seize taxing power for goods purchased within the state.

While Corcoran was exerting greater than normal taxing powers at the second prison building site, it was also trying to attract new employers by using the inverse strategy—tax abatements. Sacramento had awarded a California enterprise zone (CEZ) designation to all of Kings County east of the Kettleman Plains in 1993. CEZ status was a long way from direct subventions; Corcoran juggled the short-term remedy of taxing the second prison construction site with a risky long-term solution. The risk was that employers would come to exploit up to fifteen years of benefits and leave before they became mired in the local economy's taxable ground. The wager was that sunk costs would keep investors in place. Between 1993 and 1997, only one new employer joined the city as a result of the tax incentive program (cf. LeRoy 2005).

In housing, the city also discounted itself in the hope of future revaluation by establishing the county's lowest fees and fastest approval rate. A single development proposal emerged: one builder offered to construct ten to thirty 2,200-square-foot houses. The new houses would be aggressively marketed to COs transferring to the second prison, the key selling point being a quasi-custom feature: COs had to move to their new assignment within sixty days of CDC approval or forfeit the job (which usually entails a promotion), and the developer would finish the house within sixty days to the specifications of the purchasing CO and family.

In order to persuade COs to live in a town earlier CDC transfers had spurned, Corcoran had to figure out ways to make the local atmosphere attractive, given the difficulty of developing retail and entertainment amenities. Some of the cosmetic problems could be solved inexpensively by exploiting prison labor. The obvious contradiction in using donated labor for public works in a town plagued by unemployment is underscored by the fact that at that time the CDC "valued" prisoner labor at $7/hour, thirty-five cents above the average Corcoran hourly wage.

Corcoran did not plan to limit its diversification from cotton to corrections. The failed purpose of the CEZ status was to bring other kinds of industries to town. Susanville provided a model, because its corrections experience was positive. Thus, operating from the mistaken assumption that the Lassen County city's relative prosperity was a prison by-product, Corcoran concentrated on prison-related development. This decision says more about the path that $1 billion in CDC outlays over a decade cut through the town than about a route plotted by city professional and political planners, much less by community members. The scale and scope of the CDC enterprise provided the first significant economic alternative to the oligopolistic cotton firms, even if, from the agriculturists' point of view, the prison simply provided them with some relief from the crises arising from unproductive land and potentially politically active surplus labor.

OPPORTUNITIES AND CONSTRAINTS

The UFW failed to organize the Salyer workers in 1986, but the effort charged the city's political atmosphere. The antagonisms of race and class enacted in the struggle to fight wage cuts and outsourcing surfaced in other arenas, and Corcoran's Chicana/os began to mount a concerted attack on the city's racial hierarchy. The Salyer workers, while fighting against a severely weakened employer, were still fully caught up in the political economy of cotton, and the UFW's unsuccessful campaign showed the industry's power, amassed over more than sixty years. But if cotton had power, not all children of field workers belonged to that sector. Ironically, some activists were liberated by the coming of the prison.

In 1986, the Corcoran City Council was desegregated for the first time with the election of Daniel Léon. Léon was born in Corcoran shortly after World War II. He attended UCLA and Fresno State, where the Brown Power/La Raza Movement, inspired by the UFW and by Black Power (especially the Black Panthers), was a principal feature of the political landscape. Léon and his cohort came of age when federal and state programs had "fixed" impediments to advancement by mandating postsecondary antiracist admissions policies and funding generous student aid programs. In those times, poor kids from rural towns and inner cities who had decent grades and a modicum of decent counseling could find a place in the state's rapidly expanding postsecondary system (R. W. Gilmore 1991). Many who left did not return, seeing no opportunity to use their education and skills in Corcoran save possibly in a middle-management position in cotton or in the tiny city government.

Léon eventually moved back to Corcoran and commuted to work at Fresno's Office of Human Resources. Along with other Chicana/os who had left and returned, such as auto parts store owner Ruben Quintinilla, who attended San Jose State University, Léon began to denounce some of the town's more egregious inequities, such as school tracking. Not dependent on the cotton industry or the city government for a livelihood, the reformers were in effect insider/outsiders, their relative economic independence coupled with deep roots in the Mexicano/Chicano community.

When the prison opened, Léon became its manager of community resources. The manager performed a number of tasks, ranging from negotiating the uses of the Level I prisoner "worker bees" on city beautification projects to bringing religious and other volunteer-based city programs into the facility and awarding contracts to city vendors for the prison's locally purchased commodities. Quintinilla's auto parts store became the prison's prime supplier for items such as batteries and spark plugs. The coming of the prison enhanced vendors' economic independence and stature, because they were outside cotton and city government, yet *both* locally based *and* formally attached to a higher level of the state. Léon, Quintinilla, and several others became increasingly vocal concerning the need for structural change in the social and political arenas.

In the late 1980s, the San Francisco–based Mexican American Political Alliance (MAPA), under the leadership of the Brown Power veteran Joaquin Avila, had been scouting for jurisdictions around California where it could mount challenges to discriminatory electoral practices. In the manner of lawsuit-based

African American antiracist electoral organizing in the U.S. South during the same period, MAPA evaluated sites whose Chicano majority populations had little or no representation on elected bodies such as city councils and school and hospital boards. The localities chosen for challenge were cities like Corcoran, Dinuba, and Watsonville—places with relatively stable second- and third-generation Mexican American populations who had developed, from within, the rudiments of a professional managerial class.

In July 1993, MAPA launched an offensive against Corcoran with a letter to the city council. Rather than fight the charges, shallow-pocketed Corcoran decided to shift from at-large to electoral district representation for the council and the school board. Corcoran's failure to attract new residents along with the first prison might well have enhanced the power of Corcoran Chicana/os to wage their political struggle. The lack of immigrants meant that the city's demographic profile had stayed fairly constant, and that the social relations within the city, even if stratified, had not been diluted by growth.

While the city capitulated to the MAPA challenge without a court battle, it also instantly reenacted the national postwar racial ritual, with paternalistic expressions of denial clashing with angry denunciations of repression. Anglos suspected—not altogether incorrectly—that the new militancy was the result of Chicana/os having gone off to college and encountered La Raza (Brown Power) and other radical politics. But they failed to consider that some of the activists' family members had a local history of radical labor activism in the 1930s strikes. At the same time, the fact that the political battle was waged against the city council, rather than against the cotton elites, bespoke both a status division within the Mexicano/Chicano community and a displacement of political economic struggles from the realm of production to the realm of representation.

During a ten-year period, from 1984 to 1994, the small city experienced two scandals involving the chiefs of police: first, an Anglo accused of selective enforcement of laws by zeroing in on youth of color, and subsequently a Chicano accused of harassing an Anglo woman. The charges and countercharges were well reported in the weekly newspaper. Predictably, the Anglo seems to have enjoyed a presumption of innocence, while the Mexican American faced a cloud of presumed guilt. That difference forced particular mobilizations, with the small cadre of the city's growing Chicano professional-managerial class joining together in 1994 as the Coalition of Concerned Citizens. In response, members of the coalition were themselves accused of wrongdoing. The point here is not to judge whether or not any of the accusations were justified, but rather to look at the peculiar ways in which the topic of race and processes of racism get played out. In Corcoran, as in the larger society at that time, racism was viewed narrowly in terms of relative access, after the fact of development, to certain social and economic opportunities. In that view, those denying racism argued that antiracist activists were only trying to get "power"—conceived of as a thing, a crowbar that would pry open formerly locked doors, rather than a new set of local relationships. What fell out of the discussion was the ways in which the development of the place created the ground on which the crisis arose (cf. James Ferguson 1990). Just as the cotton oligopoly was not on the agenda in these debates, the discussion of wrongful behavior, its prevention and remedies, did not stretch to consideration of the thousands held in custody down the road. The prison at the edge of town, then, while seeming to be a relatively autonomous solution to a long-standing problem of structural inequality in the south San Joaquin Valley, might have been seen as a threat looming against the children's futures as much as a disappointing employment prospect for the city's kids.

The city's principal justification for both prisons centered on the urgent need to fashion a future for Corcoran's children. The city's high school dropout rate soared in the mid 1980s, and the city was eager to find both reason and means to persuade young people to stay in school. The coming of the first prison allowed educators, parents, and city leaders to assert that CDC jobs could be had by energetic young people who got their diplomas. Given the dearth of CDC hires of townspeople of any age, however, the school board devised a work credit program to enable students who completed the minimum course requirements to stay enrolled—and graduate—while also holding down part- or full-time jobs, although the high school lacked a full-time guidance counselor to implement it by helping young people coordinate their school and work lives and plan for their futures. When the school board sought the city council's permission to advertise for an education professional to fill the critical position, it was rebuffed by the council, which claimed to have no money in the budget to make the hire.

After more than a year of intensive, and sometimes acrimonious, negotiations between the school board and the council, and between Anglo and Chicano council members, the city manager came up with a solution. Since criminal justice was the "hot, sexy thing," and 70 percent of Corcoran's prison-derived subventions at that time went straight into an expanded city police force, supplementing, not replacing, appropriations from other revenues, the manager persuaded the council to hire a plainclothes policeman to serve full-time at the high school in the dual capacity of career and substance abuse counselor. The council justified the expense by treating secondary school guidance—rather than secondary *schooling*—as crime control. Furthermore, those enthusiastic about the new appointment expressed hope that the officer-counselor would help students learn to talk with police respectfully before they got into trouble and had to talk to less sympathetic uniformed officers. Given the apparent inevitability that Black, Brown, and other poor youth will have encounters with the law, activists against the criminalization of youth have written and distributed pamphlets and books in big cities throughout the United States advising people on how to be arrested—not how to capitulate, but rather how to achieve a favorable outcome and protect one's rights and one's life. But Corcoran's institutionalization of this activist practice changed the thrust by trying to educate youth for surveillance and deferral to authorities—an old story in an agricultural community threatened by "farm fascism" during the labor wars of the 1930s (McWilliams [1939] 1969; Bean 1973).

At that time, some students were wary of the new counselor, and many were acutely aware of their own surplus status in the California political economy as a whole. The best evidence for their collective consciousness of what was happening around them was the startling walkout of two hundred Corcoran high school students in protest against California's anti-immigrant

Proposition 187 in October 1994. These rural youths saw themselves as having few options given their understanding, on the one hand, of Proposition 187 as an attack on *all* poor Latinos—not only noncitizen workers—and the criminalizing effects of anxiety about youth gang and drug culture, as figured by the new officer-counselor, on the other. From that time on, young people started to organize, while regional governments, such as Fresno County, began enormous youth jail projects.[27]

Although in the 1980s and 1990s, Corcoran had a decrease in its already low crime rates, as did California as a whole, several million dollars in onetime state mitigation funds were used to expand the local jail and county courthouse when the first prison was built. The expansion did not signify an anticipated explosion in Corcoran crime; rather, it was a necessary external appendage to a more or less self-contained city (the prison) located in the county's criminal justice jurisdiction. Every prison operates within three spheres of sanction: CDC regulations, state law, and federal law. The CDC has its own regulations, which are approved by Sacramento but enforced by the wardens at each facility, and their application to prisoners can include restricted privileges, relocation, time in the security housing unit (solitary confinement), and other punishments. However, any indictable state law violation committed inside—whether by a CDC employee or prisoner—must be referred to the county grand jury and, if necessary, tried in the county courthouse before a locally summoned jury. Additionally, prisoners who wish to challenge the conditions of their confinement in the federal courts must first exhaust state remedies, starting in the local county courthouse.[28]

ALTERNATIVE VISIONS

Criminal justice is, literally, state power. It is the police, guns, prison, the electric chair. Power corrupts; and power also has an itch to suppress.

LAWRENCE M. FRIEDMAN, *CRIME AND PUNISHMENT IN AMERICAN HISTORY* (1993)

Contemporary prison-siting literature, exemplified in a special edition of *Crime and Delinquency* (Gibbons 1990; see also Krause 1992), approaches the problem as a fairly narrow question of whether all groups engaged in making the decision have adequate information about prisons. In this logic, the boundaries of adequacy are limited by the presumption that prisons have to go somewhere: the carceral is a given. The problem then is relegated to a calculation, a technical exercise in weighing "fear" against "finances" (Carlson 1988; see also Lake 1992), with the opposition conceived of as simple differences whose resolution derives from narrowly defined, factual expertise, rather than a redefinition of the problem to be solved. In Corcoran, the public record includes no inquiry about the state's decision to expand prison capacity. There was no nearby crime wave to give the program a locally palpable explanatory context. When asked in passing what difficulties they envisioned, most people only remembered worrying about whether prison would mitigate local and regional inequality; when they decided it might, the decision rolled forward. But as with the lack of critique concerning the need for more prisons, there was no discussion, either, about what it would mean for a small city dominated by a single-industry oligopoly to deal with inequality by bringing in an enormous new employer outside the direct control of anybody; nor did people ponder what might happen should the prison fail to do the economic job.

Indeed, insofar as prison siting, like all industrial siting, is a question of land use, it is, further, a question about horizontal and vertical social and economic planning. It is not surprising, but at least a little ironic, that "planning" has such a bad name these days; in everyday common sense, "planning" smacks of all the negatives implied in an alienating and cumbersome state bureaucracy. But as every geographer knows, "planning" is what makes "globalization" possible and powerful, and the loss of the power to plan (to have some sense of how to secure the future) is what makes small towns, small farmers, and small-income households desperate for relief.

In a number of communities around the Central Valley and elsewhere in the Golden State's rural reaches, grassroots activists have stopped prisons from coming to their communities. In general ways, these places bear strong similarities to those where prisons *have* been sited; and in some cases they are (old- and) new-era prison towns. What's compelling is how the communities have over time, in part through networking and collaboration, begun to make different assumptions about new prisons and therefore to ask, and find answers to, questions other than those that would come up in a narrowly conceived siting discussion.

The question everybody asks at first focuses on the "fear versus finances" calculation (Carlson 1988): if prisons *are* safe, then do they *also* benefit towns by distributing dollars into hands that spend locally? Corcoran's experience is in key ways typical: when measured by jobs for current residents, residential development, locally sited related industries and services, or consumer retail, prisons have not delivered even on the modest employment and growth projections derived from the CDC's categorical assurances. Indeed, the biggest single beneficiaries of retail dollars are those major shapers of the valley's development, utility companies. For other retail, prison towns' economic well-being and growth potential compare unfavorably over time with depressed rural places that did not acquire prisons (Hooks et al. 2004).[29] The second question, inseparable from the first, focuses on the goods and harms that might come to a small town that suddenly finds itself a dependent neighbor to a town of equal or greater size (a prison) whose residents are involuntary and whose employees are mostly commuters; this is a question about place—the one raised by the Corcoran prison opponent who wanted to "save" her town. The answers to this question require more evaluation than calculation: for example, it might seem better than nothing that a handful of new jobs go to old residents.

For towns with unemployment that has stayed above 25 percent during the longest economic expansion in U.S. history, a single new job is a benefit. Such was the official wisdom in Delano, former headquarters of the United Farm Workers, where the city was slated to get a hotly contested, activist-delayed (from 1999 to May 2005) second 5,160-bed prison. Delano's 1999 ten-year planning document barely mentioned the extant prison—or the community corrections facility the city manages on behalf of the CDC—other than to note that some residents wish it were not there, and made no reference to the new one, focusing instead on other economic activities that would presumably induce growth. The mayor at the time of the battle over the prison did not particularly support it, but found no grounds—no palpable harms—for opposing seventy-two new jobs (out of a projected total of 1,600 new hires). After all, in the decade after the first prison opened, unemployment climbed from 26 to 29 percent (U.S. Bureau of the Census, *Census* 1990, 2000). The struggle over the prison became a statewide and national symbol against prison expansion.[30]

In Farmersville, about an hour from Delano or Corcoran, farmworkers *and* growers lined up in 1999 to talk a prison proposal to death—to banish it from the city council's agenda. Farmersville unemployment is worse than Delano's; yet at the council meeting, two venerable and classically contradictory groupings—Tulare County family ranchers and farmworker families united under the UFW flag—agreed from a number of perspectives not only that a prison would fail to solve economic problems, but also that it would create new problems. In the residents' view, the proposed prison would likely endanger water supply and quality. They also argued that a prison would certainly aggravate race and class inequalities by fixing into the city's landscape under night-polluting lights the heightened expectations of racialized, impoverished criminality that U.S. prisons symbolize. And, finally, they expressed fears that their community would be transformed if augmented by households with higher than average rates of domestic violence—as is the case in military, police, and prison guard homes. In fact, people who organize against prisons invoke the same beneficiaries ("the kids") as those who organize *for* prisons.

In the landscape of home, the state's capacities to make the water flow, the soil yield, the workers work, and the employers finally sometimes pay resonate in the eye and the memory as materials for renovation. Thus in Tulare County, a cost-benefit analysis of incentives for young people to do well (such as graduate from high school) versus punishment for having done badly produced by the Rand Corporation in the early 1990s (Greenwood et al. 1994) circulated among farmers as an example of what could be done. In Imperial County, parents bristled at adding more COs' children to the public schools, noting an increase in their own kids' use of fear to settle differences. But also, women and men in California, along with many who self-organized to save their communities around rural America, began to tire of using fear to fight fear. Instead, they widened their scope of analysis, in large part by listening closely as various kinds of struggles came to their attention through conferences, documentaries, and chance encounters during testimony before governmental bodies. In particular, environmental justice activism emphasized the inseparability of economic well-being, physical safety, healthy workers, flourishing children, and vibrant places. This broadening view gradually replaced a one-dimensional picture of public safety with a complicated agenda based on identifying and undoing the deadly cumulative impacts of organized abandonment. Throughout the valley, new formations came together composed of all kinds of members—community people, paid activists, and college graduates employed in governmental agencies devoted to well-being. They started to ask new questions about development and control of financial and other resources and to begin to envision what grassroots planning might look like.

CONCLUSION
When people talk about the kids, about "saving" a place, what are they talking about? Far from freezing a landscape in time and place, the desire seems to be quite the opposite—one of pursuing particular kinds of change in order to produce the conditions under which social and cultural reproduction might happen. In other words, they are engaging in the tarnished practice

of planning. In lieu of technocratic expertise that "shows" how a prison might blend into a community, activists opposed to such a solution to political and economic crisis propose alternate planning criteria that must precede any industrial location decision. If industries do create places, then so does planning; and indeed, one of the rarely unacknowledged bitter ironies of the past twenty-five years is that, while planning—in California, at any rate—fell from its constitutionally mandated place on governmental agendas, the corporate and banking forces' determining the movement of capital across the land feature central planning as a fundamental activity of their institutions and organizations.

This line of argument leads away from thinking of prison location as a siting problem for development ends and toward thinking of prison as fully a development problem—or perhaps, more accurately, as an *antidevelopment* problem (cf. Ferguson 1990). Certainly, a rich literature critical of developmentalist assumptions in the planet's poorer countries highlights the ways that particular forms and relations of developmentalism serve deliberately or unwittingly (it really makes little difference in the end) to further the underdevelopment of regions. The poorer places, or global South, are also here in the global North, in both urban and rural areas "unfixed" by capital flight and state restructuring. The unfixing is not, however, an absolute erasure; what's left behind is not just industrial residue—devalued labor, land made toxic, shuttered retail businesses, the neighborhood or small city urban form—but, by extension, entire ways of life that, having been made surplus, unfix people: women, men, "the kids." In the course of crisis, ordinary people do not abandon themselves but rather renovate already existing activities. Renovation entails planning. Rural antiprison activists are increasingly taking up planning as the only means by which they can keep prisons permanently off the local agenda because the accumulating evidence shows that they are not good for the towns where they go. Furthermore, such activists are joining forces with their urban counterparts, to whose story we now turn.

FIVE

MOTHERS RECLAIMING OUR CHILDREN

Now that you have touched the women, you have struck a rock, you have dislodged a boulder, and you will be crushed.

**WOMEN'S POLITICAL CHANT, ANTI-PASS LAW MOVEMENT, SOUTH AFRICA, 1956,
QUOTED IN ANGELA Y. DAVIS, *WOMEN, CULTURE & POLITICS* (1989)**

others Reclaiming Our Children (Mothers ROC) began
to organize in November 1992 in response to a growing
crisis: the intensity with which the state was locking
their children, of all ages, into the criminal justice system. At the outset, the ROC consisted of only a few
mothers and others, women and men, led by its founder and
president, Barbara Meredith, and the life-long activist Francie
Arbol. The initial project was to mobilize in defense of Meredith's son, an ex-gangster, who had been instrumental in the historic 1992 Los Angeles gang truce. The ROC lost his case but
gained the makings of a movement. By the spring of 1993, when
the LA Four went to trial, Mothers ROC had developed a net-

work throughout greater Los Angeles and achieved recognition as an organization devoted to action rather than to commentary.[1] Mothers ROC's mission was "to be seen, heard, and felt in the interest of justice." To achieve this goal, Mothers ROC convened its activism on the dispersed stages of the criminal justice system. The group extended an unconditional invitation to all mothers and others struggling on behalf of their children, and it reached its audience in various ways. The primary method was leafleting public spaces around jails, prisons, police stations, and court-houses to announce the group's existence and purpose. When dis-tributing flyers and business cards, members engaged people in conversation to explain the purpose of Mothers ROC (whose members are known as ROCers). ROCers gave talks and work-shops at elementary and secondary schools, colleges and univer-sities, churches, clubs, and (at the outset, but with decreasing fre-quency) prisons and jails. They also appeared on regional and local radio and television programs. Using these means, Mothers ROC established a presence at many locations throughout the political geography of the penal system.

ROCers attracted hundreds of mothers to fight on behalf of their own children in the system. Many were already solitarily performing the arduous labor of being on the outside for some-one—trying adequately to switch among the many and some-times conflicting roles required of caregivers, wageworkers, and justice advocates. Some would attend one meeting and never re-turn; others have persisted, whether their loved one's case lost or won. Often newcomers brought someone to the meeting for moral support—a marriage or other partner, relative, child, or friend from church or neighborhood, and that person also be-came active. Each weekly gathering averaged twenty-five women and men. Most of them learned about the ROC from one of the outreach practices noted above, or from an acquaintance who had direct contact with a member. The rest, however, were guided to the organization by their loved ones in custody. Among the tens of thousands awaiting trial or doing time in the juvenile detention camps and centers, and in the county adult jails throughout the Southland, knowledge of Mothers ROC circulated by word of mouth, and a standard part of the message was that the women were willing to help with even apparently hopeless cases.

Every flyer proclaimed the ROC's principle: "We say there's no justice. What are we going to do about it? . . . EDUCATE, ORGANIZE, EMPOWER." Mothers ROC made no judgment about the innocence of those whose families turned to the group for help. Not a service organization, the group helped mothers learn how each part of the system works, and, as we shall see, to grasp the ways in which crisis can be viewed as an opportunity rather than a constraint. In the process of cooperative self-help, the mothers transformed their caregiving or reproductive labor into activism, which then expanded into the greater project to reclaim all children, regardless of race, age, residence, or alleged crime. Experienced ROCers teamed up with newcomers to call on investigators and attorneys. They researched similar cases, and became familiar with the policies and personalities of prosecutors and judges. In addition, ROCers attended one another's hearings or trials. They also observed courtroom practices in general, monitoring individual officers of the court or state's witnesses believed to be promoting injustice.[2] The group's periodic demonstrations outside courthouses and police stations brought public attention to unfair practices. Finally, ROCers sponsored monthly legal workshops with attorneys and requested research reports from scholar-activist members to help mothers become familiar with the bewildering details of the system in action.

Although never an exclusively Black organization, Mothers ROC presumed at first that it would appeal most strongly to African American women, because the state seemed to focus on taking their children. However, the sweeping character of the state's new laws, coupled with the organization's spatially extensive informational campaigns, brought Chicanas, other Latinas, and white women to Mothers ROC for help. A few years into its existence, the group had Black, Brown, Asian American, and white women, and some men. Most participants had loved ones in custody. People came to meetings from all over Los Angeles County, western San Bernardino and Riverside Counties, and northern Orange County, while their loved ones were locked up throughout California.

Mothers ROC consciously identified with Third World activist mothers, the name deliberately invoking South African, Palestinian, and Central and South American women's struggles. As we shall see, the organization was neither spontaneous and naive nor vanguard and dogmatic, but rather, mixing methods and concepts, it exemplified the type of grassroots organization that "renovates and makes critical already-existing activities" of both action and analysis to build a movement (Gramsci 1971: 330–31).

The material basis for their struggle was apparent: California's deep political-economic restructuring reconfigured the social reproductive landscape, as well as the world of work. The condition of surplus labor falls most heavily on modestly educated men in the prime of life from Black and other households of color in Los Angeles; such men are also overrepresented among CDC prisoners. Fully 40 percent of state prisoners come from Los Angeles County, and 70 percent from the Southland. What happens in the communities from which prisoners make their involuntary migrations? While the expansion of industrialized punishment in California has a relentless intensity, it is important not to misread the structural as also somehow inevitable. Industrialized punishment produces its own contradictions, as we saw in the conclusion to the account of the CDC's growth.

Mothers ROC's work illuminates a contradiction from another cut—that of working women who refuse the state's criminalization and sacrifice of their loved ones dispossessed by deindustrialization. Crucial here are both the state of emergency that communities such as South Central Los Angeles have been living under for more than a generation and its broader historical context. From the mothers' vantage point, we can see how prison expansion and opposition to it are part of the long history of African Americans and others whose struggle for liberation in the racial state has never achieved even a fully unfettered capacity to be free *labor*. The development of political responses to legal dilemmas indicates how profoundly incapacitation deepens, rather than solves, social crisis. This chapter is a polemic in the dramatic tradition of slave narratives; it both personalizes and generalizes the morally intolerable (Kent 1972) to highlight objective *and* subjective dimensions of the expansion of punishment and prisons, the demise of the weak welfare state, and the capacity of everyday people to organize and lead themselves.

SITUATING MOTHERS ROC: SOME STRATEGIC
HISTORICAL COMPARISONS

We think organizations have to be the first step toward a social movement.

MYLES HORTON AND PAOLO FREIRE, *WE MAKE THE ROAD BY WALKING* **(1990)**

Mothers Reclaiming Our Children is part of a rich history of twentieth-century movements whose systems, organizations, and practices resonate with the Los Angeles grassroots women's critique of social conditions and their approach to social change. The point of the following historical excursions is to show how spatially, sectorally, and temporally far-flung struggles intersect in Mothers ROC and similar grassroots organizations that rise up everywhere. Beyond a formal analytical similarity, the convergence suggests real connections between underlying causes that produce similar outcomes.

As with Mothers ROC, the organizations briefly examined in this section mingle reformist and radical ideologies and strategies; in the vision and substance of their political projects, they pose challenges to the system in question *and* to troubling hierarchies and unusefully narrow practices in organizations that are the basis of antisystemic movement. I believe such complexity expresses an organic relation between these struggles and the specific context of the crises from which they emerge. Here, I wish to differentiate specificity from a narrow conception of localism or specialization. Thus, by "organic" I mean situated—the quality of being on the ground. It is a material, not mystical, quality; and what one makes of it can be wonderful or terrible. The way conflict emerges in a social structure is not inevitable, even though it may be understood, in a general sense, to be an expression of a fundamental antagonism—such as class conflict. What happens at the local level has everything to do with forces operating at other scales, and it is my interest here to reconcile the micro with the macro by showing how the drama of crisis on the ground is neither wholly determined by nor remotely autonomous from the larger crisis. I do not wish to ascribe intentions or dimensions to people's actions where evidence indicates otherwise; rather, I wish to draw out the ways in which practical questions of method, argument, and/or structure powerfully engage crisis on the material and ideological stages where the conditions of crises unfold.

For Mothers ROC, then, the group's specific response to crisis was organized, with varying degrees of self-consciousness, around three key factors. These are the embeddedness of African American and other working-class mothers in a world only minimally shut out by home; the problem of organizing the unorganized in the United States according to categories other than singular, partial identities (e.g., occupation, race, parental status); and the potential power of "motherhood" as a political foundation from which to confront an increasingly hostile state and the polity legitimizing it.

Black Working-Class Mothers   Women whose paid labor is crucial to the household economy and who are judged in the dominant discourse and the gross domestic product according to their performance in the gender-segmented labor market embody different roles with respect to production, reproduction, and politics from women who can ignore such material and ideological constraints (Boris 1989). Such difference in the United States is further hierarchically organized by race (Fields 1990). During the Progressive Era (roughly 1893–1920), African American "club"

women who organized around issues of gender and work could
not echo, on behalf of their sisters, the rhetoric of home and
dependency espoused by white women reformers (Linda Gordon
1994; Giddings 1984). While immigrant European working-class
women ordinarily had to work for wages, the standards by which
white feminist/gender politics—dominated by native elites—
strove to produce the "true" and then the "American" woman
rested on the expectation that all such women should at the earliest
economic opportunity become dependent, full-time homemakers
(Boris 1989; Carby 1987; Fraser and Gordon 1992). The gendered
economic power of anti-Black racism made such an expectation
for African American women impossible, since there was no
likelihood either that their own paid labor would soon become
unnecessary or that their mates could ever earn a reliable family
wage (Linda Gordon 1994; cf. Dalla Costa and James 1972; W. J.
Wilson 1987). In the period, while elite civic activists developed
new state agencies to guide the transformation of immigrant
women and their families into Americans, and juvenile justice
departments initiated a particular repertoire of control-as-reform,
the simultaneous proliferation of Jim Crow laws shut out most
Black people from political or economic engagement (Mink 1995;
Schlossman 1995; Woodward [1955] 2002).

African American club activists' politics focused on ways to
ameliorate working-class women's daily experiences within and
between home and work, with the church typically serving as a
semipublic arena where such women could gather in relative
safety to organize for social change (Giddings 1984; Gilkes 1979,
1989; Long 1986; Sterling 1984). Efforts centered on life's everyday details and included lessons in such areas as grooming, liter-

acy, and better housekeeping either for wages or for family. Club women used recognizable household relations to build women's political consciousness (G. E. Gilmore 1996). The self-help lessons were strategies through which the most vulnerable members of the workforce could make themselves stronger against everyday assaults on their integrity—assaults typified by employer rape no less than paltry wages (Angela Davis 1981). Activists insisted that Black women must expect to act on a stage where no sturdy legal or customary curtain shielded the private from the public realm. The legacy of slavery (Angela Davis 1981; White 1985), the reality of Jim Crow laws (Sterling 1984; G. E. Gilmore 1996), and the discipline of lynching (Ginzburg [1962] 1988) suspended any illusion that Black women might either withdraw from the labor market—and the coercive social controls determining when and where they entered it—or turn to the state for protection or relief.

In this historical context, motherhood functioned through, and as an attribute of, the woman-as-laborer, enacted as collective, or social, rather than individualized practice (Collins 1990; see also White 1985; Kaplan 1982). Club women included mothering lessons among their outreach projects, because they rightly viewed the future of the race as depending on the children's successful preparation to participate in severely restricted, highly unstable job markets. In other words, the club women's specific conception of the politics of motherhood required good housekeeping to include, as a matter of course, deliberately raising children to survive in racially defined, conflict-riven lives. These lives would be shaped by a constantly "changing same" (Jones 1967) of negative contingencies—exemplified by the nation's territorywide, multiscalar accumulation of both Jim Crow laws and de facto segregation practices in the Progressive Era (Du Bois [1935] 1992; Marks 1989; Woods 1998). Most children might learn strictly to labor in whatever niches defined their generation's market enclave (Willis 1977). At the same time, however, the constant reorganization of labor markets—most notably during wartime—meant that mothers were also educating their daughters and sons in ways of thinking that might lead to more radical consciousness of what change without progress meant, given the material and ideological positioning of Black people in the racial state (cf. Omi and Winant 1986). While the type of organizing club women espoused seems to have fallen squarely into Booker T. Washington's Tuskegee model of cooperative apartheid, it also opened new possibilities for women to enlarge their scope of activity through emphasizing rather than minimizing Black women's visibility in the world. Although dangerous, visibility also provided Black women with peculiarly exploitable access to potentially political audiences because of their regular passage through public space. For example, women were often in the vanguard protesting state and state-sanctioned terrorism—in part because men were the ordinary (although not exclusive) victims of lynching and police brutality (Carby 1987; Ware 1992). Similarly, in later years, the Montgomery bus boycott—popularly viewed as a watershed of the post–World War II civil rights movement—gained structure and strength in large part from a church-based women's organization. These women built the scaffolding from which to dismantle U.S. de jure apartheid around the issue of public transportation for African American domestic and other workers (Powledge 1991; Kelley 1994). For both the immediate Montgomery audience and viewers of newsreels shown on televisions and in movie theaters across the United States, the boycott produced an unfamiliar and compelling image of urban Black women walking in groups to and from the job, their apparent cheerfulness belying the fearful conditions in which they confronted the most readily perceivable ways in which U.S. racism divides class and gender. In these women, foes recognized unanticipated adversaries; allies, by contrast, recognized, through the women's actions, how familiar practices of everyday life might be rearranged in order to take on previously unimaginable tasks (A. D. Morris 1984).

The Problem of Identification   Organizing is always constrained by recognition: How do people come actively to identify in and act through a group such that its trajectory surpasses reinforcing characteristics (e.g., identity politics), or protecting a fixed set of interests (e.g., corporatist politics), and instead extends toward an evolving, purposeful social movement (e.g., real class politics)?[3] This question has particular importance when it comes to the age-old puzzle of organizing unorganized workers. U.S. labor history is dominated by work site and occupational movement building, with group boundaries established by employers or by skills (Wial 1993; Johnston 1994; Stone 1981). These boundaries, of course, negatively organize—and even disorganize—people who are excluded, because U.S. work sites and occupations are historically segregated by both gender and race (Cobble 1991, 1994; Milkman 1987; Roediger 1991; Wial 1993).

In a few instances, U.S. labor movements have broadened their practices by engaging in a class rather than a corporatist approach. Whereas most such efforts resulted in failure—crushed by the capitalist state's policing and spin control, as well as by firms' engineer-driven managerialism—some attempts along this way produced surprising results (Dubofsky 1969; Phillip Foner 1970; Wial 1993). When the Communist Party (CPUSA) attempted to organize workers in the relatively new steel district of Birmingham, Alabama, during the 1930s, it ran into a sturdy wall of racism that prevented it from forging a movement in which whites could recognize themselves and Black people as equally exploited workers rather than as properly unequal Americans. However, the organizers who traveled to the urban mills and rural mines seeking out industrial laborers discovered an unanticipated audience for their arguments among predominantly Black sharecroppers. The Share Croppers Union adapted the CPUSA analysis to its own precarious conditions, and the group grew rapidly, forming a network of cells in urban and rural locations throughout the region. One needed neither to be a sharecropper nor employed nor Black to participate in the union. Upwards of 6,000 millworkers and miners, in addition to dispossessed (busy or idled) farmers, found common cause in a social movement through their understanding of their collective "equality"—which was at that time their individual interchangeability and disposability on northern Alabama's agricultural and industrial production platforms (Kelley 1990; Painter 1979; B. M. Wilson 2000).[4] State forces eventually crushed the movement, yet the submerged remnants of the union, according to its indigenous leadership, formed the already existing regional foundation for wartime organizing and postwar antiracist activism (C. L. R. James 1980).

Today, Justice for Janitors (JfJ) is a innovative labor movement in which neither work site nor occupation has served as a sufficient organizational structure in the low-wage service industry (Johnston 1994; Erickson et al. 2002). Learning from history, JfJ's strategy has been to exploit the otherwise inhibiting features of the labor market by pursuing a "geographical" approach to organization (Wial 1993; Johnston 1994). In the massive layoffs of the late 1970s and early 1980s, firms broke janitorial unions that African Americans and others had painstakingly built under the aegis of the Congress of Industrial Organizations (CIO) during and after World War II (C. L. R. James 1980). Industry subcontracted maintenance and thereby negated labor's hard-won work-site-by-work-site agreements.

The ensuing proliferation of small, easily reorganized janitorial service contractors made actual employers moving targets, and traditional forms of wage bargaining thus became impossible to carry out or enforce.[5] Furthermore, janitors working under the new arrangements, often at less than minimum wage, have not been the same people who by 1980 had fought for and won hourly wages of $10 or more (in 1980 dollars). Thus, in addition to pressing employers for contracts, JfJ's solution was to organize both the actual market for janitorial services (hotels, for example, rather than contractors) and the potential labor market for janitors. This limits employers' flexibility, because it is their actual and potential clients who agree to do business only with unionized contractors. The solution has also required that labor organizing be *community* organizing as well, as was the case with the CPUSA's work in 1930s greater Birmingham. To appeal to former janitors in target areas, and to potential janitors wherever they may might be, the JfJ approach is a bottom-up strategy to develop comprehensive regional plans that include, but are not reducible to, setting minimal standards for wages that employed individuals (janitors or not) might expect (Wial 1993; Parker and Rodgers 1995; see also Faue 1990).[6]

Public Mothers   The divisions between home and work, private and public, on the stage of capitalist culture seem for many the self-evident, natural limits to particular kinds of conflict. When political conflicts show the holes in those limits, new possibilities for organizing unfold. As we have seen, Black working-class women politicized the material and ideological distance between their paid and unwaged labor by traversing the streets. More recently, janitors around the United States have taken their clandestine exploitation public on a number of fronts, combining community-based organizing with frontline public-sphere militancy led by immigrants who gained experience as oppositional subjects of, for example, Salvadoran state terrorism (Pulido 1996).

In Argentina, under the fascist military government (1977–83), Las Madres de la Plaza de Mayo defied the presumption that women should not meddle in affairs of the state—which is to say the male, or public, sphere—by organizing on the basis of a simple and culturally indisputable claim that mothers ought to know where their children are (Fisher 1989; Bouvard 1994). The fascists' nightly abductions of teenage and adult children—most of whom were never seen again—effectively co-erced neighbors who had not yet been touched to avert their eyes and keep their mouths closed. However, a cadre of mothers, who first encountered one another in the interstices of the terrorist state—waiting rooms, courtrooms, and the information desks of jails and detention centers—eventually took their quest into the Plaza de Mayo. There, with the eyes of the nation and eventually the world on them, they demanded both the return of their disappeared and the names of those who had perpetrated the terror. The mothers dressed for recognition, wearing head scarves made of diapers, on which each had written or embroidered the name(s) of her disappeared (M. E. Anderson 1993; Bouvard 1994; Femenía 1987; Fisher 1989; Mellibovsky 1997; Sepúlveda 1996).

The Madres' fundamental position, echoing and echoed by similar movements in such places as South Africa, Palestine, and El Salvador was, and is, that children are not alienable (Harlow 1992; Tula 1994). In order to make this position politically material, in the face of continuous terror, the Madres permanently drew back the curtain between private and public, making "maternal" activism on behalf of children a daily job conducted as visibly and methodically as possible. The Madres' persistence, both before and after the official admission that the children had died horribly, transformed the passion of individual grief into the politics of collective opposition (Mellibovsky 1997). Betrayed in the early years by state and church officials alike, by military, police, bureaucrats, and priests, the Madres learned to challenge institutions as well as individuals, and, as their analysis became enriched by experience, they situated their disappeared in the context of political-economic crisis. Thus, when a redemocratized Argentina emerged, they did not return to hearth and home but rather expanded their political horizons, shifting their focus to the effects of the country's structural adjustment program, which widened and deepened poverty and reduced opportunities for young people (Fisher 1989; Sims 1996).

As we shall see, Mothers ROC emerged in a political-economic climate as hostile as that which formed each group we have briefly examined. ROC's solutions to the problems constituting the daily struggle to reclaim the children drew on the structural features of radical self-help, on the strategies of organizing on every platform where conflict is enacted, and on the argument that mothers should extend their techniques as mothers beyond the veil of traditional domestic spheres. In a word, they realized the "consciencization" (Freire 1970) of motherhood, such that one need not be a woman or a parent to participate in an action-based critique of vulnerability grounded in, but not bounded by, local conditions.

FREE GILBERT JONES: THE EARLY POLITICAL GEOGRAPHY
OF MOTHERS ROC

Mothers suffer a special pain when their children are incarcerated (lost to them). It was from this pain and suffering that Mothers ROC was born! We are an organization of Mothers (and others) whose children have been arrested & incarcerated. We fight against the police abuse, the false arrests & convictions and the unfair treatment throughout the Justice System. We educate ourselves and our young about the workings of the Criminal Justice System.

MOTHERS RECLAIMING OUR CHILDREN 1995 FLYER

Nobody disputes that on November 29, 1991, a Los Angeles Police Department officer shot George Noyes to death at the Imperial Courts public housing project, outside the homes of his mother and grandmother. The still-raging controversy concerns whether he was armed, whether he was kneeling, and whether he was begging for his life. According to members of the George Noyes Justice Committee, he was executed by a notoriously brutal policewoman. According to the LAPD, he was a gangster run amok. No charges were ever filed in the case.

The killing provoked a grassroots rearrangement of power throughout South Central Los Angeles, producing along the way both the 1992 LA gang truce and Mothers Reclaiming Our Children. Formerly an active gang member, George had recently moved to Sacramento to get out of the life. He died while home for the Thanksgiving holidays. For his family members and friends who began organizing, the nature of George's violent end epitomized their collective experience and dread of the LAPD.[7] Two of the dead man's cousins, Gilbert and Jocelyn Jones, and their mother, Barbara Meredith, initiated the work of figuring out how those most vulnerable to state violence could begin systematically to shield themselves from it. Family, neighbors, and visitors at Imperial Courts, including George's mother, grandmother, siblings, aunt, and cousins, began to testify among themselves about what they had seen, what they had heard, and how the death could only be explained as murder. Such discussion is typical wherever poor people are harassed, hurt, or killed by police (see, for examples, Piven and Cloward 1971; Hall et al. 1978). The political problem centers on what to do with the energy that fears and traumas produce. Does the state's discipline work? Does it terrorize everyone into silence, by dividing the "good" from the "bad," by intensifying anxieties that lead to premature deaths due to alcoholism and drug addictions (including cigarettes), heart disease, suicide, crimes of passion, and other killers that relentlessly stalk the urban working and workless poor (see Greenberg and Schneider 1994; R. W. Gilmore 2002a, 2002b).

In order to persuade as many residents as possible that the death concerned them all, the family formed the George Noyes Justice Committee, which met in the all-purpose room at Imperial Courts to plan ways to fight the wrongful death. To mark the moment further, Barbara, Gilbert, and Jocelyn decided to walk the neighborhood, starting with the three South Central public housing projects, and ask the gangs to declare a one-day truce so that all of George's family and friends—who lived scattered about the area—could attend the funeral. The dangers of the pilgrimage were many: Gilbert was a well-known gang member who could not pass through the streets freely. His sister Jocelyn and mother, Barbara, could not identify themselves as George's or Gilbert's relatives without simultaneously revealing their familial connections to—and therefore exposing themselves as—potential enemies. And finally, since neither Jocelyn nor Barbara lived in housing projects, residents might easily view them as outsiders making trouble in locations intensely surveilled through a number of means, including helicopters, on-site security, caseworkers from income assistance programs, and periodic LAPD raids (Mike Davis 1990).

To reassure residents that she was not an "outside agitator" but rather a grieving aunt, fearful mother, and good sister, Barbara started to hold meetings for women, especially mothers, at Imperial Courts. She explains:

> I believed we had to start taking care of our children. The police would not think they could get away with shooting our children down in cold blood if we took better care of them. So I started [what eventually became] Mothers ROC at Imperial Courts. We would meet once or twice a week. We talked about grooming, about how to brush and braid your daughter's hair. How your children should look when they leave your house. How they should talk to the police, to strangers, to each other. It seemed to me it was up to us to change things, by doing what we already knew how to do. Our mothers had taught us everything. And our grandmothers, and our aunts, and the ladies next door. They all taught us so we could have a better life. So we have to teach our children for them to have a better life. I think we let them down because we stopped teaching them and talking to them. . . . My [late] husband and I both worked, all

day, every day, so our kids could have the things we never had. We thought it was the right thing to do, to work hard and to make our children's lives easier than our lives. But we didn't make their lives easier, we made them harder. And now we have to teach them, and let them teach us where we went wrong.

Born on the eve of World War II, Barbara grew up in Louisiana, enmeshed by formal and informal community networks of family and friends (see, for example, hooks 1990, chs. 5–6). She married a career military man, lived on bases around the United States, including Alaska, and eventually settled in Los Angeles, where she was widowed as her four children reached adulthood. While many African Americans in Los Angeles achieved modest prosperity during the defense boom of World War II, their segregation from good jobs started at the war's end, and every subsequent recession has hit the community with lasting severity (Soja and Scott 1996). When the old heavy industries (steel, tire, auto, and to some degree oil) cut workers or closed plants and the waterfront mechanized, direct loss of those jobs, in combination with the disappearance of jobs reliant on that industrial core, left the city's Black working-class men without access to alternative high-wage local industries (Grant et al. 1996; Oliver et al. 1993; Peery 1994; Soja 1989).

Many women from the "stranded communities" (Jacqueline Jones 1992) concentrated in the projects enthusiastically welcomed Barbara's meetings. They could talk about themselves, their hopes and disappointments, their interrupted life plans. As many as sixty mothers and daughters (and sometimes young sons, but rarely any boys over four or five years old) might attend one of the sessions, and they eagerly put themselves to the tasks of doing each other's hair, and staging fashion shows, while talking about their loved ones who had died violently, who were in prison, or who had simply disappeared. According to Barbara, most of the women were engaged in the informal economy, selling legal goods or providing lawful services for unreported income (see, e.g., Spalter-Roth et al. 1992; Hartmann 1996). At the same time, concern about joblessness—their own, their children's fathers', their children's, and especially their sons'—dominated the discussions that did not focus on grooming, nutrition, or violent premature deaths. The women reported from experience what scholars prove again and again: in the United States, certain types of people have access to certain types of jobs. For Black people looking out from the jail-like complex of Imperial Courts, the landscape of legitimate work was bleak: an expanse of big, empty factories, minimum-wage service jobs in retail or home health care, unreliable, slow, and expensive public transportation, and bad schools leading nowhere in terms of education and skills (see also Sklar 1995). Barbara forged an alliance among women in the projects in spite of her own outsider status by appealing to a capacity the group achieved through coordinated maternal practices; they made critical the activities of mothering as necessary, social, and consequential by doing, collectively, what they already knew how to do as individuals (Collins 1990).

At the same time, Barbara, Gilbert, and Jocelyn achieved the one-day truce, by persuading the gangs—temporarily—to suture South Central's divisions and shift their everyday capacity to act as extralegal "shadow states" by realigning their practices from small-scale "interstate" rivalries to an areawide alliance.[8] They walked and talked with people in the three projects and along the streets between them, emphasizing how everyone could relate to a family who had lost a loved one and everyone could tell a tale of police violence. Rodney King's beating in March of that year provided a ready and politically charged referent that even extremely hostile listeners could recognize, and it transformed highly segmented groupings into a provisional "we" who might mediate the gang-controlled divisions of Los Angeles's streets. Little by little, the older male gang members began to acknowledge their collective power and what it could mean for Rodney King, for George Noyes, for many others, and for themselves, should they decide to allow everyone one day's free passage through the streets of South Central.

The men also agreed to a truce in the name of the grieving mothers. They extended their commonsense notion of the gangs as "families" and thereby recognized a central familial figure's claim on their care. "Mother" became, in name, George's mother, for whom Barbara, her sister, was a stand-in. Barbara's ability to speak from her heart, to express a mother's pain at losing a child, and to acknowledge her own son's gangster status without glorification or shame, touched men for whom George's death was, at least at first, of minimal importance. On behalf of Barbara, of George's mother, of "mothers," the men agreed to redirect their power and to instruct the gangs to police their streets and themselves in order for the dead man's family to gather for a big, peaceful funeral.

The two groups—mothers and gangs—quite rapidly developed a process of identification, focused, at the outset, on realizing a common interest—an ordinary funeral for a man many of them did not know. But while they came together in the name of children and of mothers, their goal became action in the context of their more general interest to struggle against the conditions that required so much organizing to precede such a homely affair as a burial. The everyday brutality that provoked Barbara and her children to bring this particular funeral to the foreground of consciousness provided material and symbolic shape for what was to follow. The interest embodied by those who attended, or who helped secure, George's peaceful services gave way to a sense of purpose not bounded by a gravesite or a day. The developing identity of purpose cast the spatially unified legal state as the legitimate object of resistance and opposition against which to organize future actions.

The next stage of organizing followed shortly after George's December 9 funeral. During the services, mothers and others who spoke in his memory called for a rally to protest the police murder. At the same time, the imam of a nearby independent mosque offered it as a sanctuary where the gangsters could work to extend the truce across time and space. The gang reconciliation first embraced the rally: more than five hundred people turned out at the 108th Street Station to accuse the police of murder and to announce the end of the community's passivity, vulnerability, and complicity with respect to the brutal treatment too often doled out by the hands of the law (Donner 1990).[9]

Throughout the winter of 1991–92, Gilbert and a number of other gang members, inspired by the turn of events, continued the peacemaking process, each day bringing in more people from a wider and wider region of South Central. Word went out through all sorts of networks, alerting Black gangsters everywhere to the possibilities of the historic moment. Barbara attended every meeting at the mosque and continued to hold the self-help discussion groups at Imperial Courts, where women from other projects would sometimes show up to see what was going on. Gang members from the truce meetings would come to report their progress, and women other than Barbara would also attend meetings at the mosque to monitor the proceedings. The George Noyes Justice Committee also continued to meet, with the object of finding an opening in fortress LAPD through which they could successfully lob their charges of wrongful death.

Shortly after 10:30 P.M. on February 16, 1992, just as a Justice Committee fund-raising dance at the Imperial Courts all-purpose room was about to end, the LAPD showed up at the door to arrest Gilbert. They charged him with taking ten dollars during an armed robbery that had allegedly occurred outside the building moments earlier. The problem of justice for George immediately widened to include his cousin Gilbert. Barbara, convinced that the purpose of her son's arrest was to stop the work she and her children had started, began to organize on his behalf as well.

While Gilbert was in custody, fighting for his freedom, the Los Angeles uprising (April 29–May 2) changed the city's political mood. Three days of "multicultural riots" (Mike Davis cited in Katz and Smith 1993) produced both new unities and new divisions. The uprising began in the afternoon, after a Simi Valley jury acquitted the four LAPD men who had beaten Rodney King, a motorist who had apparently committed several misdemeanors.[10] Millions had viewed the videotape of the beating by an eyewitness, George Holiday, which had been extensively and intensively broadcast for more than a year (R. W. Gilmore 1993; Madhubuti 1993; Gooding-Williams 1993).

Friend and foe widely attributed the truce to the uprising.

However, according to participants and witnesses, a month earlier, on March 29, the peacemakers of the Los Angeles gang
worlds met at the independent South Central mosque to sign
their historic declaration. Indeed, the riots did not produce the
truce; rather, the truce, Mothers Reclaiming Our Children, and
the uprising were all expressions of the same objective conditions
that characterized relations between the state and stranded
Black, Brown, and other poor communities throughout dein-
dustrializing Los Angeles.

Like the trial of the four LAPD officers, Gilbert's also
changed venue. But whereas the trial of the former was moved
to Simi Valley, where they were more likely to have a jury of their
peers (e.g., police or retired military), the state relocated Gilbert's
case from Compton—where seating a Black jury is quite easy—
to the Long Beach courtroom of an "antigang" judge, Marvin
Doolittle. Despite the testimony of numerous witnesses who
were with him at the time of the robbery, the jury found Gilbert
guilty, and, despite further testimony at the sentencing hearing
by former Governor Jerry Brown, Congresswoman Maxine Waters, and others concerning his peacemaking achievements, the
judge bound the young man over to the custody of the California Department of Corrections (CDC) to serve seven years for a
ten-dollar robbery.

For Barbara, the injustice in both cases made it clear that the
object of struggle was not only the South East station house of the
LAPD Southern Division. It was the state, at many levels, that
had taken her son away, just as it was the state, at many levels,
that had enabled the police to take her nephew's life. The CDC
assigned her son to Susanville, a prison located more than 500
miles from Los Angeles, where the white supremacist Aryan

Brotherhood reputedly dominated the prisoner population. This assignment terrorized the family on two accounts. First, they feared that his notoriety as a Black gang peace activist would bring him into conflict with the Aryans. Second, Barbara had suffered a heart attack during the fall of 1992, and she was not able to make the long journey to visit him. The ROC launched a successful political campaign to have Gilbert moved closer to home, and he spent about half his time in Tehachapi, about 150 miles north of home, and was released on parole after serving three years and eleven months.[11]

The project to "Free Gilbert Jones" also marked the beginning of the formal organization of Mothers ROC. In alliance with a number of other South Central mothers, many of whom had children of all ages in custody as a result of the uprising, Barbara started to hold regular sidewalk protests downtown: at the main Los Angeles County Courthouse, and at Parker Center, the LAPD headquarters. During this phase, in November 1992, Francie Arbol, a Los Angeles activist, met Barbara through the intervention of an LA-based writer who had been impressed both by Gilbert's accomplishments and by Barbara's eloquent persistence. Together, Francie and Barbara founded Mothers ROC.

FROM IMPERIAL COURTS TO THE STATE COURTS

The formation of Mothers ROC as a political group seeking justice coincided with the restructuring of the Communist Labor Party, which had organized in several U.S. cities in the 1950s. The African American revolutionary Nelson Peery founded the small party. His consciousness of race and class oppression had developed while he rode the rails as a teenage laborer during the

Great Depression and further evolved while he served in the Pacific theater during World War II (Peery 1994). The group was renowned in radical Los Angeles circles for grassroots, issue-oriented organizing with nonmembers. Francie Arbol, daughter of Syrian and Lebanese immigrants, had joined the party as a teenager in the 1960s. She had always worked on both workplace and community-based issues arising from exploitation and injustice, while raising her two daughters—mostly alone—on a bookkeeper's wages. She brought to Mothers ROC a systematic analysis of social structures and political economy, cast in colloquial terms, and a keen sense of how to get things done. Unafraid to engage in spirited debate, she also carried through on any group-chosen project, regardless of her opinion of it.

When Francie and Barbara sat together to plan the contours of an action-oriented group of mothers, it was in the garage office of the disbanded Communist Labor Party's ongoing community organization, the Equal Rights Congress (ERC). The office was about a mile north of the infamous intersection where Reginald Denny and the LA Four had their fateful encounter and seventy-five blocks northwest from the site of George Noyes's murder. The garage sits on property belonging to the Society of Friends, and the livingroom of the small front house became Mothers ROC's regular meeting place. The house has long been a location for activists to meet, a surprisingly pacific oasis in a neighborhood in constant flux. People who live in South Central, as well as those from outlying communities, are not afraid to go there because the house is not "of" any particular group's turf.

By linking Mothers ROC to the other projects of the ERC, Barbara and Francie started out with amenities others struggle long to acquire: an office, a telephone, one of the world's oldest copiers, and a convenient meeting place on neutral ground. They announced a regular Wednesday evening meeting beginning in November. African American mothers came—six, then ten, then twenty, then twenty-five or more. They came to talk about the injustice of the LAPD case compared with that of the LA Four; they came to talk about their own children's and other loved ones' cases; they came because there was someone, at last, with whom they could talk about what concerned and frightened them most.

Most of the women who had so enthusiastically participated in Barbara's mothering sessions down at Imperial Courts did not come, although Mothers ROC's central premise had not changed. Barbara remained consistent in her invocation of collective mothering as the practice from which political action springs. However, the outright politics of the formal organization apparently deterred some, especially given its dedication to confronting the state head- on. This aspect seemed dangerous to people who live intensively policed lives. Francie's role discouraged others who, perceiving her as white, would not trust her as a matter of course. And finally some came and left because rumors that communists controlled the new group spread rapidly thanks to the perhaps inadvertently strategic intervention of two Black policemen.

According to the story that circulated widely through the organization and beyond, the two policemen called on the parent of an LA Four defendant to warn her that her son's case would go much better if she disassociated herself from "those communists" in Mothers ROC. Many disputed the visit's purpose: some said the police were trying to break up the group, and others maintained they were trying to help a struggling Black woman, known personally to one of them, who did not understand the consequences of her activism.[12] The news provoked a crisis in the ROC. Some women wanted Francie expelled; others, including the mother in question, quit. Barbara and Francie held special meetings one weekend at several locations in the city and county, where they fielded questions and engaged in fiery debates about communists, racism, and justice.

Francie candidly discussed her reasons for having become a communist, and also described how the party had, in her view, outlived its usefulness. She also refused to quit the ROC and made clear to those who planned to flee her influence that if she was the biggest problem in their lives, they would not have joined Mothers ROC in the first place. The brutality of the police, the menace of prosecutors, and the meanness of judges with respect to their children was not a response to communism. But could the specter of communism make things worse? Barbara reminded the group that the ROC's purpose did not preclude any kind of person from joining and being active—as long as they worked toward the goal of justice.

The debates followed an intricate pattern, demonstrating the rich complexities of common sense in this particular time and place (cf. Gramsci 1971; Stuart Hall 1986). The systematic critique of state power with respect to criminalized children required the mothers also to question the authority of the state's representatives—police, judges, and prosecutors and other lawyers. Setting communism aside for the moment, the mothers would agree in one voice that their problem was, indeed, violence and systemic injustice. Yet when confronted by the fact of a (former) communist in their midst—even as the Soviet Union was collapsing—many of the women absolutely embraced the government's definition of the collective enemy, for whom Francie, a tiny activist, was a stand-in. Most of the women had attended elementary school during the Cold War buildup in the 1950s, and the lessons they had learned—whether lining up for civil defense drills or studying the geography of "the free world"—informed their current evaluation of possibility and danger. Furthermore, the connection of communism with atheism sat ill with women for whom, as we shall see, God and prayer are vital sources of guidance and strength.

What Barbara and Francie and their allies had to do was help the women see and say that their own children—not the "communists"—were the new official enemy now (R. W. Gilmore 1993). Even if the policemen represented authentic African American anticommunist fears, rather than the designs of the county prosecutor, the outcome would not change. Others versed in radical traditions spoke up during the agonizing debates, but the heat stayed mainly on Francie, who stalwartly took it. She was not the only apparent Anglo in the group at the time, but the combination of her ascribed race, radical roots, and refusal to yield—plus her blunt confrontational style—kept Francie downstage center during the crisis.

The crisis resolved into a truce among those who stayed, forcing the group to mature quickly into an organization *for* itself despite substantial internal differences. The process heightened suspicions but also enhanced everybody's sense of political identity. That is, while disagreeing with the "politics" figured by Francie and others, the women enacted an alternative political vision by remaining in the fight as the ROC. They made clear to all who inquired that mothers, not some hidden cadre of white or Black communists, openly and deliberately set the agendas for action. Severance of the ROC from the Equal Rights Congress gave symbolic emphasis to the organization's insistence on autonomy, even though the meeting place, office, and telephone number did not change.

In this period, the group's actions, formerly centered on the Gilbert Jones and LA Four cases, became generalized so that the ROC could act quickly and consistently on new cases. Members set up systems of court monitoring and legal workshops. Mothers would attend court sessions, either for the cases of other mothers or randomly to see what was happening to defendants. Over time, this system became a palpable presence in the halls of Southland county courthouses—especially in Los Angeles. Bailiffs, prosecutors, public defenders, and judges began to recognize that, in Bernice Hatfield's words, "nice Negro ladies with big handbags" were watching and noting. Indeed, some judges ordered the women *not* to write while court was in session. They would scribble a clandestine note or two and then write up or dictate the proceedings afterward. Judges who issued such orders got more, rather than fewer, observers in their courtrooms. Some mothers who had difficulty with the written word would simply pretend to take notes and rely on their substantial memories to reconstruct events at the end of the legal day.

Mothers also monitored relations between defendants and their attorneys—usually public defenders—and began to hold workshops with activist lawyers in order to learn about the best way to work with legal representation. The workshops became primary centers for people to learn about topics such as acting as one's own lawyer; sentence enhancement; and related issues. One recurring issue was the belief that a private attorney is better than a public defender—the belief is rooted in the commonsense American notion that "you get what you pay for." The fact that working people including the ROCers "pay" for all the public defenders via taxation is invisible in this schema. However, in the ROC, automatic distrust of public defenders (known on the street as "public pretenders") gradually gave way to a view of how rapid growth in industrialized punishment produced both overworked public defenders and a concomitant expansion of unscrupulous private lawyers looking to make a sure dollar.[13] This critique further sharpened the ROC's perception of the crisis as a political question—what should the state be like?—as well as a legal question—how do we correct wrongs in the courtroom?

The shift in location and project—from the meetings at Imperial Courts to the full-fledged Mothers ROC poised to take on the state courts—represented a change in the social position of the women as a group. Nearly all the ROCers worked for wages in the formal economy; and those who did not were disabled (generally by ailments exacerbated by poverty and stress, such as diabetes, heart disease, and cancer) or retired. Many noted the bitter irony that in order to become full-time mothers for the first time, they had to lose one or more children to the system. More than half were homeowners living in modest stucco or frame bungalows, or condominiums. They were all keenly conscious that they had something to lose. The structure of Mothers ROC gave them a framework for hope as well as for action, encouraging an expansion of political scope from immediate legal remedies to a wider exposition and assault on the criminal justice system as a whole.

A MOTHER'S PLEA FOR HELP: LAW, SPACE, AND SOLIDARITY

Early on a Thursday morning in 1992, just before that year's long Independence Day weekend, a dozen officers from the San Bernardino and Los Angeles County Sheriff's Departments and the West Covina Police kicked in Bernice Hatfield's front door. Hearing what sounded like an explosion, followed by footsteps, falling furniture, and shouting, Bernice rushed to the top of the stairs in her modest suburban condominium, and looked down on a vision of terror. Guns drawn, the police stood in the knees-bent, two-hands-on-the pistol crouch that tells every television viewer that bullets are sure to fly. The officers were calling for the surrender of her seventeen year-old son, "Stick," and they hollered at her to put her hands where they could see them. Bernice raised her hands over her head and edged down the stairs, trembling as she asked over and over again, "What are you doing here? What do you want?" As it turned out, they wanted to charge Stick with six counts of attempted murder. The officers took the teenager away that morning; and for the next decade, Bernice fought against what in her periodic newsletter, *A Mother's Plea for Help,* she called "the legal kidnapping of my child."

Never a naive woman, Bernice grew up Black and working class in a postwar southern New England city, living inequality and racism in generally unremarkable ways. Determined not to be poor all her life, she studied hard in school, became a nurse, and worked for twenty years to care for and reassure the sick and suffering. Bernice thought she knew about how the justice system worked. While she did not expect it to be truly unbiased, she did expect that when someone is charged with a crime, there is probably some evidence, whether genuine or bogus. The "people's" case against her son consisted of contradictory testimony and there were no injuries, no gun, no motive, and no clear reason for him to have been brought up on charges in the first place. Yet he was charged, and as a gang member.

The powers of and pressures on the principal players in the criminal justice system were augmented by the California Street Terrorism Enhancement and Prevention Act (STEP Act) of 1988, and a host of related laws. California declared war on gangs during the first phase of the prison expansion program in the mid 1980s, and specifically targeted Los Angeles County, where Bernice and her family lived, as the region where new programs would be developed. Sacramento directed local law enforcement agencies to identify all gang members in their jurisdictions so that the state could develop a comprehensive, centralized gang database.

Stick had never before been in custody, but about a year earlier, after he was pulled over for a motor vehicle infraction, his name had been entered into the state's gang database. In early 1993, after he and his mother rejected a plea bargain offering him six years in the Youth Authority, the prosecutors decided to try him on the six counts. With sentence enhancements, or extra time per charge, due to his gangster status, the state assured him that he faced ninety-one years in prison. Stick, who by then had turned eighteen, decided to accept the bargain, which required him to confess guilt and to waive any rights to an appeal; in the interim, the prosecutor increased the minimum term from six to nineteen years, even though nothing in the case had changed except Stick's age. Bernice could not legally intervene, because the child had reached majority. In her view, he had been coerced into the confession by those who promised him a lifetime behind bars if he went to trial and lost. Young and scared, he tried to act hard and worldly. Although Stick was a minor at the time of his arrest, the sentencing judge bound him over to the custody of the California Department of Corrections (CDC) Adult Authority. The morning the police first took her younger son away, Bernice stepped into a role she could never have imagined herself playing: that of a mother who would reach out to strangers and ask anyone who might listen to help her get her child back. At first she did everything herself, driving fifty miles round-trip to her nursing job each day in addition to traveling forty miles round-trip in the opposite direction for Stick. She visited with her son, met with the public defender, checked up on the private investigator, confronted the prosecutor, interrogated the psychiatric evaluators, and sat stony-faced at the hearings.

Bernice found that while she was struggling to free her child, because his arrest was simply a mistake, the state was working systematically to hold onto him, because his arrest was part of a program to take people "like him" off the streets. For Bernice, the crucial given was that her son had never been in trouble with the law before; for the state, the crucial given was his prior identification as a gang member. For a long time, she refused to engage the state on its own terms, because she thought things should work out fairly: "I believed I had constitutional rights. I mean, I *really* thought I had constitutional rights. But I found out . . . in the courtroom . . . that I am a second-class citizen. The Constitution does not apply to me."

For African Americans there is nothing new in realizing, once again, second-class citizen status (Du Bois [1935] 1992; Sykes 1988; Fields 1990). But while repetition is part of the deadly drama of living in a racial state, the particular challenge is to work out the specific realignments of the social structure in a period of rapid change.

Toward the end of one of her long, lonely days, before the confession and plea-bargain deal was struck, Bernice drove toward home from a visit with Stick, frightened that they were losing and unable to understand why. She happened to tune in a radio program about the trial of the LA Four and heard a defendant's mother talking about ROC. While Bernice had thrown herself into her child's case because she was his mother, she had never thought about forming alliances with parents in similar circumstances. Keenly aware that being able to claim her maternal relation to Stick made some difference—court officers and bureaucrats might return a mother's call or respond to one who spends hours waiting on molded plastic seats in anterooms or standing in corridors—Bernice decided to attend a Mothers ROC meeting to see if they could help her.

The ROCers encouraged her to get her story out, to start a chapter over in her part of the county, and to reach out to other mothers like herself in the places where she spent so much time on Stick's behalf. Bernice promptly wrote the first edition of *A Mother's Plea for Help*. She visited a number of copy shops looking for affordable rates and found an establishment run by a man who became sympathetic with her cause after she explained her plight. He agreed to let her use his machines at a discounted rate; and she began to produce her news on brightly colored paper (usually orange, sometimes startling blue) to catch the prospective reader's eye. Combining narrative, scripture, and cartoons, Bernice's two-to-six-page broadsides attracted the attention of mothers and others engaged in the unwaged reproductive labor of reclaiming the future by saving their children.

Eventually, Bernice established a regional meeting in the Inland Empire (the area straddling the nexus of Los Angeles, San Bernardino, and Riverside Counties). Every Saturday, new mothers and others arrived at a Pomona coffeehouse with a broad range of problems; some were trying to stop drug dealers on their streets; others had lost their children to the Department of Youth and Family Services and wanted them back. Men from churches, the Nation of Islam, and several local Black fraternal organizations came to observe and offer help. They also came to let the ROCers know that city and street politics were already under the informal jurisdiction of the old urban coalition organizations such as the NAACP and the churches; thus any new organizing required the blessing of particular power brokers. It quickly became clear that the stages and stakes of the old struggles—churches, city hall, the schools, the civil service—would be helpful but hardly adequate to the new struggle. The implicit caution and challenge from the old civil rights elites, then, came to nothing for two reasons. First, their highly developed localism availed little against a state-organized criminalization project consisting of combined and overlapping jurisdictions. Second, under the weight of the region's ongoing political-economic crisis, the golden-age Black-white coalitions were crumbling, while at the same time Chicana/os' achievement of elected and appointed positions signaled certain, if unpredictable, changes to come (cf. Sonenshein 1993).

The ROCers determined to find out about the STEP Act under which Stick had been charged and sentenced. One Saturday afternoon, a group gathered in a California lawyer's library to read up on the law. None of the participants was an attorney, but they had extensive experience in research and writing, and they assumed it would take them an hour or two at most to find the statute and write a statement about it for a flyer. Several hours into their quest, they all realized that the arcana of legal letters starts at the most fundamental level of organization; an outsider could not simply slide her finger down a table of contents or index to find a law. A subcommittee of the group found the law's text the following week by talking their way into a library with an electronic legal database service, and doing electronic subject searches.[14]

The STEP Act, and the events leading up to its implementation, made abundantly clear what the mothers feared: the "system" had for years been designating a profile of young persons whose rights and prospects were statutorily different from those of others in their cohort. The Task Force on Youth Gang Violence had stipulated that the region most in need of surveillance and control was in the Southland, and that Black and Brown youths were most likely to be gang members (California State Task Force 1986). While it had stretched the analysis of gang violence to encompass suicidal propensities among white middle-class "Heavy Metal" and "Satanic" gangs, the task force absolutely ignored, for instance, the growing skinhead and neo-Nazi gangs concentrated in the Southland (R. W. Gilmore 1993b).

The act's directive compelling local enforcement to identify all gang members in their jurisdictions seemed to the mothers likely to produce indiscriminate listings that would include people based on race and space, and that this, in turn, would transform any kind of youthful stepping out of line into major confrontations with the system. Acting on their new knowledge about the STEP Act, the ROCers decided to expand their stage of activism in order to prepare audiences and future actors for what the drama was really all about. They produced a flyer titled *MOTHERS WARN*

YOUR CHILDREN, alerting principal caregivers to forbid their dependents to sign papers or allow their pictures to be taken by police on the street. Minors should insist that their parents be called. Adults should politely but firmly demur. The flyers were extremely effective ways to start conversations at bus stops, in the blistering sun at the county jail parking lot, and outside schools, courthouses, and police stations. Both men and women took the flyers—often promising to duplicate and distribute them at church or work. New people arrived at the Inland Empire meeting, flyer in hand, to learn more about the act.

Bernice had to expand her daily activities. The combined events of Stick's confession and the discovery of the STEP Act increased her labor; in addition to duties of home, job, and the court/jail complex, she now had to learn more about how the act and related laws worked, politically and juridically, and whether anyone had successfully opposed the statutes. Chastened by the afternoon in the lawyer's library, she started spending her free days in the library at the UCLA Law School. By browsing and asking the reference librarian strategic questions, Bernice discovered how to find summaries of recent cases and judgments, how to find the full arguments of those cases, and how to compare the growing stacks of paper to Stick's case.

In the short run, neither new knowledge nor new comrades made Bernice's struggle easier; on the contrary, she realized that she would have to work longer and harder hours as the mother of a kidnapped child. Since Stick's accomplices were never charged with anything, since people not enrolled in gang databases charged with similar offenses receive far lighter sentences, and since young people from different racial, class, or regional positions are often diverted to rehabilitation programs, Bernice set out to make the case of discriminatory prosecution, augmented by other claims, such as ineffective counsel. Indeed, Bernice perceived what had once been a state-identified chink in its own armor a generation earlier, when the first set of postwar federal antigang street crime acts was enacted between 1968 and 1970.[15] At that time, law enforcement hesitated to exercise the statutes because of civil rights concerns—especially in the area of discriminatory prosecution.

However, more than two decades of political-economic crisis, coupled with intensive and extensive crime sensationalism in the media (political campaigns, news programming, reality-based shows, movies, and television series), had produced the notion that some people's rights should be restricted based on prior patterns of behavior, which was now perceived as common sense.[16]

The intensification of Bernice's anxieties and labors on behalf of her son, coupled with her new occupation helping out and reassuring other mothers in similar predicaments, impeded her nursing. She had always derived great satisfaction from caring for sick people. However, not long before Stick's troubles began, a racist patient in the regional hospital where she had worked for several years had informed a floor supervisor that he did not want the Black nurse to touch him. Bernice decided to find a new job serving a predominantly African American clientele, and she loved looking after "my Black patients," most of whom suffered from chronic, and often terminal, ailments. As is the case with so much "women's" work, nursing requires physical, intellectual, and emotional labor (Cobble 1991; Duffy 2005). This, on top of Stick's plight, wore Bernice out—especially emotionally. Ironically, she gave up "women's" paid work in order to do "women's" unpaid work, her inability to nurse enabling her to become a full-time mother. But full-time mothering meant being a "co-mother"

(Tula 1994) with the ROCers, an advocate for her son and all the others—adults and children—caught up in the system.

The web of laws and mandates the ROCers found themselves tangled in was so complex that it seemed to many mothers as though the public defenders who *could* take the time to explain things were spinning tales. Eventually, however, the stories revealed patterns to investigate. Gilda Garcia's testimony exemplified many sociospatial constraints of everyday life for ROCers and their families:

> And then she [the public defender] said, "The reason the prosecutor can add the extra time is because your son was within 500 feet of a school when he was picked up." My son went to bring his little brother home from school! That's why he was at the school. *La migra* waits by schools to catch people without green cards, and they detain anybody who looks like us. Anybody. We sent our son because he doesn't have a job, so if they stop him we don't lose any money. We're just making it. We can't afford to miss work just because INS needs to look good to . . . I don't mean any offense, but . . . they need to look good for the white people. They don't care about us, that we have jobs. It's all a show. But in the morning, as soon as my husband and I drive away to work, the [city] police are on our street, starting stuff, making our kids mad, telling them they are going to get them. One day I went back because I forgot something, and the police were there, outside of their cars. I asked them, "What is wrong? What do you want here?" And this one cop, his name is ——— [knowing laughter in the room], told me, "We're going to get your son," and he called my son names. He told me my son was in a gang. But see, I know he isn't in a gang, because the gang they said he was in is in another neighborhood. My son could not live with us and be in that gang. I have relatives in that gang, who have an auto body shop, and sometimes my son does some

work for them to make a few dollars. But he could never join that gang, because of where we live. Everyone knows that.

As the newcomers like Gilda shared their stories, and began to help each other on cases, Bernice began to understand why she had been so perplexed. While there had been no doubt in her mind that she and Stick were up against a *system,* it became clearer and clearer how the system specifically targeted children like hers, and Gilda's, and Barbara's. She had imagined the criminal justice system was on the other side of a fixed line of law, rather than that the law had moved to include her and her family in its legal and social space.

California's expanding criminal justice system overlaid the state's restructuring landscape with new prisons, new laws targeting people in specific areas, new mandates for law enforcement, prosecutors, and judges; these territorial and discursive regions constituted the system's political geography that the mothers were trying to find their way through. Their techniques of mothering, in and as Mothers ROC, extended past the limits of household, kinship, and neighborhood, to embrace the political project to reclaim children of all ages whose mothers were losing them, at a net rate of fifty-five statewide per business day, into the prison system.

ONE STATE + TWO LAWS = THREE STRIKES

[W]hen the woes of the poor press most dangerously upon the rich, then an age searches most energetically to pierce the future for hope.

PETER LINEBAUGH, *THE LONDON HANGED* (1992)

Prayer framed every Mothers ROC meeting. At the beginning and end of each session, the group held hands in a circle to ask for protection and guidance. The women who led the prayers had a gift for preaching. Their invocations set and summarized the seemingly endless agenda of reclaiming the children within a material context of spiritual hope realized through human action. Prayer helped span the visible and invisible social distances among people for whom, in most cases, organized religion was a vital aspect of life. Prayer also figured the power of attentive listening for group-building. During prayer, anyone in the group might comment affirmatively on the leader's devotional trajectory, and such encouragement of the speaker encouraged the collectivity, as one and then several voices would rise, lifting the speaker's higher. And finally, by emphasizing the difficulty and urgency of the situation that had brought them together, prayer renewed and strengthened the mothers' provisional unity. Individual differences, which occasionally produce incidents, did not need to become persistent organizational impediments—in a house of worship or in the ROC.

The group meditation on power and powerlessness established the scene in which mothers are able to identify with one another in a fast-changing world. In 1994, the FBI recorded 11,500,000 arrests by federal, state, and local law enforcement. In 1995, the number increased to 14,500,000 (U.S. Bureau of the Census, *Statistical Abstract,* 1995, 1996). Arrest and incarceration are common in the United States, yet those who are touched by law enforcement are so segregated, in many different ways, that the experience of confrontation with the legal system does not of itself produce any kind of strong social identification. In the ROC and elsewhere, the similarity of mothers' stories could produce a sense of commonality, but without guarantees that such a sensibility might serve as the basis for collective action. Within a social order of wide and deep inequality—most forcefully expressed as racial inequality—the mothers were cautious, because not all children are equally vulnerable to the law's harsh punishments.

When Pearl Daye's thirty-one-year-old son called from the police station to say he had been arrested for allegedly shoplifting a package of razor blades from a discount drugstore, she was confused—he had a steady job—and distressed—he had not been in any kind of trouble for more than eight years.

Going to the station to post bail, Pearl found it set at an absolutely unattainable $650,000, because the Los Angeles County District Attorney's office had charged Harry Daye with a third-strike felony rather than a petty theft misdemeanor. Suddenly, the African American man faced a mandatory minimum sentence of twenty-five years to life without possibility of parole.

As Pearl related the compounding events of Harry's arrest and accusation at her first Mothers ROC meeting, she often had to pause because of the breathtaking anxiety of revealing seemingly unbelievable adverse family circumstances to strangers. However, the roomful of women recognized the Dayes' drama as neither bureaucratic error nor bad dream, but rather as an increasingly ordinary conflict between families like theirs and the law. The plot had already become so familiar, one year into implementation of California's three strikes act, that at certain moments, a number of women, as though they were a chorus, recited with Pearl what the public defender and others had told her—especially the guaranteed sentence of twenty-five years to life without the possibility of parole, known on the street more briefly as "twenty-five to . . . without."

Harry Daye faced the death of freedom because at that time

the Los Angeles County district attorney's written policy was to enforce the three strikes law vigorously. Such vigor included charging defendants to ensure the longest possible prison sentences, regardless of the current character of the defendant's life. Harry's alleged petty theft constituted what California law designates a "wobbler"—a charge that can be treated as either a misdemeanor or a felony. Three strikes and other minimum-mandatory-sentence laws, conventionally portrayed to work with a machinelike disregard for individual circumstance, actually explicitly allow prosecutors and judges to use discretion "in the furtherance of justice." However, throughout California—especially in the southern counties that produce most prisoners—the practice of prosecutorial or judicial discretion in favor of second- or third-strike defendants was throughout the 1990s so rare as to be newsworthy (see, e.g., Gorman 1996).

Pearl ended her introductory testimony to Mothers ROC with an observation about the entire system: "The way I see it there are two laws, one for the Black, and one for the white." Leticia Gonzales, a Chicana whose husband had started a "twenty-five to . . . without" sentence some months earlier, disagreed. "No. I think there is one law for the people of color, and another law for the white." By this time, everyone was talking. Francie Arbol proposed another structure: "Poor people and rich people." But poor versus rich failed to explain the state versus O. J. Simpson. Why was the Los Angeles County District Attorney's Office spending so much time and money to convict one Black defendant?[17] Therefore, the distinction could not be rich versus poor. At the same time, because virtually all the prisoners anyone in the room knew or could imagine were people of modest means from working-class families, the money question could not simply be dropped. Anti-Black racism seemed to explain a great deal, but could not account for all poverty, powerlessness, and vulnerability before the law. In the year or so before Pearl Daye brought her case to ROC, Latino (mostly Chicano and Mexicano) prisoners surpassed African Americans as the largest group in absolute numbers in CDC custody.[18] The unevenness in outcome for people of color lies in both patterns of policing and the offense with which defendants are charged. For example, in Los Angeles County, white defendants would be far more likely to have charges reduced from felonies to misdemeanors or dropped completely, while people of color are more likely to have the harshest possible charge leveled against them (Schiraldi and Godfrey 1994; see also Nasar 1994). Both federal and California laws allow radically different treatment of people who have done essentially the same thing. Such police, prosecutorial, and judicial capacity—which, since its introduction in the early 1980s, has remained fundamentally impervious to challenges based on "equal protection" and other constitutional principles—provides both the means and the encouragement for application of substantively different rules and punishments to various kinds of defendants (see, e.g., Butler 1995).

It is not surprising, then, that the ROCers had a hard time developing a summary of how the law discriminates against and among those who are most vulnerable to the system. The law's ability to wobble made routinely unequal punishments possible. At the same time, the wobble made developing a commonsense definition of how such inequality is achieved and reproduced on

a case-by-case basis very difficult indeed. Everyone who spoke—
nearly everyone in the room—had no doubt that the system operated on a dual track. But how is each defendant routed?

Leticia Gonzales could match Pearl's story horror for horror.
Her husband had been tried and convicted for shoplifting a pair
of pants during the Christmas shopping rush. She was convinced
that either nobody took anything, or that somebody else, who
looks like her husband, took the items. "Why would he take
some pants? He could buy them. And at Christmas, there are
guards everywhere around at the stores. He's not stupid." However, since in his deep past he had been convicted on two counts
of robbery, the petty theft of a pair of inexpensive trousers became, in his case, robbery, sending him away for "twenty-five
to . . . without."

Leticia heard about the ROC from her husband, who had
learned about it in the county jail. She was afraid to come to the
meeting at first, because she did not know anybody, lived down
in San Pedro, and was afraid she might not be welcome. Much to
her surprise, the group, still composed predominantly of African
Americans, did welcome her, and as the months went by, more
and more Latinas showed up at the door. Mothers of sixteen-
year-olds charged with murder. Wives of second- and third-
strike defendants. Grandmothers of kids charged under the
STEP Act. Indeed, the Black and Brown cadres of *abuelas* began
to hold occasional caucuses—after the manner of the grandmothers of Argentina's Plaza de Mayo—to discuss their unique
problems, which often centered on their status as undocumented
primary caregivers to their children's children.

The number of Latinas attending meetings increased, as the
Los Angeles County prosecutor extended vigorous enforcement

of California's 1,200 new pieces of criminal legislation to Brown as well as Black defendants. The night of Pearl Daye's first visit, the ROC's debate about the law's unequal application continued well into the evening and spilled out onto the sidewalk after the regular meeting came to a close. The crucial issue in resolving the question had to do with maintaining organizational solidarity, which the closing prayer emphasized as the session's unfinished business. Finally, one of the women proposed a solution. There are, as Pearl had said, two laws—one for Black people and one for white people. Given how the prosecutors had started charging more and more Brown and other poor defendants under the new laws, especially the three strikes act, then perhaps the explanation could be put this way: You have to be white to be prosecuted under white law, but you do not have to be Black to be prosecuted under Black law. The resolution satisfied that evening's debaters, because it provided a way for the women to recognize one another through the extension of prosecutorial practices without ignoring African Americans' indisputable experience of the new laws' most intensive application.

Not long after discovery of the Black/white law solution, a local power broker came calling on the ROC. The African American man, who had made a small fortune running secured (locked-down) drug rehabilitation units for the state, wanted the ROC's blessing to build a private prison (owned by him) in the neighborhood where the CDC would send selected prisoners to serve the final year of their sentences. He assured the women that the prison would be run in accordance with community wishes, since the city would not grant a conditional use permit for the location without community approval. For many ROCers, this visit crystallized the dynamic contradiction in the system they had taken on. If the ROC was right, then the prison was unnecessary. If the prison came in, accompanied by "jobs," then part of the ROC's critique—poverty—would seem to have been addressed by expanding the specific object of the ROC's opposition—cages. As the carceral entrepreneur—himself an ex-prisoner—explained how much good the prison would bring to South Central, the ROCers listened closely. Then, in an orderly show of political passion, each one told him why, from her perspective, the ROC would never endorse the facility. His claim that somehow the community could control the inner workings of a prison because of its location struck them as ludicrous; they had learned that distance is not simply measured in miles, and that the prison would not be a neighborhood or community facility, but rather a state incapacitation facility run according to state rules. His promise that perhaps their own children might be in the prison elicited, at first, an emotional moment of hope on the part of some women, who drove fifteen-year-old cars four hundred miles round-trip on Saturdays to see their sons. But the record of failures in many of the campaigns to have children moved closer to their families indicated that the people in the proposed South Central prison would not likely come from the area. The ROC told the entrepreneur, over and over, that they would not remedy the disappearance of jobs at GM, Firestone, and Kaiser by putting half the population into prisons so the other half could make money watching them. They sent him on his way, somewhat bruised by their blunt words.

The visit provoked the members to ask themselves what else they should be doing to stop the prison from going up in South Central. They knew that the prison would go up somewhere—the power broker had assured them of that—and so protesting at the local level would not solve the problem. Clearly, the ROC had to expand its activities to an adequate scale. At the next meeting, they decided to take on the brutal three strikes law in order to build a statewide coalition of people who would be likely to help fight the expansion of prisons as California's all-purpose solution to social problems involving the poor. That project, inaugurated in January 1996, built slowly over a year, eventually culminating in a "Three Strikes Awareness Month" during which teach-ins, radio and television appearances, and leafleting outside court-houses raised consciousness of the legislation's effect. Although the scale of activity grew, so did uneasinesses and antagonisms as the ROC entered a new organizational phase, in which the place where it had begun life in the ERC's office might remain the symbolic, but not necessarily the political, center of the group.

YOU CAN'T MAKE ANY MONEY HOLDING BAKE SALES: NEW SITUATIONS, NEW STRATEGIES

While Mothers Reclaiming our Children started off with the kinds of amenities—office, telephone, fax, copier—that most fledgling grassroots groups lack, the meager initial advantage created the basis for future needs. In particular, the organization's capacity to plan outreach and strategy around the three strikes law rested on the fact that it had a place, could make and receive telephone calls, produce flyers, and get communiqués to and from other concerned activists—including a few inside key state offices—printed reasonably rapidly. To some ROCers, however, this flurry of activity—while important—threatened the Mothers' core purpose and constituency both by diverting material resources and by turning so much attention toward one category of defendant/prisoner.

In order to achieve stability in the newest crisis, ROCers from both tendencies agreed to formalize as a not-for-profit organization. Across the divide, the activists agreed that a mission statement would be an objective standard against which all collective undertakings could be measured, and they also agreed that current and future projects would require substantial income. The agreements produced sustained disagreement as factions tried to fashion mission statements commensurate with what they thought the group should become. The debate shifted a good deal of everyday work from the politics of organizing to the politics of organization. In other words, reworking themselves into an institution—with written rules, a governing board, and detailed expenditures—became, for a while, *the* ROC activity.

The astonishing suppleness of the ROC's earlier days gave way in this period to slower and more deliberate methods; it was as if the structural imperative everyone wished to satisfy ruled out a future in which the women and men could depend on ad hoc summonings of sense, experience, and spirit to work through problems and differences. What they hoped to gain in return for the sacrifice of spontaneity was the sturdiness of reproducibility: not an ad hoc future, but a predictable one. Of course, to guarantee a future meant to become legitimate, to seek shelter in one corner of the state while doing battle in many others. But being so sheltered also meant getting "legal"—following rules, no less than laws, with the specter of noncompliance standing in as a shadow policeman. Poverty and underdevelopment persist because the way out is across the very infrastructured barriers that make it possible to identify poor regions, or neighborhoods, or races, or genders, in the first place; being locked in and locked out are two sides of the same coin. A good deal of the early excitement

at the prospect of becoming a registered not-for-profit organization centered on the hopeful misunderstanding that achieving
tax-exempt status under Section 501(c)(3) of the Internal Revenue
Code was in itself a development plan—as though eligibility for
certain kinds of money were a fiscally magnetic force. Those with
different understandings—from prior experience or present
study—began to think quite practically about fund sources, given
the ROC's potential range of not-for-profit practices. Grants?
Speaker fees? Services? T-shirts?

A consultant who specialized in helping grassroots groups incorporate encouraged the group to think creatively, while cau-
tioning that they could not make any significant money from
holding bake sales. The reminder that neighborly voluntarism
could not guarantee the ROC's future forced everyone to think
about the array of funding options that might realistically be
forthcoming. In other words, whenever the work focused on
budget building—the "business" of legally legitimate activism—
discussions gravitated toward the cooperative self-help mode
that gave the ROC its early local appeal and strength, setting
aside more expansive political strategies the three strikes faction
struggled to realize.

Polled separately and informally, every ROCer wanted to save
everybody caught up in the criminal justice system, but polled collectively and formally, most said their organizational attention
ought to concentrate on youth. By the mid 1990s, organizing on
behalf of young people "at risk" had gained cachet among the
kinds of small regional foundations from which the ROC might
get seed money. At the same time, governmental agencies, such as
the U.S. Department of Justice, dangled money for community-
based organizations in cities that agreed to trade "weeds" (crimi-

nalizable adults or juveniles) to law enforcement for "seeds" (grants).[19] Deindustrialization and crumbling welfare state institutions combined to create emergencies that were addressed by the official sector—if at all—either through the expanding system of criminalization or, in a smaller way (at least when measured by expenditure per youth, if not in absolute numbers), through the interventions of not-for-profit organizations fueled by pre- or posttax dollars. The ROC did not predicate its future on what was fundable. However, it incorporated at a time when the public abandonment of young people applied increased pressures throughout the quasi-private caring community. Therefore, to join that community "officially" meant taking on that pressure and, as a result, "naturally" taking up that work.

Although popular, the campaign to overturn the three strikes law had less natural appeal than saving kids among those most intent on establishing the ROC's formal structure. The arduous work of coalition building—any campaign's first step—requires constant deal making and compromise, even as the character of the struggle is redefined in the practice of producing consent. Or, as the singer-activist Bernice Johnson Reagon liked to put it: "If you're in a coalition and you're comfortable, you're not in . . . a coalition" (Reagon 1983). Since the ROC was in process of defining itself, negotiating externally seemed precisely to threaten the stability and autonomy that members sought to solidify internally.

The strain of give-and-take should have strengthened the core, as it had in the past, particularly because the ROC was the undisputed force behind the new, slowly coalescing, anti–three strikes movement. In a way, the challenge did prove to be strengthening, but not in anticipated or previously experienced ways. At the end of the day, the Mothers rolled down as two boulders: the new, incorporated, youth-oriented ROC; and the heart of an emerging statewide organization (which itself incorporated after two years of struggle) called Families to Amend California's Three Strikes (FACTS).

In the scramble to institutionalize an identity—to secure a reliable, reproducible, public face—the stresses and strains sometimes degenerated into personality conflicts. Accusations of disrespect flew furiously, and it was fairly common during meetings for people to step outside, caucus in the driveway, and return with hardened faces and steely glares. As happened in the early days around the communist scare, some police made informal, friendly suggestions to ROCers about how they could enhance their legitimacy by distancing themselves from extremists.

What constituted extremism? For the police, extremism meant any willingness to face off with (and mouth off at) authority, particularly uniformed authority. But within the group's logic, extremism seemed also to mean any combination of ambition and compromise. Thus, each side saw the other as extreme. The anti–three strikes contingent denounced as "unwilling to do anything" those who emphasized conserving identity through the articles of incorporation and the local, reproducible, repetitive work that would come from success in the endeavor. The latter group, in turn, shook their heads and wagged their tongues at the anti–three strikes faction's seemingly impossible scheme to implant family-based opposition to draconian laws and the media-enhanced fears that produced them into the vastness of California.

While those working on the anti–three strikes campaign initially strove to form a coalition of already existing organizations, the outreach that generated the most stable chapters around California used the ROC methods. It should not be surprising to realize that people who drive long distances to see loved ones will make small talk in parking lots and discover an identity in their immediate purpose, which then might be amplified in open-ended organizing and advocacy. What is surprising, perhaps, is that the temporary camaraderie of those emotional encounters became the basis for trust enabling the newly formed collectives of people with modest resources, mostly women, to do things on a less-than-modest scale. They learned to make plans long distance, use library email capacities, devise agendas, collect signatures on petitions, and eventually come together, lobby elected officials, hold rallies in Sacramento, and, within two years, form a new entity—this time a 501(c)(4) nonprofit organization with an expressly, if narrowly, political purpose.

While FACTS was amassing membership around the state—including many among the (by 1998) more than 50,000 prisoners in the CDC's custody on second or third strikes—the ROC moved office twice. The first time was uptown, across the freeway, out of South Central, to Wilshire Boulevard. Fancy as the address sounds, the location is one where a number of low-budget not-for-profits have concentrated in buildings once the exclusive domain of high-wage service providers such as law and accounting firms. Mid Wilshire, for the moment, was a remnant of the old space economy, with beautiful art deco buildings decaying in capital limbo before their rediscovery by the next round of investment.

Although the ROC meetings continued every Wednesday at the original place, the relocation of the office, while only a short distance away, severely disrupted the group's cohesiveness. In retrospect, it seems that the layers of formalities—becoming a 501(c)(3) organization and settling into a businesslike office—invigorated a few while alienating many. People just didn't go there.

Barbara Meredith, who continued as president throughout the transition, found the new setup discouraging after a while. The last thing she ever wanted to do was sit alone in a big office waiting for something to happen. What happened was that energy drained from the ROC; some people drifted away, while others, including Francie Arbol, transferred most of their activism to building FACTS.

With her son Gilbert finally released from prison, Barbara Meredith decided that her daily work ought to reach back to those among whom she had done her earliest organizing—the young people (parents as well as kids) at Imperial Courts, whom she saw as tomorrow's strikers, especially given the increased use of zero tolerance and police in public schools and the increasingly common resort to lawmaking and enforcement, rather than informal sanctions, when young people acted out. After she and Gilbert persuaded the Housing Authority to grant them an apartment for on-site activism, Barbara Meredith closed down the Wilshire office and opened the new one a hundred blocks south, where they had walked the streets nearly ten years earlier to accomplish the one-day truce. And while, by day, Gilbert worked for a state senator, he worked around the clock to maintain the gang truce in honor of his dead cousin and the many men and women serving long sentences, as he had done.

FROM THE CRISIS OF PLACE TO THE POLITICS OF SPACE
Arrest is the political art of individualizing disorder.
ALLEN FELDMAN, *FORMATIONS OF VIOLENCE* (1991)

For millions of people in the United States each year, the individual nature of arrest produces fragmentation rather than connection, because each person and household, dealing with each arrest, must figure out how to undo the detention—which appears to be nothing more than a highly specific confrontation between the individual and law enforcement. The larger disorder is then distorted to reflect only a portion of social fragilities, and measured, like unemployment, as though its changing rate in a society were a force of nature (see, e.g., Greenwood et al. 1994; Wilson and Herrnstein 1985). ROCers gradually but decisively refused to be isolated and began to develop oppositional political arts centered on creating an order different from the one built by the state out of more and bigger prisons. They arrived at their art through critical action. Action, crucially, includes the difficult work of identification—which entails production, not discovery, of a "suture or positioning" (Stuart Hall 1990).

By enlivening African American practices of social mothering, the ROCers engaged a broadening community in their concern for the circumstances and fate of prisoners. That social opening provided avenues for all kinds of mothers (and others) to join in the work, because the enormous labor confronting each mother tended to encourage all of them both to accept and extend help. I make no claim for "social mothering" as an exclusively or universally African American cultural practice; it is neither. However, Barbara Meredith's commonsense invocation of mothering as collective action made possible the group's integration of mothers with similar or quite different maternalist assumptions (Kaplan 1982; Collins 1990; see also Traugott 1995). In other words, techniques developed over generations on behalf of Black children and families within terror-demarcated, racially defined enclaves provided contemporary means to choreograph interracial political solidarity among all kinds of caregivers losing their loved ones into the prison system. These mothers and others identified one another in the tight public spaces between their socially segregated residential living places and the unitized carceral quarters in which their loved ones are caged. Some were shy about jumping into the process, while others came to the ROC for help on their individual cases only; but all who persisted practiced the "each one teach one" approach.[20]

The process of integrating different kinds of mothers and others into the ROC involved extensive outreach designed to permeate the social organization of space. These projects also caught people in the "betweens" of segregated lives: at work, for example, or on the bus. Like the Justice for Janitors Los Angeles crusade, however, this approach raised a more general problem of identification. The ROCers easily recognized one another in the spaces of the criminal justice system. Outside those areas, how do people resemble each other? If we are not all Black, and if all activists are not mothers, and if all prisoners are not (minor) children, then who are we? Poor people who work. As a community of purpose, Mothers ROC acted on the basis of a simple inversion: we are not poor because our loved ones are in prison; rather, our loved ones are in prison because we are poor. It followed that outreach should target working poor people and their youth. Class, then, while the context for this analysis and action, cannot displace or subsume the changing role and definitions of race: poor people of color have the most loved ones in prison.

As a matter of fact, the primacy of class is thoroughly gendered: women who work to support their families and to free their loved ones encounter one another as laborers with similar triple workdays—job, home, justice. Moreover, mothers who reject the disposal of their children and ask why they themselves should not be compensated for struggling against the state raise a challenge to both their children's and their own devaluations from the vantage of the declining welfare state and the perils of reproductive labor (Dalla Costa and James 1972; Fortunati 1995; Quick 1992).[21] The communist organizational and analytical influences in the ROC kept these complicated interrelated issues in the foreground of activism. In the context of shared opposition, the activists "discovered" (Kaplan 1982)—which is to say, created—shared values; in turn, that collective work produced community solidarity, or political integration, enabling further action. Solidarity increased with increased knowledge about the complexity of how power blocs have built the new state by building prisons. Thus an individual police precinct house no longer loomed as the total presence of the state, shrinking back toward its real position—the neighborhood outpost of what both the ROCers and FACTS characterized as a military occupation.[22] If it takes a village to raise a child, it certainly takes a movement to undo an occupation. As Mothers ROC went deep and FACTS went broad, both sought to immerse themselves in other communities of activism, reaching out nationally and internationally to similar organizations.[23] Such motion then and now heightens the potential for connections between women struggling against prison expansion and women throughout the global workforce who struggle daily against the actual processes and effects of worldwide structural adjustments.[24]

Mothers ROC critically used the ideological power of motherhood to challenge the legitimacy of the changing state. All prisoners are somebody's children, and children are not alienable (see Cornell 1995). The racial and gendered social division of labor required mothers of prisoners to live lives of high visibility; ROCers turned that visibility to a politically charged presence, voice, and movement against injustice, such that their activism became the centerpiece of their reproductive—and socially productive—labor (see Fisher 1989). As with mothers' movements in Latin America, South Africa, and Palestine, Mothers ROC's frontline relation to the state was not as a petitioner for a share in the social wage but rather as an opponent of the state's changing form and purpose with respect to the life chances of their family members and those like them. The insistence on the rights of mothers to children and children to mothers was not a defense of traditional domesticity as a separate sphere; rather, it represented political activation around rising awareness of the specific ways that the contemporary working-class household is a site saturated by the neoliberal racial state.

Mothers Reclaiming Our Children evolved from a self-help group that formed in response to a crisis of place—a police murder in South Central Los Angeles—into a pair of political organizations trying to build a powerful movement across the spaces of domestic militarism.

A small, poor, multiracial group of working-class people, mostly prisoners' mothers, mobilized in the interstices of the officially abandoned, heavily policed, declining welfare state. They came forward in the first instance because they could not let their children go. They remained at the fore, in the spaces created by intensified imprisonment of their loved ones, because they encountered many mothers and others in the same locations eager to join in the reclamation project. And they pushed further, because from those breaches they saw and tried to occupy positions from which collectively to challenge their political, economic,

and cultural de-development brought about by the individualized involuntary migration of urban "surplus population," and
the potential values that go with that population, into rural prisons. For the ROC and FACTS successfully to oppose the disposal
of their loved ones, they organized to challenge the fullest possible reach of state (and civilian) powers arrayed against them.
Working through cases, they built alliances of and as multiracial
groups that create and sustain solid centers of activism throughout and across the "nested scales" (Smith 1992) of the rising
prison state. Thus both groups demonstrate the possibilities and
the urgent difficulties of organizing across the many boundaries
that rationalize and reinforce apartheid America. Indeed, their
work might well exemplify what utopia is these days—social
perfectibility recognizable in something as modest as people getting on a bus.

SIX

WHAT IS TO BE DONE?

he patient reader has traveled a long way in a short book. The journey, like the one undertaken by the bus riders in the Prologue, is an adventure of possibility rather than certainty. While the outcomes to cooperative human efforts are never ever guaranteed, I certainly believe this: the lessons I've drawn from researching and writing these pages while simultaneously engaging in political work advise us to quit the divisions, old and new, that trap us in doomed methods of analysis and action. There are obvious divisions that, as we have seen throughout the Central Valley Mother's ROC chapters, can and should be overcome. Most urgently, we must lift our ability to recognize how to craft campaigns that both create solid organizations and foster robust coalitions among already existing organizations. The following theses—which suggest themes for amplifying the work—are a modest attempt to propel us to a different scale by showing both myriad locations where activism can take root and flourish and the potential for connecting those sites into something bigger. The outcome of this adventure might be simply a more general, and therefore more comprehensive, way of acting on problems in the political-economic geography that currently prevails. Or a different scale might signal the development of innovative social and spatial relationships and capacities for action—just as the "Third World" and "Pan-Africanism" did for earlier generations.

The proliferation of antiprison groups during the decade when this book was in progress indicates how many kinds of people understand that prison is not a building "over there" but a set of relationships that undermine rather than stabilize everyday lives everywhere. Unfortunately, many remedies proposed for the all-purpose use of prisons to solve social, political, and economic problems get caught in the logic of the system itself, such that a reform strengthens, rather than loosens, prison's hold. In a sense, the professionalization of activism has made many committed people so specialized and entrapped by funding streams that they have become effectively deskilled when it comes to thinking and doing what matters most. What are the possibilities of nonreformist reform—of changes that, at the end of the day, unravel rather than widen the net of social control through criminalization?

If we take to heart the fact that we make places, things, and selves, but not under conditions of our own choosing, then it is easier to take the risk of conceiving change as something both short of and longer than a single cataclysmic event. Indeed, the chronicles of revolutions all show how persistent small changes, and altogether unexpected consolidations, added up to enough weight, over time and space, to cause a break with the old order. Certainly, the political forces that hold governmental power in the United States of the early twenty-first century figured this out and persisted for decades until they won. With persistence, practices and theories circulate, enabling people to see problems and their solutions differently—which then creates the possibility of further, sometimes innovative, action.

Such change is not just a shift in ideas or vocabulary or frameworks, but rather in the entire structure of meanings and feelings (the lived ideology, or "taking to heart") through which we actively understand the world and place our actions in it (Williams 1961). Ideology matters along its entire continuum, from common sense ("where people are at") to philosophies (where people imagine the coherence of their understanding comes from: Jesus, Mohammed, the Buddha, Marx, Malcolm X, the market).

The bottom line is this: if the twentieth century was the age of genocide on a planetary scale, then in order to avoid repeating history, we ought to prioritize coming to grips with dehumanization. Dehumanization names the deliberate, as well as the mob-frenzied, ideological displacements central to any group's ability to annihilate another in the name of territory, wealth, ethnicity, religion. Dehumanization is also a necessary factor in the acceptance that millions of people (sometimes including oneself) should spend part or all of their lives in cages.

In the contemporary world, racism is the ordinary means through which dehumanization achieves ideological normality, while, at the same time, the practice of dehumanizing people produces racial categories. Old races die, through extermination or assimilation, and new races come into being. The process is not biological, however, but rather the outcome of fatal encounters that ground contemporary political culture. This culture, in turn, is based in the modern secular state's dependence on classifica-

244 WHAT IS TO BE DONE?

tion, combined with militarism as a means through which classification maintains coherence. A sign of militarism's ideological embrace is the fact that all kinds of U.S.-based people believe without pause that, in a general way, "the key to safety is aggression" (Bartov 1996; R. W. Gilmore 2002a). Where classification and militarism collide is in the area of identifying an enemy. "The Japanese are an enemy race" wrote a State Department wonk in 1941, at the height of both Jim Crow and universal military conscription, as prelude to the internment of 120,000 people in concentration camps in the South and the West.

Sadly, even activists committed to antiracist organizing renovate commonsense divisions by objectifying certain kinds of people into a pre-given category that then automatically gets oppressed. What's the alternative? To see how the very capacities we struggle to turn to other purposes *make* races by making some people, and their biological and fictive kin, vulnerable to forces that make premature death likely and in some ways distinctive. The racialization of Muslims in the current era does double duty in both establishing an enemy whose being can be projected through the allegation of unshakable heritage (fundamentally, what the fiction of race is at best) and renewing the racial order of the U.S. polity as normal, even as it changes. Given these practices, it should not be all that surprising that hundreds of thousands of white men are also in prison; while they might be, as Pem Buck poignantly describes such people, a "reserve army of whiteness" (Buck 2001; see also Roediger 2002), I wouldn't count on it—not when the twenty-first century hasn't quite wrapped up what I call the age of human sacrifice. Such men, and their diverse caged brethren, might alternatively be, as Staughton Lynd's Lucasville prisoner activists novelly named themselves, the "convict race" (Lynd 2004). As ever, solidarity in the present is a precondition for any future less bleak than the past quarter century.

TEN THESES

1. A new kind of state—an antistate state—is being built on prison foundations. The antistate state depends on ideological and rhetorical dismissal of any agency or capacity that "government" might use to guarantee social well-being. Beginning with the premise that social wages in the shape of tax dollars belong to all of us, inasmuch as we produced them, people can organize at some political-geographic levels to take charge of resources and turn them to life-enhancing use.

2. Capitalists are not equally footloose, and the employment of working people's future surplus (what repayment of public debt is) is a political decision. Public sector financiers had a crisis in the 1980s—growing pools of investable cash but shrinking outlets that could only be resolved in the *political* arena. The problem is not, then, debt, but rather the uses to which public borrowing is put.

3. Starting in the 1980s, the federal government reduced its participation in state and local government funding of social programs, thereby passing along to lower-level administrative units the task of making up for federal tax cuts granted to big firms and rich individuals. This practice endures into the early twenty-first century, and scaling back—"devolution"—characterizes economic relations between states and their constituent cities and counties. These rollbacks demand attention to the dynamics of abandonment and the possibility of activism, and demand action to foster greater alliances between currently geographically and politically nonaligned impoverished places.

4. The compensatory implementation of regressive taxes such as sales tax and user fees has helped ensure that as local governments drew down their reserves and then tightened their belts, the poor would have higher relative costs and fewer services than their richer neighbors. As this complicated jumble of fiscal apartheid failed adequately to produce the desired goals, certain kinds of dead-end redevelopment schemes based in fiscalization of land plus tax breaks suggest a new regionalization of production and services, inviting activists to consider ways and means to intervene in decision making.

5. Voters and legislators decided to lock immigrants out of social services, to lock more people into prison for part or all of their lives, and to put a personal lock on opportunities in public sector education, employment, and contracts. This triple-pronged attack on working people demonstrates the potential for identifying linkages between immigrant, labor, and antiprison activism. In particular, if public sector and low-wage unions have made the greatest strides in the past twenty years, then their members are constrained by the growth of prisons. Prison jobs are few next to the plethora of non-cage-based employment possible when public sector investment is maximized for social goods such as schools, parks, museums, and mass transport.

6. In a place where research indicates that other outcomes might have occurred, Mothers ROC built an organization that spurred the founding and growth of even larger organizations. The ability to reach across social and spatial divides came from the Mothers' use of the ideological power of motherhood to challenge the legitimacy of the changing state. This activism, rooted in earlier rounds of antiracist work by both these women and their prior generations, shows how using the familiar opens the

possibility of identification through the crafting of purposeful action by continual revision.

7.   Mothers ROC's frontline relation to the state was not that of petitioners for a share of the available social wages, but rather in opposition to the state's form and purpose with respect to the life chances of the mothers' family members and those like them. By thinking through the general details of this antagonism, we can see how other kinds of oppositions become possible. Such imaginative responses then open the way to new solidarities based in recognition of the life-threatening harms that new and old racist structures produce in all kinds of households of all races and ethnicities.

8.   The places where prisons are built share many similarities with the places prisoners come from. Rural communities stuck in economies that have languished for more than twenty years have not profited from prisons as expected; rather, they continue to struggle for the same kinds of opportunities and protections that the urban mothers want for their biological and fictive kin. These forgotten places, and their urban counterparts, can be understood to form one political world, abandoned but hardly defeated.

9.   Racism is the state-sanctioned and/or extralegal production and exploitation of group-differentiated vulnerability to premature death. Prison expansion is a new iteration of this theme. Prisons and other locally unwanted land uses accelerate the mortality of modestly educated working people of all kinds in urban and rural settings and show how economic and environmental justice are central to antiracism.

10.   Power is not a thing but rather a capacity composed of active and changing relationships enabling a person, group, or institution to compel others to do things they would not do on

their own (such as be happy, or pay taxes, or go to war). Ordinarily, activists focus on *taking* power, as though the entire political setup were really a matter of "it" (structure) versus "us"
(agency). But if the structure-agency opposition isn't how things
really work, then perhaps politics is more complicated, and
therefore open to more hopeful action. People can and do *make*
power through, for example, developing capacities in organizations. But that's not enough, because all an individual organization can do on its own is tweak Armageddon. When the capacities resulting from purposeful action are combined toward ends
greater than mission statements or other provisional limits, powerful alignments begin to shake the ground. In other words,
movement happens.

ANOTHER BUS

▌n 2001, a group of people boarded another bus in South Central Los Angeles, this time bound for Fresno and a conference called Joining Forces: The Fight for Environmental Justice and against Prisons. Fewer rode this time, but their determination was no less fierce. They were headed to the second small conference in California bringing together rural people trying to stop the building of prisons and urban activists trying to stop the production of prisoners. Meeting was not easy, because for quite some time each group imagined that the other, in a general way, was the reason for its struggles. City people presumed everyone in rural towns wanted prisons, and rural activists feared that nobody in urban centers was trying to get at the root causes sending so many people into cages.

The recognition that forged solidarity between unlikely allies from Farmersville and Los Angeles was not spontaneous. However, something like magic seemed to happen. At the conference, activists talked about how their organizations identified problems, shaped good questions, searched for causes, and em-barked—often in fits and starts—on courses of action. Juana Gutierrez, the founder of Mothers of East Los Angeles, a group that stopped Sacramento from building a prison in their neigh-borhood, described how she and the other "crazy women" she worked with started to raise questions about why so many people presumed their kids would wind up in prison.

Guitierrez laid out the scenario—identifying what tech-nocrats would call "risk factors"—and paused at each one to raise a question about the problem. School, for example. Kids who miss a lot of school generally do not graduate, and young people without high school diplomas are more likely than those with credentials to wind up in cages. She and her friends asked why their kids were more likely to miss school, and through ob-servation, arrived at a cause: They were sick a lot. What kind of illnesses? Asthma. Why would kids in East Los Angeles have higher than normal rates of asthma; in other words, why is asthma a disease of the poor? Their reasoning took them further, and in studying about the breathing disorder, they discovered that restricted airway disease is caused by certain environmental contaminants—toxic substances that are common in their area, which abuts on LA's mini-steel-mill district.

Farmworkers, prisoners' families, immigrant rights activists, environmental justice organizers, and prison abolitionists all rec-ognized in Gutierrez's argument some fundamental practices and welcome truths. As Guitierrez showed, urban and rural households struggle from objectively similar but subjectively different positions across the prison landscape. They can and will join forces when the purpose is a common one, and the issue is not just local. Most of those fighting in the trenches have little time for activism motivated solely by abstract political or ethical rhetoric. Rather, they are fighting for their lives, their families, and their communities. The remedy for cumulative negative impacts must be bigger and more compelling than a simple technocratic fix. A principled sense of mortal urgency gets grassroots activists to go to meetings, makes them board buses, and inspires hope. Perhaps this is what class politics *should* be, in contradiction to the Golden Gulag's prison-lit but starless night.

NOTES

ONE. INTRODUCTION

1 The total number of adult lockups has fluctuated over the past five years or so. The CDC built twenty-four new prisons, but it closed an 800-bed women's prison in Stockton in 2003. The agency wanted to reopen the building as a men's prison, but this has met with strong local opposition. A total of sixteen community corrections facilities opened over the past fifteen years, but in the face of strong opposition to privatization by the California Correctional Peace Officers' Association, the number has shrunk. The total number of adults in prison did not shrink with the closures, however, and advocates within the CDC and in the private sector lobby have worked hard to reopen the facilities. The trend is toward putting as many people as possible in the most massive prisons. And finally, on January 5, 2006, Governor Arnold Schwarzenegger proposed two *new* prisons in his State of the State Address (www.governor.ca.gov/state/govsite/gov_html display.jsp?sCatTitle = Speeches&sFilePath = /govsite/selected_speeches/20060105_StateoftheState.html [accessed January 2006]).

TWO. THE CALIFORNIA POLITICAL ECONOMY

1 The distinction made here represents tendencies rather than absolute differences.

2 In 1967, the U.S. Supreme Court struck the law down. So much for the efficiency of the market.

3 In addition to free tuition in the public colleges and universities, the state also guaranteed tuition scholarships for financially needy students attending the state's private colleges and universities in California. In the first fifteen years after the establishment of California state scholarships—until the early 1970s—the grants were generally sufficient to pay the average tuition at any independent school; and the income cutoff for means testing was set at a then-generous $30,000 per year. The master plan "articulated" (a key word in California postsecondary education) community college (2-year), state college (4-year and graduate nonresearch), and university (4-year and graduate research) curricula with the explicit intention that students could pass from one level to another until they achieved their ultimate educational goals. This plan lifted traditional class, gender, and, to a lesser degree, racial barriers by transforming community colleges from dead ends into gateways. And the financial incentive encouraged the independent sector to seek out students in the wide, deep pool of potential applicants (R. W. Gilmore 1991).

4 Chief Parker's warnings about the "Negro" threat to Los Angeles issued throughout his career (see, e.g., Sonenshein 1993; Herbert 1997) are instructive of the hegemonic formation of the LAPD as a force of the racial state, regardless of the race or intentions of individual officers. Daryl Gates, Parker's successor-but-one, who was notorious for his overt anti-Black racism, actually betrayed no unique virulence, given his training and the ambient apartheid of Los Angeles and the police who maintained the city's social and spatial divisions (cf. Fanon 1961).

5 The mystification had much to do with a dominant theme of neoclassical economics and Chicago school sociology, which was that urbanization would break down racism—seen as a relic of slavery, alleged rural backwardness among southern whites, and the theoretically suspect concept of hard-wired fear of darkness among Europeans (Jordan 1968). Economists asserted that racism's marginal utility would prove to be trivial, and that therefore everyone willing to work hard and acquire the appropriate skills would progress—a position that even Nathan Glazer (1997) has finally retreated from. The sociologist Robert Park wrote in 1950: "America and, perhaps, the rest of the world, can be divided between two classes: those who reached the city, and those who have not yet arrived" (cited in Cell 1982: 5).

6   In 1967, the objective of California gun control was to disarm the Black Panther Party for Self Defense. When the Panthers took to the streets toting shotguns and lawbooks, they were legally armed (Bean 1973). It is somewhat difficult to understand the recent gun control movement as being structurally tied to this law. The irony underlying the ethos of nonviolence that dominated much of the postwar antiapartheid struggle in the South was that everybody in the region—Black and white—was always already armed. The question—a matter of power—was not *whether* to have guns, but rather if, how, and when to *use* them (Powledge 1991; Dittmer 1994).

7   In his popular textbook on urban planning history, *Cities of Tomorrow* (1988), Peter Hall sneers at the notion of "institutional racism" and drags out a convenient colored commentator—complete with photograph—to say that racism is not the real problem. Hall goes on to aver that the challenge for tomorrow's planners is the challenge of how to plan for (or around) Black teenagers on drugs—complete with photograph of looters.

8   Strikes in 1974 included rail; communications (May); Northern California construction; West Coast dock; telephone; second rail (July); steel (averted, July); Teamsters' walkout in Northern California against building contractors (in response to federal undermining of the Davis-Bacon Act; August); East and Gulf Coast longshoremen (October) (CDF-CEI October 1977: 16ff.).

9   The point here is not to wax nostalgic for Keynesianism, much less for Keynes. As Lynn Turgeon (1996) explicates in his recent book, the title quoting Joan Robinson, all Keynesianism is *Bastard Keynesianism*. But with disappearance of the congeries of policies that to some degree guaranteed effective demand and provided—however haphazardly and stingily—incomes and services for the most vulnerable workers in the racial state, some other form of social control will, indeed *must,* step into the breach, as we shall see (cf. Piven and Cloward 1971).

10   There were six major strikes that capital took note of: the air traffic controllers, whom Reagan fired (1981); the United Airlines Pilots' Association (1985); two steel strikes—the first in a quarter of a century—followed on democratization of the union (1985, 1986); and in 1989, the machinists struck Eastern Airlines and Boeing in Seattle (CDF-CEI 1989).

11   California's promotional web site www.commerce.ca.gov, which was advertised on airlines' inflight news programs, exemplified this in 1997.

12   For readers who wish it, here's the longer version: Insofar as capitalist accumulation is based in the private appropriation of socially produced value, the system is necessarily prone to crisis. The potential for crisis derives from the fact that the portion of socially produced value privately retained by capital—profit—is necessary for further accumulation; and yet the means available to secure profit also contain the conditions for undermining its growth. The summary effect of this contradiction, according to Marx, is that inbuilt in capitalism is the tendency for the rate of profit to fall.

What is profit, and why does its *rate* tend to fall? Not uniquely among political economists of his era, Marx believed that all value is produced by labor. However, he put this insight at the center of his analysis and argued that the changing proportion of labor power to all other inputs in commodity production affects the structure of profit and therefore the structure of capitalism. All value that workers produce but do not retain as wages is retained by capital as "surplus"; the difference between capital's fixed costs and the gross surplus retained equals gross profit.

To increase profit, capital requires that labor produce more value; but the challenge is to retain the additional value as surplus, rather than to pay it out in more wages. One way to resolve this difficulty is for capital to require workers to put in longer days; another is for capital to put more investment into fixed means of production—such as machinery—in order to increase labor's productivity (Braverman 1974; Bowles 1986). In the latter scenario, while capital does not pay out significantly greater wages, it does incur greater fixed costs that, while amortizing over time, negatively affect the *rate* of profit. The rate of profit is calculated as the return on capital investment; thus, the rate declines even if the mass of profit increases due to greater output (Shaikh 1983). In Marx's logic, this proportional shift is due to the fact that while more commodities might be produced given greater technological capacity, each one congeals less labor, thus less value. And since profit is derived from value, its rate can go nowhere but down if value diminishes (Marx [1867] 1967).

Systemic imbalances result from the dynamics that determine the tendency for the rate of profit to fall. In the first instance, capitalists may retain greater and greater masses of surplus value, thus bringing about greater concentration of capital in their collective hands. However, in order to do so, they must individually make sectorally determined investments (Shaikh 1983). Firms that become overextended by such investment get swallowed up by other firms capable of buying machinery; or they are driven out of business because of an inability to compete on unit price in the market. As a result, concentration also creates the conditions for centralization, in which there are fewer firms in any given sector over time, leading to oligopoly if not monopoly (Smith 1984; Markusen 1985).

At the same time, if the total output for a given political economy equals the value of all the commodities produced, then they all must be sold for capital to reproduce itself, which is to say to complete the circuit M-C-M'—transforming money (M) through commodities (C) into more money (M'). However, if capital is making more with a static or shrinking wage bill, then overaccumulation can result because, in part, the mass buying capacity of all those workers is less than the mass value of goods for sale. Unlike labor in the aggregate, businesses do not spend all they take in (Baran and Sweezy 1966). Firms and rich people save, and the savings constitute, in the aggregate, unrealized sales. The overaccumulation of commodities leads to a cutback in production, leaving the system with unused, or surplus, productive capacity (David Gordon 1996). Productive capacity spans the entire range of the forces of production, and includes *both* capital's inputs—such as machinery and money, *and* workers' inputs—which is to say labor power (Marx [1867] 1967).

Radical theorists of crisis have tried to isolate the precise causes for the rate of profit to fall. There are two general kinds of explanation. One focuses on underconsumption, which can be understood as overproduction—the scenario in which incomes are insufficient to buy all products, unemployment rises, and economies stagnate (Baran and Sweezy 1966; Brenner 2002). This theory has been characterized as the "declining strength of labor" argument (Sherman 1997). Another class of explanation emphasizes the effect that rising wages (or low unemployment) have on the total costs of production, arguing that wages squeeze profit (Bowles 1986); this theory constitutes the "rising strength of labor" perspective (Sherman 1997). For Sherman (1997; see also Hunt and Sherman 1972), Shaikh (1983), and others the two strands of argument do not cancel each other out but rather reveal the contradictory nature of crises at different moments along the cycle, just as Marx argued ([1867] 1967).

13 Unless otherwise noted, the data in this paragraph are culled from Edward M. Gramlich's (1994) review essay on public infrastructure in the United States.

14 The exception to the rule is that debt can be created pledging the state's full faith and credit in time of war or to suppress insurrection (California State Public Works Board 1985: C-2).

15 In technical terms, such profit is called "the underwriter's spread."

16 The Peripheral Canal was defeated by a strange alliance of growers, environmentalists, and tax rebels. The growers, dominated by cotton powers J. G. Boswell and Salyer American—who figure prominently in chapter 4—fought the canal because the law to enact it stipulated that all other Northern California rivers would be forever protected from damming and diversion (Gottlieb 1988; Reisner 1986).

17 The California Land Conversion (or Williamson) Act of 1965 protects farmers from enforced disinvestment due to tax effects of encroaching suburbanization via voluntary, ten-year, renewable contracts stipulating that the county and city will assess and tax farmland at rates tied to farm income, rather than real property assessment, as long as the land is used for agriculture. Sacramento subvents a portion of local income forgone, but poor counties and towns are not able to make up the difference, while the state has not increased its share (Sokolow and Spezia 1992; Landis 1992).

18 Marx's concept of "immiseration" is not tied to a singular vision of ab-

solute poverty and mass starvation. That is a piece of the vision, amply illustrated by events around the world. Another key aspect of "immiseration" is what Marx described as an "accumulation of misery, agony of toil, slavery, ignorance, brutality, mental degradation" for workers whether their "payment [be] high or low." The present project is trying to account for *this* immiseration (Marx [1867] 1967: 645).

19 People in jail are likely to be included in another category, because few are in jail for a full twelve months and those who get out on probation who do not have jobs waiting are required to register with the Employment Development Department and therefore are included in the unemployment count.

20 A concept dating from the early 1970s, "underclass" was taken up by William Julius Wilson (1987) in the 1980s to describe poor people who are socially and spatially isolated from legitimate employment opportunities *and* from people who work in the formal economy (cf. Massey and Denton 1993). The term gained popularity—without the analytical complexity that Wilson attached to it—because it gave observers a word to describe the increasingly visible social phenomenon of people carrying on lives apart in deindustrialized inner cities. Wilson's error, in my view, was to reinforce U.S. racial hierarchy by proposing a novel, racially demarcated stratum ("underclass") and then arguing that those consigned to it should be reintegrated into the stratum (working poor) from which they have been expelled. It was an easy move for Charles Murray (1984) and Murray and Richard Herrnstein (1994) to take up the stratum as an object of analysis, but with the crucial twist that in their view the underclass consisted of the stupid, the dependent, and the lazy, whose rightful (and highest) place is among the working poor. Wilson did not even intend for "underclass" to refer only to Black people; however, his particular research and policy interest gave others the opening—even as he was roundly criticized for underplaying the power of race in the order of U.S. society. Caveat theorist.

21 Los Angeles, San Bernardino, Riverside, Orange, and Ventura Counties.

22 Chicanos and Chicanas are native-born Mexican Americans.

23 As MacKinnon (1989: 163) puts it, "Law, as words in power, writes soci-

ety in state form and writes the state onto society. The rule form, which unites scientific knowledge with state control in its conception of what law is, institutionalizes the objective stance as jurisprudence" (cf. Bartov 1996).

24   Of course, anarchism rejects the state form categorically. But short of anarchism, other quasi-antistate movements, such as libertarianism and the posse comitatus, actually do recognize legitimate scales of, and uses for, socialized wealth and power.

25   Everyone's hair stands on end when I claim that Proposition 13 was "labor's" round of disinvestment in the state. It is true that landlords, led by wealthy apartment building owners, bankrolled the proposition. However, it would be naive to ignore the fact that for most of the people who voted for Proposition 13, their homes were their chief asset; they were wage and salary workers with nothing else to fall back on and much to lose. They decided that protecting their wealth was eminently sensible in a period when double-digit inflation and unemployment made every worker wonder how else she might envision retirement security. The legal gutting of pension plans since 2001 under bankruptcy laws underscores how widespread organized abandonment of a broad range of workers has become since the early 1980s.

THREE. THE PRISON FIX

1   The federal Counter Terrorism and Effective Death Penalty Act of 1996 has drastically narrowed the ability of state prisoners to use the federal courts to review the circumstances of their arrest, charge, conviction, sentence, or confinement; the new law amounts to a de facto repeal of the right to file a writ of habeas corpus (the U.S. Constitution forbids de jure dismantling of the right). The new rules, which require petitioners to meet stringent time, evidence, and other criteria to qualify for review, make nearly impossible the kinds of cases that resulted in success for prisoners around the United States who filed writs of habeas corpus before 1996 (Counter Terrorism and Effective Death Penalty Act of 1996).

2   Indeed, California's oldest prison, San Quentin, was designed to hold

48–50 prisoners. Before it opened, the state's temporary prison, sited in a ship in the Sacramento River, held 150 people rounded up from five counties around the state (Bookspan 1991: ch. 1).

3   As should be evident from the first epigraph to this section, mainstream historians of prison use the word "cage" to describe the particular quality of this institution of social control; in other words, "cage" is a technical term.

4   Prison capacity is measured in beds. The number of beds is not equal to the number of cells, because there are different numbers of beds in cells depending on the security level of the cell in question. We return to this topic below in notes 27 and 31.

5   See "Gang Truce Leader: From Peacemaker to Prisoner," *Los Angeles Times,* December 20, 1992, B-1.

6   I learned a great deal about the JLCPCO from conversations with chief staffers R. Bernard Orozco (July 1995 and July 1996), Gwynnae Bird (various dates, 1999–2003), and John Lum (2003).

7   There were already precedents for assigning work to specialists; for example, the California Student Aid Commission could hired financial aid experts to analyze students' applications for state funding without advertising or bidding out the work.

8   The LAPD is a highly capitalized police force. Cost control centered on equipment, not salaries and benefits. As Bradley told one scholar, LAPD "asked for everything from a tank to a submarine to an airplane and I took those out of the budget" (Sonenshein 1993: 158).

9   There are two ways a person on parole goes back to prison. The first is by committing a new crime; that is, classically speaking, recidivism. The second is by violating the terms of parole, through commission of status rather than criminal offenses. A status offense is something that is illegal or demands *prison* time only because of the condition of the person charged. In 2000, for example, the single largest class of admissions to CDC custody—45 percent—were (status) parole violators, outnumbering those who had committed new crimes by more than 3:1 (Coalition for Effective Public Safety 2004).

10   Although Gomez did not become director until 1990, he took charge of

CDC's budgetary and bureaucratic maneuvering under Directors Daniel McCarthy (1983–87) and James Rowland (1987–90). McCarthy and Rowland had been career correctional officers—the old way to work up to head warden. Gomez was the first technocrat to run the department (Morain 1994). By 1994, Gomez's planning staff numbered 216 people, plus Kitchell Capital Expenditures Management, the outside consultant that has overseen the planning, design, budget systems, and evaluation of all CDC building projects since 1981 (Morain 1994; SPWB 1993).

11   L. F. Rothschild, Unterberg, Towbin went out of business because of trading excesses—unrelated to the municipal finance sector—that put the company in a perilous position after the 1987 stock market crash. When LFRUT closed, it was the leader in underwriting tax-exempt debt in California. Prager went on to form his own company, which leads the state in higher-education facilities debt issues. The balance of this section was shaped in part from interviews generously granted by the following: Fred Prager (July 1996), Tom Dumphy (July 1996), and Dan Morain (July 1995); see also Morain (1994a, 1994b, 1994c, 1994d, and 1994e).

12   One of the contradictory consequences of skyrocketing interest rates in the early 1980s was an increased willingness on the part of consumers to borrow money whenever interest rates were favorable. That was because inflation had stayed so high for so long that it seemed wise household strategy to borrow rather than pay full costs out of current income or savings, the theory being that the present discounted value of future dollars would always pay off in the midrun (the average term to retire a major consumer loan). In addition, consumer interest payments were fully tax deductible up through 1986 (Grant 1992).

13   This section was shaped in part from interviews generously granted by Andrew Parks (July 1995), Berndt Beutenmuller (July 1995), R. Bernard Orozco (July 1995 and July 1996), and Don Pauley (July 1995 and July 1996).

14   The balance is held for future expansion (Mike Davis 1995), although it is sometimes used, in the interim, for state prison industry agricultural products such as vegetables or cotton (Andrew Parks, interview, 1995; PIA 1995).

15   The Los Angeles prison was never canceled; the legislature made the mistake of writing into law that no new prisons authorized after the LA Prison Act could be put into operation until the LA prison was activated. The legislature got around its own stumbling block by deliberately failing to appropriate funds for the site. Before the legislature devised this strategy, several completed prisons sat empty while East LA and Sacramento went toe to toe (Jacobs and Wolinsky 1986; Baker 1987; Sussman and Howard 1987).

16   These include smaller farmers concerned about water scarcity; ex-urbanites eager to keep living in the small fishing town they moved to— even if most fishermen have given up; and so forth.

17   The targeted communities are remarkably similar to those profiled by Cerill Associates (1984) as ideal (i.e., easily exploitable) locations for waste plants (see also Cole and Foster 2001).

18   Lancaster is exceptional in every way. It was the political compromise in the battle to site a prison in Los Angeles County. The region has been economically dominated by Edwards Air Force Base. It is also rapidly suburbanizing, trying deliberately to form a "pro-business" development edge on Los Angeles County's northern perimeter. Extremely conservative politics, dominated by retired and active police and military, brought the town around to accepting the prison once residents heard that escapes are extremely rare.

19   R. Bernard Orozco, interview, July 1996.

20   Because this book is about expansion of the Adult Authority, the STEP Act might seem an extraneous item for discussion. However, while the STEP Act came out of the Youth Gang Violence Task Force, there is no age limit for those who fall under the act's enhancements. Thus, anyone over eighteen years old can be charged under the STEP Act and remanded to the Adult Authority. In some cases, younger defendants upon convictions are assigned to the Adult Authority but spend the first part of their sentences in the Youth Authority. Proposition 21 in 2000 expanded on both the STEP Act and "three strikes" laws.

21   The ballot initiative campaign was set in motion by an angry and bereaved Anglo father, Fresno photographer Mike Reynolds, whose teenage daughter, Kimber, was murdered during an armed robbery in 1992. A more notorious case—the kidnap-murder of young Polly Klaas—is credited by many with having put the initiative over the top, although her father testified against the law as written (Reynolds et al. 1996). As in the 1988 Willie Horton case, the combination of white female victims and the random viciousness of the crimes threw into stark ideological relief the need, and indeed the ease, by which society could separate the guilty from the innocent, although in both the Reynolds and the Klaas murders, the killers were Anglo (D. C. Anderson 1995; Reynolds et al. 1996). The former California assemblyman and then state senator Jim Costa (D–Fresno) was co-author with the Fresno Republican farmer-turned-politician Bill Jones (who served in the assembly and became secretary of state) of the 1994 "three strikes" bill (AB 971). Earlier in his Sacramento career, between 1985 and 1991, Costa was politically key in siting four prisons in his region: Avenal, Corcoran I and II, and Coalinga (LAO 1986).

22   "Wobblers" are offenses that can be charged as misdemeanors or as felonies. Prosecutors have the discretion to charge either way. In Los Angeles County, the district attorney instructed staff always to wobble misdemeanors to felonies in order to invoke second and third strikes on defendants (Buttitta 1994). It is through prosecutorial use of the "wobble" that defendants whose controlling offense is shoplifting an inexpensive item have been sentenced to eight years (second strike) or twenty-five years to life without possibility of parole (third strike). See chapter 5.

23   One of the most notorious, and relatively successful, struggles was waged by the former Los Angeles County sheriff Sherman Block; responsible for the county jails that hold misdemeanor offenders, felony defendants, and convicts awaiting transport to the state prisons, Block gained funding to build a new jail by letting 23,000 inmates go home one week. Block failed, however, to get enough funding to run the new jail, which was built with municipal bond funds in the heart of downtown Los Angeles in the courthouse district. The CDC director wanted Sacramento to reclaim the jail as state property because the county had failed to use the facility in accord with the debt agreement. However, the CDC was stymied in its efforts because it seemed impolitic, according to the chief consultant of the

JLCPCO, for the CDC to undermine LA County when that jurisdiction alone produces nearly 40 percent of the annual commitments to the CDC (R. Bernard Orozco, interview, 1996).

24 Starting with the Reagan "War on Drugs" legislation in 1984, the United States has offered financial aid to state and local law enforcement for particular kinds of activities. For example, under drug interdiction, the federal zero-tolerance statute allows seizure of any property alleged to have been obtained through, or used for, drug manufacturing, transport, storage, or sale; if and when local law enforcement makes a "federal" case out of a drug bust, by bringing in federal personnel and allowing defendants to be charged in federal rather than state court, the local jurisdiction gets half the money of all assets seized in relation to the action (Baum 1996). Other subventions are more direct; for example, under the 1994 Violent Crime Control and Law Enforcement Act, California local law enforcement (cities and counties) has received more than $100 million for new personnel; and the CDC has received $80,000,000 toward the cost of new prisons (LAO 1996).

25 The LAPD developed SWAT (Special Weapons and Tactics) teams specifically to police Black political activists (Bean 1973; Donner 1990; Newton 1996) and was among the first metropolitan police forces to use battering rams to smash into houses—a sight now common on televised police shows such as *COPS*.

26 See www.corr.ca.gov/ReportsResearch/MonthlyTpop1aArchive.html (accessed January 25, 2006).

27 Prisoners are classified according to a rating, or points, system that evaluates them on the basis of the nature of the crime(s) for which they are currently committed, prior criminal history, and a psychological profile (Rudman and Berthelsen 1991). Prisoners are then assigned to one of four levels, from I (minimum security) to IV (maximum security). Level I prisoners live in dormitories and generally work on the prison grounds and in the towns where the prisons are sited; it is not uncommon to encounter complaints about the "shortage" of Level I prisoners. Level II prisoners also live in dormitory-style setups, but do not participate in extramural work; this classification is used sparingly. Level III prisoners are under

full-time surveillance, and live in cages most of the time, although they have access to public rooms in the facility. Level IV prisoners live in cages twenty-three hours per day, seven days per week. Very few CDC commitments are classified Level II, and many Level III facilities have been upgraded by the CDC to Level IV, at the encouragement of the correctional officers' union (CCPOA) (BRC 1990; Rudman and Berthelsen 1991; CCPOA 1996).

28 The CDF Performance Review did not, however, touch the underlying issue of CO pay—the political power of the guards' union, the CCPOA.

29 In truth, the university has been neither; but in representation lies the drama of politics and power.

30 San Joaquin Delta College, outside Sacramento, made the mistake of boasting how little it spends on its CO training program compared with the income it generates, only to be excluded from future participation on the recommendation of the Legislative Analyst (LAO 1996). The boast was not made clandestinely. It seemed perfectly sensible to the administration to trumpet the college's efficiency. Since the surplus from the guard program was recirculated through other, more expensive programs at the college, there was no apparent larcenous intent.

31 During a six-year battle with a statewide coalition of community, labor, civil rights, environmental justice, antiprison, and other opponents, the CDC briefly averred that the North Kern State Prison (Delano II) would be its last. However, even before the activist-delayed prison, originally scheduled for 2001, finally opened in June 2005, Sacramento was firmly forecasting new needs. By January 2006, new prisons featured prominently in the governor's developmental agenda (see chapter 1, note 1). The wildly erratic forecasts produced by the department never improved in accuracy, due to the political pressures on, rather than the statistical skills of, those in charge of crunching the numbers. The statistical branch is not directed to lie, but it is directed to use criteria and parameters that always reinforce claims of imminent shortage.

32 James Gomez served as deputy executive director of California's Public Employee Retirement System (CalPERS), the largest such pension fund in the United States until 2002, and then became a health care industry lobbyist.

33 More "local" control varies widely by jurisdiction and should not be understood as synonymous with more *direct* control. For example, Los Angeles County is the largest substate governmental unit in the United States, and residents are far further removed, numerically, from the county supervisors than they are from State Assembly and Senate representatives (Mike Davis 1993b).

34 The reader will note that the Lockyer plan rewards county and local criminal justice jurisdictions for doing exactly what San Joaquin Delta College was punished for doing.

35 Tom Hayden (D–Los Angeles) did vote for the measure, arguing on the Senate floor that while he did not like the idea, he believed that privatizing prisons was the only way to save public education (JLCPCO, April 10, 1996). Hayden's presumption of two classes of Californians, those bound for prison and those headed to college, is not very distant from that of former State Treasurer Kathleen Brown (Jerry's sister), who in 1994 devised a tax-exempt college bond that parents could buy for their children; the proceeds of the bond sale would go to building prisons for, presumably, other people's children (Morain 1994d).

36 The more it changed, the more it stayed the same. When Deukmejian took over from Jerry Brown and decided to embark on a much larger and more ambitious prison program, he termed the facilities he would approve "megaprisons."

37 Voters rejected GOBs in the 1990s, and they also approved diversion for first- and second-time drug convictions (Proposition 36) in November 2000. In addition, multiple statewide polls found likely voters demanding prison cuts (Coalition for Effective Public Safety 2004).

38 Wackenhut emerged from the CIA, for example, and GE, Lockheed, and other defense contractors are trying to get a piece of the domestic military action (Neumann 1996). This is a Cold War "conversion" development explicitly called for by Markusen and Yudken (1992).

FOUR. CRIME, CROPLANDS, AND CAPITALISM

1 Eli Whitney invented the cotton gin in 1793, and its proliferation throughout the U.S. South radically increased the demand for field slaves and thereby stepped up the international slave trade. Upon legal termination of the international trade, an intra-U.S. trade between Virginia and the Deep South grew and flourished through the Civil War (Tadman 1990). The big cotton ranchers in the southern San Joaquin Valley all owned gins (Weber 1994). It was not until 1942 and after that innovations in raw product production began to reduce cotton's dependence on human labor, with the introduction of the mechanical harvester (Bergman 1969).

2   Until the 1965 Williamson Act, California taxes on farmland were assessed against potential profits; thus, the productivity of the larger growers squeezed the smaller ones indirectly as well as directly (Goldman 1991).

3   Reorganized in 1930, the Bank of Italy became the Bank of America.

4   In different regions and sectors of California, agriculture arrangements of capital and labor differ. For example, Miriam Wells (1996) documents how contemporary Salinas Valley strawberry growers combine sharecropping, tenant farmer, and wage labor relationships to establish political security over crop production. However, for the vast commodity farms of the San Joaquin Valley, agricultural labor was proletarianized both before, and as a consequence of, the rise of corporate cotton production (Weber 1994; Daniel 1981).

5   Surface-water irrigated farming in the Central Valley long predates European settlement there (Caughey 1940; Preston 1981), but its expansion since the onset of Anglo immigration in the mid nineteenth century is also the story of battles between direct producers (whether small farmers or wage labor) and capital (Norris 1987; Bean 1973; Pisani 1984). The two decades following the 1880 Mussel Slough shootout near Hanford, the Kings County seat, marked the rise of intensive farming in the area (Bean 1973; Pisani 1984). The shootout resulted from the Southern Pacific Railroad's pricing scheme for its federally granted lands that small farmers had contracted to buy. The sales took nearly five years to complete, during which time the farmers had irrigated their plots; when the railroad included the value of sweat equity improvements in the purchase price, it dispossessed those who had been working the land in favor of larger landholders who had sufficient capital to buy at the higher prices. Between

1880 and the turn of the century, most irrigation districts were privately owned, with everything from sweat equity to local cooperative investment to absent national and international capital sunk in their dams and ditches (Bean 1973; Pisani 1984).

6   The idea behind the married couple rule was not to grant women equal property rights, but rather to allow married men to accumulate more, because their responsibility as husbands would presumably make them more reliable farmers (Pisani 1984). Pisani's argument shows a key contradiction within the capitalist class, with San Francisco lenders who held bad paper in 1898–99 wanting the big farms broken down so that the "boom-bust" cycle that sent capitalist growers into ruin would be mitigated by mixed (subsistence and commodity) family farmers who could be more flexible when it came to market or climate fluctuations (Pisani 1984). The act's rules, which were easily and regularly broken, not only imposed acreage limitations but also, to prevent speculation, required those obtaining reclamation water to sell off their surplus acreage at *pre-project* prices. The disputes over the Bureau of Reclamation acreage limitations raise interesting questions for future research concerning the desire for, and failure of, land redistribution (downward) in the United States in the mid–twentieth century compared with its U.S. military–organized, top-down enforcement in East Asia after World War II (Pisani 1984; Amsden 1985; Hart-Landsberg 1993; cf. Woods 1998).

7   The 1982 reauthorization of the Reclamation Act purported to close these loopholes, and raised the maximum farm size to 960 acres. A political settlement that preceded (and delayed) the new regulations, which were not promulgated until 1987, ensured that they would not directly address the methods by which large landowners got around the acreage restriction; therefore, the regulatory "oversight" voided the original and extended purpose of the law (Gottlieb 1988).

8   The nationalization of surplus water was not established without struggle, and the sovereignty question has never been fully resolved: How can the United States "claim" California surplus as a U.S. rather than California public good (Hundley 1992)?

9   The Corps' political success in this project (Reisner 1986), coupled with the

postwar rise of the Department of War (renamed Defense) into an enormous and insulated entity (G. Hooks 1991), gave the Corps power to displace the bureau on all major postwar western water projects (Reisner 1986).

10 Walker and Storper calculated that for 1.8 million acre-feet of water the growers received as surplus, farmers paid $6 million and Met customers paid $170 million (Reisner 1986; Gottlieb 1988). Central Valley cities and towns can also contract for Met surplus, but they pay the cost of production.

11 Almost immediately after the drought ended, California winters, starting in 1978, became inordinately wet (Reisner 1986; Cooke 1984; Gottlieb 1988); 1983 was central California's wettest recorded year (*Coalinga Record,* May 2, 1984).

12 There are several methodological problems inherent in pinning down these "facts." First, Boswell is privately held and divulges nothing about its employment practices, valuations, and so forth. And California does not have reliable records on seasonal and migrant farmworkers. "Nonfarm" employment is the ordinary indicator of jobs for a given region. The invisible workers in the "factories in the field" (McWilliams [1939] 1969) seem as erased from the official story as they do from the agricultural vistas that Don Mitchell (1996) deconstructed with his labor theory of landscape.

13 The balance of this section was shaped in part from interviews generously granted by Don Pauley (July 1995 and July 1996), Jeanette Todd (July 1995), Melissa Harriman (July 1996), Charley Trujillo (May 1999), and many anonymous Corcoran residents who talked with me during my research visits to the town.

14 Nobody talks about the great taboo of African Americans marrying anybody but African Americans; valley Okie Merle Haggard's song "Irma Jackson" is a down-home critique of the unspeakable.

15 CDC job classifications in 1987 at salaries of from $873 to $1,730 a month included automobile mechanics, carpenters, electricians, plumbers, truck drivers, maintenance mechanics, account clerks, account technicians, bakers, bookkeeping machine operators, cooks, office assistants, telephone op-

erators, library assistants, dental assistants, medical technical assistants, medical transcribers, and X-ray technicians.

16 Susanville's second prison was sited in 1991, and the town has not recovered. When tiny Lake County, Oregon, found itself an unwilling host city for a prison whose site was chosen by the Governor's Office, the Susanville City Council wrote an apparently unsolicited letter to Lake County warning it of the significant disadvantages of host city life.

17 Certainly, Okies, Mexicans, and Africans who had come to Corcoran earlier in the century as migrant workers did not universally experience the unqualified welcome the rancher credited Corcoran with extending. My own travels to Corcoran supported her sentiment—but I attribute some of the positive reception I got to the fact that I came as a researcher interested in the social and economic health of the place; that is, I came in peace, and I was not going to stay. It is also true that shortly upon my arrival in town, each visit, I participated in a brief ritual. In the cool of the morning I would review my notes at a picnic table in a Boswell-built park, until the *Corcoran Journal* office across the street opened for business. The patrol car on duty would slowly cruise the park perimeter (one relatively small city block), its officer checking me out. I would fuss with my papers, change my glasses a few times, and look very busy. The policeman would drive away. Every time.

18 In 1942, the state's rate of imprisonment was lower than at any time during the twentieth century. In the final scene in *If He Hollers, Let Him Go,* Chester Himes's brilliant novel about Black Los Angeles, the warfare industry, and racism in World War II, a judge sentences the narrator, who has been framed for rape, to Uncle Sam's rather than the CDC's uniform (Himes [1945] 1986; cf. C. L. R. James 1980).

19 SPWB 1986b; BRC 1990; *Corcoran Journal,* May 28, 1987.

20 The balance of this section was shaped in part from interviews generously granted by Don Pauley (July 1995 and July 1996), Jeanette Todd (July 1995), R. Bernard Orozco (July 1995), and anonymous residents.

21 *Corcoran Journal,* June 16, 1987.

22 The more isolated, or islandlike, a prison town, the more economic activity appears to stick locally, as measured by, for example, sales tax revenue.

However, the appearance may well be an illusion. Far-flung Blythe's (see map) relative tax pull seems to be more an effect of constant building (following the prisons, the town has experienced construction of one of a proposed series of power plants) than of any prison-related activity. Blythe, like Crescent City and Ione, is also a spot where tourists spend money for food, lodging, and supplies.

23 The utilities maintained a low profile during siting struggles. It is stunning, in retrospect, that the 1985 study by Lofting and Linton underestimated CDC expenditures in the county by failing to include utilities as a budget item.

24 *Coalinga Record,* February 20, 1985.

25 By comparison, in Avenal the water issue demonstrates how the prison directly *undermines* local development efforts. Having been forbidden to use groundwater as a result of the farmers' lawsuit, the CDC negotiated with Avenal to take a portion of the city's contracted State Water Project–Met water. The negotiations included no mitigating funds, or provisions should the prison cage more inmates than anticipated. As the prison designed for 2,700 took in more than 6,000 prisoners, it consumed water at more than twice the projected rate. Avenal buys water from the SWP–Met at the price of production (about $35 per acre-foot), and, with a very poor resident population, cannot afford to increase its contracted amount. As a result, the city has not been able to recruit manufacturing or other promising employers, because it cannot guarantee sufficient water for industrial or expanded residential use, due to the CDC drain (Melissa Harriman, interview, 1996).

26 For all but three of the state's twenty-four new prisons, the allied towns have had to annex the sites (R. Bernard Orozco, interview, 1995).

27 Fresno County rolled out a Juvenile Jail Complex in 2003; the four-stage project will not be completed until 2040, meaning the county planned a jail for children whose parents had not yet been born.

28 Prisoners challenging the conditions of their arrest, conviction, or sentences would return to the jurisdiction where the event(s) occurred.

29 Robert Puls, a hardworking and prosperous Tulare County rancher, did his own study to support his group, Stop This Outrageous Prison (STOP),

which fought back five prisons between 1989 and 1998 (interview, September 1998).

30   The origin and circulation of the number of projected jobs—72—sheds interesting light on the geopolitics of knowledge. In the spring of 2000, I combed through the Delano II prison's Supplemental Environmental Impact Report to figure out what the CDC's forecasters thought would happen. A little basic math produced 72 out of 1,600 jobs. In August, Evelyn Nieves of the *New York Times* interviewed me at length concerning the controversial prison. She subsequently interviewed Delano's then mayor, Napoleon Madrid, sharing the finding with him, and he is the source of the number in her story (Nieves 2000). Joan Didion cites him, as reported by Nieves, in her 2003 book *Where I Was From*.

FIVE. MOTHERS RECLAIMING OUR CHILDREN

1   The LA Four were the young African American men charged with the widely televised beating of a white truck driver, Reginald Denny, on April 29, 1992, the first day of the uprising. Opposition to the LA Four trial centered on the ideological use of the case to justify acquittal of the four LAPD officers for the televised beating of Rodney King. Reginald Denny himself objected to the railroading of his assailants *and* to the state and media's deliberate ignoring of the dozens of Black people who saved him. (Note: In most cases the names in this chapter have been changed.)

2   Officers of the court include judges, prosecutors, prosecution and defense attorneys, and bailiffs; untrustworthy witnesses include police and jailhouse informants who trade time for testimony.

3   I am thankful to Doracie Zoleta-Nantes for the conversations through which these concepts emerged.

4   In the United States, the word *equality* seems often to connote an upward leveling. Fortunati (1995) helpfully points out that other forms of "equality" (e.g., slavery) have analytical weight that requires political and organizational attention.

5   Outsource companies can disappear overnight, thanks to no fixed capital or other constraints holding them in place. Labor thus lacks the leverage it had when, for example, janitors negotiated contracts directly with the

former employers (owners of hotels, restaurants, office buildings, factories, and so forth) who are now outsource firms' clients.

6   According to a presentation given by a JfJ organizing committee in Los Angeles in March 1993, organizing has in some cases stretched back to immigrant janitors' towns of origin in Mexico and El Salvador. Insofar as it is common for people from a particular region to migrate to both the same area and labor-market niche as their friends and families who precede them, JfJ started to work backward along the migratory path in an attempt to incorporate the wider-than-daily labor market into the movement's sphere of influence. During this same presentation, when challenged by a Sandinista cadre who asked an apparently simple question ("What became of the people who used to be janitors?"), JfJ acknowledged that its organizing had not extended to the former workers. JfJ pledged to expand its Southern California scope of activity and reach out to former janitors in the community, who are, as noted above, mostly African Americans, in a project that many hoped would revive submerged knowledge from earlier labor and antiracist struggles.

7   Bear in mind that the LAPD invented the Special Weapons and Tactics (SWAT) Team specifically to police politically organized Black people (cf. Bean 1973; Sonenshein 1993; Mike Davis 1990). But the premier symbol of Los Angeles's capitalized, militarized police force is the helicopters that pulse and hover overhead day and night, coordinating motorized ground forces from a flexible vantage point—a mobile panoptic lacking the stealth Bentham envisioned. The dread is renewed daily by the noise as well as by individual encounters with police.

8   Jennifer Wolch (1989) developed the "shadow state" concept to theorize state-sanctioned nongovernmental organizations (NGOs); I use it here to emphasize how gangs constitute territorially bounded rule-making bodies for a mosaic in-filling vast regions that the legal state has abandoned except in the form of militarized occupation and social services–based surveillance (R. W. Gilmore 1993; Mike Davis 1990; Vigil 1996; see also Fanon 1961). The point is not to romanticize gangs, but rather to emphasize that all social formations—even stranded communities in deindustrialized urban centers—develop some means for maintaining order

(Mann 1988); sometimes it is necessary to look beneath the surface of apparent *disorder* to grasp the logic of a particular system of order. Furthermore, as Tilly (1985) argues, war making, state making, and organized crime are distinct with reference to those who produce and enforce the "law" but not so different in terms of actual practices, relations, and outcomes.

9   Notably, attendees at the rally—or "coming together" as many participants termed it—included survivors from the prior generation's social movements, such as the Black Panther Party for Self Defense. Thus, the "coming together" commingled community members—who were developing their political consciousness in that particular moment of powerfully focused anger and grief—with activists representing theoretical tendencies and traditions that were forged in earlier struggles against state, and state-sanctioned, violence.

10   Simi Valley is a conservative suburban town where many active and retired military and police make their homes. When the trial was moved there from downtown Los Angeles, skepticism of any outcome save acquittal dominated casual discussions about the case in South Central.

11   Prisoners are "unitized"—which is CDC jargon for "segregated." While individual wardens have power over the social organization of their prisons, the general policy is to keep prisoners in each facility separated by "race." CDC demographic analyses use four basic categories: white, Black, Latino, and "other." "Others"—Asian-Pacific Islanders and Native Americans—are not housed separately but distributed among the three principal groups, such that, for example, Samoans are usually Black; Filipinos are Latino; people of Chinese, Hmong, Lao, or Vietnamese descent might be white or Latino, but not Black; and Native Americans are usually Latino but sometimes Black. According to the testimony of some prisoners, "unitizing" helps produce and reinforce animosities, keeps internal hierarchies intact, and discourages any kind of substantive cross-racial organizing on behalf of, for example, prisoners' rights. In February 2005, the U.S. Supreme Court objected to the CDC's oft-denied practice and ordered a lower court to subject the department's motives to "strict scrutiny" (Savage and Warren 2005).

12 A recurring irony in Mothers ROC cases—especially African Americans'—is how frequently the (extended) family knows, or is related to, a police, probation, parole, or corrections officer (the frequency is related, of course, to the historical battle by Black people to gain access to state jobs, which became a relatively secure labor market niche until the attack on government size launched in the past two decades). The irony has been quite useful in helping mothers take a systemic, rather than individualized, view of their struggle. Knowing, as they do, that their friend/relative is not a bad person, and probably not a racist (although anti-Black racism among Black people is not uncommon), they then have to figure out another explanation for what is happening to their children, in which they can account for people "like" themselves on the other side (cf. Guérin 1994).

13 Many new Mothers tell the same story—they mortgage the house or sell the car in order to pay a lawyer only to discover that the contract limits the services to the most routine rounds of court filings and appearances. Furthermore, the question of mortgaging or selling has its own racialized contradictions. Oliver and Shapiro (1995) show the ways that, for Black people, residential apartheid and lender redlining effectively limit access to (as well as growth of) the fundamental source of U.S. household wealth: home equity. In the case of the ROCers who mortgage, they leverage lower-than-average equity at higher-than-average loan costs in order to—at best—maintain the status quo (a loved one kept out of prison) rather than to "invest" in the future in the form of education or other potentially remunerable family or personal development.

14 That library has since restricted access; people with no formal affiliation with the institution must pay to get in the door, and the legal database is restricted to faculty and students, who must have a personal access code, assigned by the university, to use it.

15 The Crime Control and Safe Streets Act of 1968, signed by Lyndon Baines Johnson, and the Organized Crime Control Act of 1970, signed by Richard M. Nixon. These acts were designed to deal with the urban rioters of the 1960s, revolutionary organizations such the Black Panther Party for Self Defense, and the Mafia, and indeed to merge these differently disruptive groupings into an undifferentiated enemy. Given FBI director J. Edgar Hoover's centrality in these deliberations and his coalition with certain elements of (white) organized crime, we can see in this pair of laws the state's internal conflict and contradiction. See Donner 1990.

16 The Willie Horton syndrome, which I am tempted to call rational choice fascism. Stuart Hall (1986), following Antonio Gramsci (1971) and others, argues that common sense merits the closest attention in any study of or movement for social change (progressive or repressive). At the current moment, there has been a terrifying elision in common sense across three conceptual stages: the protection and promotion of groups whose rights and opportunities have been historically undermined or suppressed (the usual list) are now vilified for unmerited favoritism and handouts, for which the proper remedy is at best judged to be individually evaluated merit, privacy, and so forth. Turning on this individualized pivot, however, is the notion that certain persons have decided to become members of outlaw groupings (again, the usual list); it follows that all such groupings, regardless of individual differentiation within them, should be uniformly coerced, sanctioned, and incapacitated. The scariest part, of course, is that the members the former group and those of the latter share striking demographic similarities—because of an objective, if not strategic, continuum from the "war on poverty" to the "war on crime."

17 The Simpson criminal trial had not been resolved during this discussion; but even his acquittal and the aftermath supported the ROCers' sense that a Black man's trial is completely unlike a white man's trial.

18 Between 1977 and 1982, the number of white prisoners increased 50 percent, while Black prisoners doubled, producing nearly equal absolute numbers between the two groups; from that time forward Black prisoners exceeded all other groups until 1994, when the steady increase in Latino incarceration shifted the balance. See table 5.

19 Thanks to a surprisingly successful grassroots campaign, the city of Los Angeles turned down the DOJ "Weed and Seed" funding, which it had been inclined to accept before ordinary people lambasted the program and its nefarious implications at public hearings in neighborhoods likely to bear the brunt of the "weeding" (Urban Strategies Group 1992).

20 A recurrent theme in discussions among many of the shyer mothers was their avowal of, and explanation for, their own unfitness. They refused the dominant explanations—they don't take drugs, rely on welfare, or work in the sex industry. But what lingered was a doubt whether they as women (and men) who might have trouble reading or who have been afraid to stand up to the law can ever be fit mothers for loved ones caught in a system in which book knowledge and various types of intimidation—intellectual as well as physical—feature centrally in the outcomes of cases. Many asked me to accompany them to meetings with officials because they felt stronger knowing that I know all the *words*—as well as the demographics, statistics, history, and so on. As they taught one another what they learned, all of the ROCers gained confidence; indeed, those who could not read well flourished by using their substantial memories to chart and compare cases (cf. R. W. Gilmore 1991 on the boys in the California Youth Authority).

21 Cf. Catherine MacKinnon's (1989) stridently clear exposition of gender displacement/subsumption. The integrations are, of course, fragile; everything is at risk, and old structures and habits of inequality easily fill social spaces left vulnerable by uncertainty. For example, at a number of Mothers ROC meetings, men who had not been active in the organization would often steamroller discussions when the ROCers are trying to figure something out; and the ROCers let it happen, reenacting other relations of love, respect, and fear.

22 Markusen and Yudken's (1992) analysis of the Cold War economy must be extended to the domestic warfare economy; see also Fanon 1961. At the same time that Mothers ROC has expanded, the LA gang truce has done so as well. By mid 2003, the LA truce included a number of Central City, Eastside and Westside Chicano and other Latino gangs. The Fourth Anniversary T-shirt (1996) featured a drawing of Malcolm X and Emiliano Zapata, the legend beneath their representations reading "X y Z." Also note, gangs engaged in peacemaking have, on a national basis, changed their moniker from "gangs" to "street organizations."

23 For example, a fairly recent newcomer to Mothers ROC was an immigrant Salvadorena who worked nights as a janitor; as noted above, core

cadres among militant labor organizers in Los Angeles include Salvadorena refugees who are experienced in dealing with state terror and
with challenging state legitimacy.

24 According to the UN International Labor Organisation, women do two-
thirds of the world's work, receive 5 percent of the income, and own 1 percent of the assets. Margaret Prescod of the Wages for Housework Campaign interprets these figures as illuminating both sexism and racism on a
global scale (R. W. Gilmore 1993).

BIBLIOGRAPHY AND REFERENCES

A list of people interviewed during the writing of this book follows the main bibliographical list.

Abramovitz, Mimi. 1988. *Regulating the Lives of Women: Social Welfare Policy from Colonial Times to the Present.* Boston: South End Press.

Abu-Jamal, Mumia. 1995. *Live from Death Row.* Reading, Pa.: Addison-Wesley.

Acoli, Sundiata. 1992. *A Brief History of the New Afrikan Prison Struggle.* Harlem: Sundiata Acoli Freedom Campaign.

Acuña, Rudolfo F. 1984. *A Community under Siege: A Chronicle of Chicanos East of the Los Angeles River, 1945–1975.* Los Angeles: Chicano Studies Research Center Publications, UCLA.

————. 1996. *Anything but Mexican: Chicanos in Contemporary Los Angeles.* New York: Verso.

Adams, Jane, ed. 2003. *Fighting for the Farm: Rural America Transformed.* Philadelphia: University of Pennsylvania Press.

Adams, John. 1990. Institutional Economics and Social Choice Economics: Commonalities and Conflicts. *Journal of Economic Issues* 24 (3): 845–59.

Agamben, Giorgio. 1999. *Remnants of Auschwitz: The Witness and the Archive.* Translated by Daniel Heller-Roazen. New York: Zone Books.
————. 2000. *Means without End.* Minneapolis: University of Minnesota Press.

Ahmad, Ajaz. 1992. *In Theory.* New York: Verso.
————. 1995. Politics, Literature and Postcoloniality. *Race & Class* 36 (3): 1–20.

Ahmed, Eqbal. 1992. Fundamentalism, Secularism and the War. *Polygraph* (5): 240–41.

Aho, James. 1990. *The Politics of Righteousness.* Seattle: University of Washington Press.

Albert, Michael, and Robin Hahnel. 1992. Yes, Socialism without Markets! *Socialist Review* 22 (3): 131–38.

Allen, Robert. 1969. *Black Awakening in Capitalist America.* Trenton, N.J.: Africa World Press.

Allen, Theodore W. 1994–97. *The Invention of the White Race.* Vol. 1: *Racial Oppression and Social Control;* vol. 2: *The Origin of Racial Oppression in Anglo-America.* New York: Verso.

Almaguer, Tomás. 1994. *Racial Fault Lines: The Historical Origins of White Supremacy in California.* Berkeley: University of California Press.

Althusser, Louis. 1991. On Marx and Freud. *Rethinking Marxism* 4 (1): 17–30.

American Lockdown: The Prison Struggle and Revolution. 1994. *People's Tribune* (Chicago), August 21, 1.

Amin, Samir. 1992. US Militarism in the New World Order. *Polygraph* (5): 13–37.

Amott, Teresa L., and Julie A. Matthaei. 1991. *Race, Gender, and Work: A Multicultural Economic History of Women in the United States.* Boston: South End Press.

Amsden, Alice. 1985. The State and Taiwan's Economic Development. In *Bringing the State Back In,* ed. Peter B. Evans, Dietrich Rueschemeyer, and Theda Skopol, 78–106. Cambridge: Cambridge University Press.

Anderson, Benedict. 1983. *Imagined Communities: Reflections on the Origin and Spread of Nationalism.* New York: Verso.

Anderson, David C. 1995. *Crime and the Politics of Hysteria: How the Willie Horton Story Changed American Justice.* New York: Times Books.

Anderson, Martin Edwin. 1993. *Dossier Secreto: Argentina's Desaparecidos and the Myth of the "Dirty War."* Boulder, Colo.: Westview Press.

Anderson, Susan. 1996. A City Called Heaven: Black Enchantment and Despair in Los Angeles. In *The City: Los Angeles and Urban Theory at the End of the Twentieth Century,* ed. Allen J. Scott and Edward W. Soja, 336–64. Berkeley: University of California.

Arax, Mark, and Rick Wartzman. 2003. *The King of California: J. G. Boswell and the Making of a Secret American Empire.* New York: Public Affairs.

Archer, Dane, and Rosemary Gartner. 1984. *Violence and Crime in Cross-National Perspective.* New Haven, Conn.: Yale University Press.

Armstrong, Louise. 1989. *Solomon Says: A Speakout on Foster Care.* New York: Pocket Books.

Arnesen, Eric. 1993. Following the Color Line of Labor: Black Workers and the Labor Movement before 1930. *Radical History Review* 55: 53–87.

Arnold, Robert K., and Stephen Levy. 1992–2001. *The Outlook for the California Economy.* Palo Alto, Calif.: Center for the Continuing Study of the California Economy. Published annually.

Arrighi, Giovanni. 1994. *The Long Twentieth Century: Money, Power, and the Origins of Our Times.* New York: Verso.

Arrighi, Giovanni, Terence K. Hopkins, and Immanuel Wallerstein. 1989. *Antisystemic Movements.* New York: Verso.

Ashley, David, and Melvin Ramey. 1996. *California Prison Capital Cost Reduction Study.* Berkeley: University of California, Office of the President.

Austin, James. 1990. *America's Growing Correctional-Industrial Complex.* Washington, D.C.: National Council on Crime and Delinquency.

Baker, Bob. 1987. Jobless Turnkeys Punished by Delay in Prison Openings. *Los Angeles Times,* June 16, 2–2.

Baldwin, Sidney. 1968. *Poverty and Politics.* Chapel Hill: University of North Carolina Press.

Balibar, Etienne. 1991. For Althusser. *Rethinking Marxism* 4 (1): 9–12.

———. 1992. Europe after Communism. *Rethinking Marxism* 5 (3): 29–49.

Bandele, Asha. 1999. *The Prisoner's Wife.* New York: Scribner.

Barak, Gregg, ed. 1991. *Crimes by the Capitalist State.* Albany: State University of New York Press.

Baran, Paul A., and Paul M. Sweezy. 1966. *Monopoly Capital: An Essay on the American Economic and Social Order.* New York: Monthly Review Press.

Barrera, Mario. 1979. *Race and Class in the Southwest: A Theory of Racial Inequality.* Notre Dame, Ind.: University of Notre Dame Press.

Bartik, Timothy J. 1990. The Market Failure Approach to Regional Economic Development. *Economic Development Quarterly* 4 (4) (November): 361–70.

———. 1991. *Who Benefits from State and Local Economic Development Policies?* Kalamazoo, Mich.: W. E. Upjohn Institute for Employment Research.

Bartov, Omer. 1996. *Murder in Our Midst: The Holocaust, Industrial Killing, and Representation.* New York: Oxford University Press.

Baum, Dan. 1996. *Smoke and Mirrors: The War on Drugs and the Politics of Failure.* Boston: Little, Brown.

Bayley, David H. 1985. *Patterns in Policing.* New Brunswick, N.J.: Rutgers University Press.

Bean, Walton E. 1973. *California: An Interpretive History.* 2nd ed. New York: McGraw-Hill.

Beckett, Katherine. 1997. *Making Crime Pay: Law and Order in Contemporary American Politics.* New York: Oxford University Press.

Beckett, Katherine, and Theodore Sasson. 2000. *The Politics of Injustice: Crime and Punishment in America.* Thousand Oaks, Calif.: Pine Forge Press.

Benaria, Lourdes, and Shelley Feldman, eds. 1992. *Unequal Burden: Economic Crises, Persistent Poverty and Women's Work.* Boulder, Colo.: Westview.

Benjamin, Walter. 1978. *Reflections: Essays, Aphorisms, Autobiographical Writings.* Translated by Edmund Jephcott. New York: Harcourt Brace Jovanovich.

Bennett, William J., John J. DiIulio, and John P. Walters. 1996. *Body Count.* New York: Simon & Schuster.

Benton, F. Warren. 1983. State Prison Expansion: An Explanatory Model. *Journal of Criminal Justice* 11: 121–28.

Bergman, Peter M. 1969. *The Chronological History of the Negro in America.* New York: Harper & Row.

Berlin, Ira, and Herbert Gutman. 1983. Natives and Immigrants, Free Men and Slaves: Urban Workingmen in the Antebellum American South. *American Historical Review* 88 (December): 1175–1200.

Berman-Santana, Déborah. 1996. *Kicking Off the Bootstraps: Environment, Development, and Community Power in Puerto Rico.* Tucson: University of Arizona Press.

————. 2002. Resisting Toxic Militarism: Vieques versus the U.S. Navy. *Social Justice* 29 (1–2): 37–47.

Bin-Wahad, Dhoruba, Mumia Abu-Jamal, and Assata Shakur. 1993. *Still Black, Still Strong: Survivors of the War against Black Revolutionaries.* Brooklyn, N.Y.: Semiotexte.

Bing, Léon. 1991. *Do or Die.* New York: Harper Perennial.

————. 1993. *Smoked: A True Story of Murder and the American Dream.* New York: HarperCollins.

Black, Jack. [1926] 2000. *You Can't Win.* Edinburgh: AK Press.

Black Panther Collective. N.d. *It's On!!! Steps to Dealing with the Pigs.* New York: Black Panther Collective Pamphlet.

Blaut, James. 1993. *The Colonizer's Model of the World.* New York: Guilford Press.

————. 2000. *Eight Eurocentric Historians.* New York: Guilford Press.

Blee, Kathleen. 1991. *Women of the Klan: Racism and Gender in the 1920s.* Berkeley: University of California Press.

————. 1998. *No Middle Ground.* New York: New York University Press.

Bluestone, Barry, and Bennett Harrison. 1982. *The Deindustrialization of America.* New York: Basic Books.

Boland, Mary L. 1997. *Crime Victim's Guide to Justice.* Naperville, Ill.: Sourcebooks.

Bonczar, Thomas P., and Allen J. Beck. 1997. *Lifetime Likelihood of Going to State or Federal Prison.* Special Report NCJ-160092. Washington, D.C.: U.S. Dept. of Justice, Office of Justice Programs, Bureau of Justice Statistics.

Bookspan, Shelley. 1991. *A Germ of Goodness: The California State Prison System, 1851–1944.* Lincoln: University of Nebraska Press.

Boris, Eileen. 1989. The Power of Motherhood: Black and White Activist Women Redefine the "Political." *Yale Journal of Law and Feminism,* Fall 1989, 25–49.

Bortner, M. A., and Linda M. Williams. 1997. *Youth in Prison: We the People of Unit Four.* New York: Routledge.

Bouvard, Marguerite Guzman. 1994. *Revolutionizing Motherhood: The Mothers of the Plaza de Mayo.* Wilmington, Del.: Scholarly Resources, Inc.

Bowles, Samuel. 1986. Power and Profits: Social Structure of Accumulation and the Profitability of the Postwar U.S. Economy. *Review of Radical Political Economics* 18 (1 & 2): 132–67.

Bradshaw, Ted K. 1992. Growth Control and the Failure of Planning. *California Policy Choices,* vol. 8, ed. John J. Kirlin, 61–83. Annual published by the Sacramento Public Affairs Center, School of Public Administration, University of Southern California, Los Angeles.

————. 1993. In the Shadow of Urban Growth: Bifurcation in Rural California Communities. In *Forgotten Places: Uneven Development in Rural America,* ed. Thomas A. Lyson and William W. Falk, 218–56. Lawrence: University Press of Kansas.

Braithwaite, John. 1993. Crime and the Average American. *Law & Society Review* 27 (1): 215–31.

Braverman, Harry. 1974. *Labor and Monopoly Capital: The Degradation of Work in the Twentieth Century.* New York: Monthly Review Press.

Brenner, Robert. 2002. *The Boom and the Bubble: The U.S. in the World Economy.* New York: Verso.

Brewer, Cynthia A., and Trudy A. Suchan. 2001. *Mapping Census 2000: The Geography of U.S. Diversity.* Redlands: ESRI Press. Originally published in June 2001 by the U.S. Bureau of the Census as part of the Census 2000 Special Reports Series.

Brimelow, Peter. 1995. *Alien Nation: Common Sense about America's Immigration Disaster.* New York: Random House.

Broadway, Michael J. 1994. Hogtowns and Rural Economic Development. *Rural Development Perspectives* 9 (1): 44–50.

———. 2000. Planning for Change in Small Towns, or Trying to Avoid the Slaughterhouse Blues. *Journal of Rural Studies* 16: 37–46.

Brody, David. 1992. *In Labor's Cause: Main Themes on the History of the American Worker.* New York: Oxford University Press.

———. 1993. *Workers in Industrial America: Essays on the Twentieth-Century Struggle.* Oxford: Oxford University Press.

Brown, Richard Maxwell. 1975. *Strain of Violence: Historical Studies of American Violence and Vigilantism.* New York: Oxford University Press.

———. 1991. *No Duty to Retreat: Violence and Values in American History and Society.* Norman: Oklahoma University Press.

Brown, Warren H. 1942. A Negro Looks at the Negro Press. *Saturday Review,* December 19, 5–6.

Brown, Wendy. 1994. *States of Injury: Power and Freedom in Late Modernity.* Princeton, N.J.: Princeton University Press.

Brown, Wilmette. 1992. *No Justice, No Peace: The 1992 Los Angeles Rebellion from a Black/women's Perspective.* London: International Black Women for Wages for Housework.

Browne, Harry, and Beth Sims. 1993. *Runaway America: U.S. Jobs and Factories on the Move.* Albuquerque: Resource Center Press.

Buck, Pem Davidson. 2001. *Worked to the Bone: Race, Class, Power, & Privilege in Kentucky.* New York: Monthly Review Press.

Bullard, Robert D., J. Eugene Grigsby III, and Charles Lee, eds. 1994. *Residential Apartheid: The American Legacy.* Los Angeles: University of California at Los Angeles Center for African American Studies.

Bulosan, Carlos. [1943] 1973. *America Is in the Heart.* Seattle: University of Washington Press.

Bunker, Edward. 2000. *Education of a Felon.* New York: St. Martin's Press.

Butler, Paul. 1995. Racially Based Jury Nullification: Black Power in the Criminal Justice System. *Yale Law Journal* 105 (3): 677–726.

Butterfield, Fox. 1995. New Prisons Cast Shadow over Higher Education. *New York Times,* April 12, A21.

Buttitta, Sandra L. 1994. AB 971: "Three Strikes and You're Out" Bill. General Office Memorandum 94–20. Office of the District Attorney of Los Angeles County.

Calavita, Kitty. 1992. *Inside the State: The Bracero Program, Immigration, and the I.N.S.* New York: Routledge.

Calavita, Kitty, Henry Pontel, and Robert Tillman. 1997. *Big Money Crime: Fraud and Politics in the Savings and Loan Crisis.* Berkeley: University of California Press.

Calhoun, Craig. 1993. Civil Society and the Public Sphere. *Public Culture* 5 (2): 267–80.

California. Blue Ribbon Commission on Inmate Population and Management. 1990. *Final Report.* Sacramento: BRC.

California Correctional Peace Officers' Association. N.d. [1996]. *Meeting the Challenge of Affordable Prisons: A Plan to Reduce the Cost of Building and Operating California Prisons to Ensure Incarceration of Violent and Habitual Offenders without Bankrupting Taxpayers.* West Sacramento: CCPOA.

California. Department of Corrections. 1971–2002. *Characteristics of Population in California State Prisons by Institution.* Sacramento: CDC. Published annually.

———. Department of Corrections. 1992. *Historical Trends, 1971–1991.* Sacramento: CDC.

———. 1993. *California Prisoners and Parolees, 1991.* Sacramento: CDC.

———. 1994a. *Proposed Medium/Maximum Prison Project.* Sacramento: CDC.

———. 1994b. *Population and Fiscal Estimate of the "Three Strikes" Initiative.* Sacramento: CDC.

California. Department of Finance. 1975–2000. *California Economic Indicators.* Sacramento: CDF. Published six times annually.

———. 1996. *A Performance Review of California Department of Corrections.* Sacramento: Performance Review Unit, CDF.

———. 2000. *A Performance Review of California Department of Corrections.* Sacramento: Performance Review Unit, CDF.

California. Department of Justice. Criminal Justice Information Services Division. http://caag.state.ca.us/cjsc/publications/candd/cd03/tabs/ (accessed January 23, 2005).

California. Governor's Commission on the Los Angeles Riots. 1965. *Violence in the City—An End or a Beginning?* Los Angeles: Governor's Commission on the Los Angeles Riots.

California. Legislative Analyst's Office. 1986. *The New Prison Construction Program at Midstream.* Sacramento: LAO.

———. 1994. *Proposition 172: How Did It Affect Spending for Public Safety? Policy Brief.* Sacramento: LAO.

———. 1994. *Bonds and the November 1994 Ballot. Policy Brief.* Sacramento: LAO.

———. 1995a. *Accommodating Prison Population Growth. Status Check.* Sacramento: LAO.

———. 1995b. *Accommodating the State's Inmate Population Growth. Policy Brief.* Sacramento: LAO.

———. 1996. *Judiciary and Criminal Justice.* Sacramento: LAO.

California. Prison Industry Authority. Annual reports, 1994–99. Folsom, Calif.: PIA.

California. Prison Reform Conference Committee. 1996. *Report to the Prison Reform Conference Committee.* Sacramento: PRCC.

California. State Board of Equalization. 1970–2000. *Taxable Sales in California.* Sacramento: Board of Equalization.

————. 1990–2000. *Top 25 Sales and Use Tax Accounts by City.* Sacramento: State Board of Equalization.

California. State Controller. 1982–2000. *Annual Report.* Sacramento: Office of the Controller of the State of California.

California. State Legislature. Joint Legislative Committee on Prison Construction and Operations. 1996. *California Senate debate on SB 2156, April 16.* Sacramento: Joint Legislative Committee on Prison Construction and Operations.

————. Joint Select Committee on Corcoran. 1998. *Hearings.* August–October. State Capitol, Sacramento.

California. State Public Works Board. 1985. *Lease Revenue Bonds (Department of Corrections) 1985 Series A (Southern Maximum Security Complex). Official Statement.* Sacramento: SPWB.

————. 1986a. *Lease Revenue Bonds (Department of Corrections) 1986 Series A (State Prison—Amador County). Official Statement.* Sacramento: SPWB.

————. 1986b. *Lease Revenue Bonds (Department of Corrections) 1986 Series A [sic] (State Prison—Corcoran). Official Statement.* Sacramento: SPWB.

————. 1987. *Lease Revenue Bonds (Department of Corrections) 1987 Series A (State Prison—Del Norte). Official Statement.* Sacramento: SPWB.

————. 1990. *Lease Revenue Bonds (Department of Corrections) 1990 Series A (State Prison—Madera County). Official Statement.* Sacramento: SPWB.

————. 1991. *Lease Revenue Bonds (Department of Corrections) 1991 Series A (State Prisons—Imperial County). Official Statement.* Sacramento: SPWB.

————. 1993a. *Lease Revenue Refunding Bonds (Department of Corrections) 1993 Series A (Various State Prisons). Lease Revenue Bonds (Department of Corrections) 1993 Series B (California State Prison—Fresno County, Coalinga). Official Statement.* Sacramento: SPWB.

————. 1993b. *Lease Revenue Refunding Bonds (Department of Correc-*

tions) 1986 Series C (Del Norte). Official Statement. Sacramento: SPWB.

———. 1993c. *Lease Revenue Bonds (Department of Corrections) 1993 Series D (California State Prison—Lassen County, Susanville). Official Statement.* Sacramento: SPWB.

———. 1993d. *Lease Revenue Bonds (Department of Corrections) 1993 Series E (California State Prison—Madera County (II)). Official Statement.* Sacramento: SPWB.

———. 2001. *Lease Revenue Bonds (Department of Corrections). 2001 Series A (California State Prison—Lassen County Susanville), and 2001 Series B (California Substance Abuse Treatment Facility and State Prison at Corcoran [Corcoran II]). Official Statement.* Sacramento: SPWB.

California. State Task Force on Youth Gang Violence. 1986. Final Report. Sacramento: California Council on Criminal Justice.

Carby, Hazel V. 1987. *Reconstructing Womanhood: The Emergence of the Afro-American Woman Novelist.* Oxford: Oxford University Press.

———. 1992. Policing the Black Woman's Body in an Urban Context. *Critical Inquiry* 18 (4): 738–55.

Carlson, Katherine. 1988. Understanding Community Opposition to Prison Siting: More Fear Than Finances. *Corrections Today,* April, 84–90.

———. 1992. Doing Good and Looking Bad: A Case Study of Prison/ Community Relations. *Crime and Delinquency* 38 (1): 56–69.

Carr, James. 1975. *Bad: The Autobiography of James Carr.* New York: Carroll & Graf.

Castells, Manuel. 1989. *The Informational City: Information Technology, Economic Restructuring, and the Urban-Regional Process.* Oxford: Basil Blackwell.

Castells, Manuel, and Peter Hall. 1994. *Technopoles of the World: The Making of 21st Century Industrial Complexes.* New York: Routledge.

Caughey, John Walton. 1940. *California.* New York: Prentice-Hall.

Cell, John W. 1982. *The Highest Stage of White Supremacy: The Origins of Segregation in South Africa and the America South.* Cambridge: Cambridge University Press

Central California Futures Institute Staff. 2000. *Five Cities Economic Development Authority: A Study of Agriculturally Related Businesses.* Fresno, Calif.: Central California Futures Institute.

Cerrill Associates. 1984. *Political Difficulties Facing Waste-to-Energy Conversion Plant Siting 43.* Prepared for the California Waste Management Board. Los Angeles: Cerrill Associates.

Chabotar, Kent John. 1985. Financing Alternatives for Prison and Jail Construction. *Government Finance Review* 1 (3): 7–14.

Chabram, Angie C. 1990. Chicana/o Studies as Oppositional Ethnography. *Cultural Studies* 4 (3): 228–47.

Chabram, Angie C., and Rosa Linda Fregoso. 1990. Chicana/o Cultural Representations: Reframing Alternative Critical Discourses. *Cultural Studies* 4 (3): 203–12.

Chabrán, Richard. 1990. The Emergence of Neoconservatism in Chicano/Latino Discourses. *Cultural Studies* 4 (3): 217–27.

Chambliss, William J. 1994. Don't Confuse Me with Facts: Clinton "Just Says No." *New Left Review* 204: 113–26.

———. 1999. *Power, Politics, and Crime.* Boulder, Colo.: Westview Press.

Chandler, Alfred D. 1977. *The Visible Hand: The Managerial Revolution in America.* Cambridge, Mass.: Harvard University Press.

———. 1990. *Scale and Scope: The Dynamics of Industrial Capitalism.* Cambridge, Mass.: Harvard University Press.

Chapman, Jeffrey I. 1991. The Fiscal Context. *California Policy Choices,* vol. 7, ed. John J. Kirlin and Donald R. Winkler, 13–36. Annual published by the Sacramento Public Affairs Center, School of Public Administration, University of Southern California, Los Angeles.

Cheng, Lucie, and Edna Bonacich, eds. 1984. *Labor Immigration under Capitalism: Asian Workers in the United States before World War II.* Berkeley: University of California Press.

Chinitz, Benjamin. 1960. Contrasts in Agglomeration: New York and Pittsburgh. *American Economic Association Papers and Proceedings,* 279–89.

Chinn, Sarah E. 2000. *Technology and the Logic of American Racism.* New York: Continuum Press.

Chomsky, Noam. 1991. International Terrorism: Image and Reality. In *Western State Terrorism,* ed. Alexander George, 12–38. New York: Routledge.

Christaller, Walter. 1966. *Central Places in Southern Germany.* Englewood Cliffs, N.J.: Prentice-Hall.

Christian, Barbara. 1987. The Race for Theory. *Cultural Critique* 6: 51–61.

Christianson, Scott. 1998. *With Liberty for Some: 500 Years of Imprisonment in America.* Boston: Northeastern University Press.

Christie, Nils. 1993. *Crime Control as Industry: Towards Gulags Western Style?* New York: Routledge.

Christopher, Warren. 1991. *Report of the Independent Commission on the Los Angeles Police Department.* Los Angeles: The Commission.

Churchill, Ward, and Jim Vander Wall. 1990. *Agents of Repression: The FBI's Secret Wars against the Black Panther Party and the American Indian Movement.* Boston: South End Press.

———, eds. 1990. *The Cointelpro Papers: Documents from the FBI's Secret Wars against Dissent in the United States.* Boston: South End Press.

Clark, Gordon. 1984. A Theory of Local Autonomy. *Annals of the Association of American Geographers* 74: 195–208.

———. 1991. *Unions and Communities under Siege.* Cambridge: Cambridge University Press.

Clark, Gordon, and Michael Dear. 1981. The State in Capitalism and the Capitalist State. In *Urbanization and Urban Planning in Capitalist Society,* ed. Michael Dear and Allan Scott, 45–61. New York: Methuen.

Clark, John, James Austin, and D. Alan Henry. 1996. *"Three Strikes and You're Out": A Review of State Legislation.* Research in Brief. NCJ 165369. Washington, D.C.: U.S. Department of Justice, National Institute of Justice.

Clark, Septima. 1986. *Ready from Within: Septima Clark and the Civil Rights Movement.* Navarro, Calif.: Wild Trees Press.

Clarke, Stuart Alan. 1991. Fear of a Black Planet: Race, Identity Politics and Common Sense. *Socialist Review* 21 (3 & 4): 37–59.

Clear, Todd. 2002. The Problem with "Addition by Subtraction": The Prison-Crime Relationship in Low-Income Communities. In *Invisible Punishment,* ed. Marc Mauer and Meda Chesney-Lind, 184–94. New York: New Press.

Clear, Todd, Dina R. Rose, Elin Waring, and Kristin Scully. 2001. Coercive Mobility and Crime: A Preliminary Examination of Concentrated Incarceration and Social Disorganization. *Justice Quarterly* 20 (1): 33–64.

Coalition for Effective Public Safety. 2004. *Lower Costs, Greater Safety: A Common-Sense Plan to Reform the California Department of Corrections to Save Money and Make Our Communities Safer.* Sacramento: Coalition for Effective Public Safety.

Cobble, Dorothy Sue. 1991. *Dishing It Out: Waitresses and Their Unions in the Twentieth Century.* Urbana: University of Illinois Press.

———. 1994. Making Postindustrial Unionism Possible. In *Restoring the Promise of American Labor Law,* ed. Sheldon Friedman et al., 285–302. Ithaca, N.Y.: ILR Press.

———, ed. 1993. *Women and Unions: Forging a Partnership.* Ithaca, N.Y.: ILR Press.

Cohen, Lizabeth. 1990. *Making a New Deal.* Cambridge: Cambridge University Press.

Cohen, Mark. 1988. Pain, Suffering and Jury Awards: A Study of the Cost of Crime to Victims. *Law and Society Review* 22: 537–55.

Cohen, Robin. 1987. *The New Helots: Migrants in the International Division of Labour.* Aldershot, Hants, UK: Avebury; Brookfield, Vt.: Gower Pub. Co.

Cole, David. 1996. Courting Capital Punishment. *Nation,* February 22, 1996, 20–22.

Cole, Luke, and Sheila Foster. 2001. *From the Ground Up.* New York: New York University Press.

Collins, Patricia Hill. 1990. *Black Feminist Thought.* Boston: Unwin Hyman.

Comfort, Megan. 2002. "Papa's House: The Prison as Domestic and Social Satellite." *Ethnography* 3 (4): 467–99.

Connery, Robert H., ed. 1969. *Urban Riots: Violence and Social Change.* New York: Vintage Books.

Conover, Ted. 2000. *Newjack: Guarding Sing Sing.* New York: Random House.

Cook, Fred J. 1962. *The Warfare State.* New York: Macmillan.

Cooke, R. U. 1984. *Geomorphological Hazards in Los Angeles.* London: Allen Unwin.

Corbridge, Stuart. 1994. Plausible Worlds: Friedman, Keynes and the Geography of Inflation. In *Money, Power and Space,* ed. Stuart Corbridge, Nigel Thrift, and Ron Martin, 63–91. Oxford: Basil Blackwell.

Cornell, Drucilla. 1995. *The Imaginary Domain: Abortion, Pornography & Sexual Harassment.* New York: Routledge.

Cox, Oliver C. 1987. *Race, Class, and the World System: The Sociology of Oliver C. Cox,* ed. Herbert M. Hunter and Sameer Y. Abraham. New York: Monthly Review.

Critical Resistance–INCITE. 2002. *Gender Violence and the Prison-Industrial Complex.* www.incite-national.org/involve/statement.html (accessed August 2005).

Critical Resistance Publications Collective, ed. 2000. Critical Resistance to the Prison-Industrial Complex. Special Issue of *Social Justice* 27 (3).

Cruikshank, Barbara. 1994. The Will to Empowerment: Technologies of Citizenship and the War on Poverty. *Socialist Review* 23 (4): 29–55.

Cullenberg, Stephen. 1994. *The Falling Rate of Profit: Recasting the Marxian Debate.* London: Pluto Press.

Cummins, Eric. 1994. *The Rise and Fall of California's Radical Prison Movement.* Stanford: Stanford University Press.

Curry, Janel M. 2000. Community Worldview and Rural Systems: A Study of Five Communities in Iowa. *Annals of the Association of American Geographers* 90 (4): 693–712.

Curtin, Mary Ellen. 2000. *Black Prisoners and Their World, Alabama, 1865–1900.* Charlottesville: University Press of Virginia.

Dalla Costa, Mariarosa, and Selma James. 1972. *The Power of Women and the Subversion of the Community.* London: Falling Wall Press.

Daniel, Cletus E. 1981. *Bitter Harvest: A History of California Farmworkers, 1870–1941.* Berkeley: University of California Press.

Davis, Angela Y., ed. 1971. *If They Come in the Morning: Voices of Resistance.* A Joseph Okpaku Book. New York: Third Press.

———. 1981. *Women, Race & Class.* New York: Vintage Books.

———. 1989. *Women, Culture & Politics.* New York: Random House.

———. 2003. *Are Prisons Obsolete?* New York: Seven Stories Press.

Davis, Christopher, Richard Estes, and Vincent Schiraldi. 1996. *"Three Strikes": The New Apartheid.* San Francisco: Center on Juvenile and Criminal Justice.

Davis, David Brion. 1986. *From Homicide to Slavery: Studies in American Culture.* New York: Oxford University Press.

Davis, Mike. 1986. *Prisoners of the American Dream.* New York: Verso.

———. 1990. *City of Quartz.* New York: Verso.

———. 1992a. Blacks Are Dealt Out. *Nation,* July 6, 1992, 7–10.

———. 1992b. The L.A. Inferno. *Socialist Review* 22 (1): 57–80.

———. 1993a. Uprising and Repression in Los Angeles. In *Reading Rodney King, Reading Urban Uprising,* ed. Robert Gooding-Williams, 142–54. New York: Routledge.

———. 1993b. Who Killed Los Angeles? A Political Autopsy. *New Left Review* 197: 3–28.

———. 1993c. Who Killed Los Angeles: Part Two: The Verdict Is Given. *New Left Review* 199: 29–54.

———. 1995. Hell's Factories in the Fields. *Nation,* January, 32–37.

———. 1998. *Ecology of Fear.* New York: Metropolitan Books.

Dawson, Robert, and Gray Brechin. 1999. *Farewell, Promised Land: Waking from the California Dream.* Berkeley: University of California Press.

Dayan, Joan. 1999. Held in the Body of the State. In *History, Memory, and the Law,* ed. Austin Sarat and Thomas R. Kearns, 183–248. Ann Arbor: University of Michigan Press.

De Certeau, Michel. *The Practice of Everyday Life*. Berkeley: University of California Press.

De Janvry, Alain. 1981. *The Agrarian Question and Reformism in Latin America*. Baltimore: Johns Hopkins University Press.

De Landa, Manuel. 1991. *War in the Age of Intelligent Machines*. New York: Zone Books.

de Sousa Santos, Bonaventura. 1980. Law and Community: The Changing Nature of State Power in Late Capitalism. *International Journal of the Sociology of Law* 8: 379–97.

Delone, Miriam Anne. 1992. Labor and County-Level Punishment Patterns in Florida during the 1980s. Ph.D. diss., Florida State University.

Derber, Charles. 1996. *The Wilding of America: How Greed and Violence Are Eroding Our Nation's Character*. New York: St. Martin's Press.

Derrida, Jacques. 1986. But, beyond . . . (Open Letter to Anne McClintock and Rob Nixon). *Critical Inquiry* 13 (1): 155–70.

Deutsche, Rosalyn. 1990a. Architecture of the Evicted. *Strategies* (3): 159–83.

———. 1990b. Men in Space. *Strategies* (3): 130–37.

———. 1992. Art and Public Space: Questions of Democracy. *Social Text* (33): 34–53.

Dickens, Edwin. 1995. U.S. Monetary Policy in the 1950s: A Radical Political Economic Approach. *Review of Radical Political Economics* 27 (4): 83–111.

———. 1996. The Federal Reserve's Low Interest Rate Policy in 1970–72: Determinants and Constraints. *Review of Radical Political Economics* 28 (3): 115–25.

Didion, Joan. 2003. *Where I Was From*. New York: Knopf.

DiIulio, John J. 1991. *No Escape: The Future of American Corrections*. New York: Basic Books.

———. 1994. The Question of Black Crime. *Public Interest*, Fall, 3–32.

———. 1997. Are Voters Fools? Crime, Public Opinion, and Representative Democracy. *Corrections Management Quarterly* 1 (3): 1–5.

Dill, Bonnie Thornton. 1994. *Across the Boundaries of Race and Class: An*

Exploration of Work and Family among Black Female Domestic Servants. New York: Garland.

Dittmer, John. 1994. *Local People: The Struggle for Civil Rights in Mississippi.* Urbana: University of Illinois Press.

Doherty, Joe, Elspeth Graham, and Mo Malek, eds. 1992. *Postmodernism and the Social Sciences.* London: Macmillan.

Donner, Frank J. 1980. *The Age of Surveillance: The Aims and Methods of America's Political Intelligence System.* New York: Knopf.

———. 1990. *Protectors of Privilege: Red Squads and Police Repression in Urban America.* Berkeley: University of California Press.

Don't Talk! 1980. Reprint of *Revolutionary Worker,* no. 42. New York: Revolution Books.

Dowd, Doug. 1997. *Blues for America: A Critique, a Lament, and Some Memories.* New York: Monthly Review Press.

Downey, Sheridan. 1947. *They Would Rule the Valley.* San Francisco: Office of Senator Sheridan Downey.

Drew, Jerry. 1984. New Prison. *Coalinga Record,* February 1, 1.

Dubofsky, Melvyn. 1969. *We Shall Be All: A History of the Industrial Workers of the World.* Chicago: Quadrangle Books.

———. 1994. *The State and Labor in Modern America.* Chapel Hill: University of North Carolina Press.

DuBois, Page. 1991. *Torture and Truth.* New York: Routledge.

Du Bois, W. E. B. [1935] 1992. *Black Reconstruction in America, 1860–1880.* New York: Atheneum.

Duff, Antony, and David Garland, eds. 1994. *A Reader on Punishment.* Oxford: Oxford University Press.

Duffy, Migon. 2005. Reproducing Labor Inequalities: Challenges for Feminists Conceptualizing Care at the Intersections of Gender, Race and Class. *Gender and Society* 19 (1): 66–82.

Dugger, William M. 1988. A Research Agenda for Institutional Economics. *Journal of Economic Issues* 22 (4): 983–1002.

Duncan, James, and Trevor Barnes, eds. 1992. *Writing Worlds: Discourse, Text and Metaphor in the Representation of Landscape.* New York: Routledge.

Dunne, Bill. 1997. *The New Plantation.* Fairfield, Conn.: Free Your-selves Collective. Pamphlet.

Dyer, Joel. 1998. *Harvest of Rage: Why Oklahoma City Is Only the Begin-ning.* Boulder, Colo.: Westview Press.

———. 1999. *The Perpetual Prisoner Machine: How America Profits from Crime.* Boulder, Colo.: Westview Press.

Edid, Marilyn. 1994. *Farm Labor Organizing: Trends and Prospects.* Ithaca, N.Y.: ILR Press.

Edsall, Thomas. 1988. *The New Politics of Inequality.* New York: Nor-ton.

Edwards, Richard, and Michael Podgursky. 1986. The Unravelling Ac-cord: American Unions in Crisis. In *Unions in Crisis and Beyond: Per-spectives from Six Countries*, ed. Richard Edwards, Paolo Garonna, and Franz Todtling, 14–59. Dover, Mass.: Auburn House.

Egerton, John. 1994. *Speak Now against the Day: The Generation before the Civil Rights Movement in the South.* New York: Knopf.

Eitzen, D. Stanley, and Maxine Baca Zinn. 1989. *The Reshaping of America: Social Consequences of the Changing Economy.* Englewood Cliffs, N.J.: Prentice-Hall.

Ekland-Olson, Sheldon, et al. 1992. Crime and Incarceration: Some Comparative Findings from the 1980s. *Crime and Delinquency* 38 (3): 392–416.

El-Ashry, Mohamed T., and Diana C. Gibbons, eds. 1988. *Water and Arid Lands of the Western United States.* A World Resources Institute book. New York: Cambridge University Press.

Engelhardt, Tom. 1995. *The End of Victory Culture: Cold War America and the Disillusioning of a Generation.* New York: Basic Books.

Engler, Robert. 1994. Progress and Power Post-Industrial Style. *Monthly Review* 46 (3): 114–22.

Epstein, Edward Jay. 1990. *Agency of Fear.* Rev ed. New York: Verso.

Erickson, Christopher L., Catherine Fisk, Ruth Milkman, Daniel J. E. Mitchell, and Kent Wong. 2002. *California's Revolt of the Bottom of the Wage Scale.* www.sppsr.ucla.edu/calpolicy02/page1.cfm (accessed August 2005).

Escobar, Arturo. 1992. Imagining a Post-Development Era? Critical Thought, Development and Social Movements. *Social Text* 31/32: 30–56.

———. 1995. *Encountering Development*. Princeton, N.J.: Princeton University Press.

Esteva, Gustavo, and Madhu Suri Prakash. 1998. *Grassroots Post-Modernism: Remaking the Soil of Cultures*. London: Zed Books.

Ethington, Philip J. 2000. *Segregated Diversity: Race-Ethnicity, Space, and Political Fragmentation in Los Angeles County, 1940–1994*. Final Report to the John Randolph Haynes and Dora Haynes Foundation. Los Angeles: Haynes Foundation.

Eu, March Fong. 1993. *California Ballot Initiatives*. Sacramento: Office of the Secretary of State.

Families against Mandatory Minimums [FAMM]. 1995. Crack and Marijuana Top Sentencing Commission Agenda. *FAMMgram*, 1.

Fanon, Frantz. 1961. *The Wretched of the Earth*. New York: Grove Press.

Farr, Kathryn Ann. 1990. Revitalizing the Drug Decriminalization Debate. *Crime & Delinquency* 36 (2): 223–37.

Farrigan, Tracey L., and Amy K. Glasmeier. 2002. The Economic Impact of the Prison Development Boom on Persistently Poor Rural Places. www.onenation.psu.edu/products/publications/prison_development/prison_development.pdf (accessed August 2005).

Faue, Elisabeth. 1990. *Community of Suffering and Struggle: Women, Men and the Labor Movement in Minneapolis, 1915–1945*. Chapel Hill: University of North Carolina Press.

Feldman, Allen. 1991. *Formations of Violence: The Narrative of the Body and Political Terror in Northern Ireland*. Chicago: University of Chicago Press.

———. 1994. On Cultural Anesthesia: From Desert Storm to Rodney King. *American Ethnologist* 21 (2): 404–18.

———. 1999. The Event and Its Shadow: Post-Ethnographic Receptions of Violence. *Transforming Anthropology* 8 (1–2): 4–18.

———. 2001. Philoctetes Revisited: White Public Space and the Political Geography of Public Safety. *Social Text* 19 (38): 57–89.

————. 2002a. Ground Zero Point One: On the Cinematics of History. *Social Analysis* 46 (1): 110–17.

————. 2002b. Strange Fruit. *Social Analysis* 46 (3): 234–65.

Feldman, Daniel L. 1993. Twenty Years of Prison Expansion: A Failing National Strategy. *Public Administration Review* 53 (6): 561–70.

Femenía, Nora Amelia. 1987. Argentina's Mothers of the Plaza de Mayo: The Mourning Process from Junta to Democracy. *Feminist Studies* 13 (1): 9–18.

Ferguson, Ann. 1990. The Intersection of Race, Gender, and Class in the United States Today. *Rethinking Marxism* 3 (3–4): 45–64.

Ferguson, James. [1990] 1994. *The Anti-Politics Machine: "Development," Depoliticization and Bureaucratic Power in Lesotho.* Minneapolis: University of Minnesota Press.

Fernandes, Leela. 1997. *Producing Workers: The Politics of Gender, Class, and Culture in the Calcutta Jute Mills.* Philadelphia: University of Pennsylvania.

Ferrari, Paul L., Jeffrey W. Knopf, and Raúl L. Madrid. 1987. *U.S. Arms Exports: Policies and Contractors.* Washington, D.C.: Investor Responsibility Research Center.

Fields, Barbara Jeanne. 1990. Slavery, Race and Ideology in the United States of America. *New Left Review* 181: 95–118.

Fischer, Michael M. J. 1993. Is There a Difference between Public Culture 1789 and 1989? A Reply to Greg Urban. *Public Culture* 5 (2): 39–44.

Fisher, Jo. 1989. *Mothers of the Disappeared.* Boston: South End Press.

Flanigan, James. 1996. A Contradictory Economy Driven by Steady Investors. *Los Angeles Times,* January 14, D-1.

Flateau, John. 1996. *The Prison Industrial Complex: Race, Crime & Justice in New York.* New York: Medgar Evers College, CUNY/DuBois Bunche Center.

Fogelson, Robert M. 1989. *America's Armories: Architecture, Society, and Public Order.* Cambridge, Mass.: Harvard University Press.

————. [1967] 1993. *The Fragmented Metropolis.* Berkeley: University of California Press.

Foglesong, Richard E. 1986. *Planning the Capitalist City: The Colonial Era to the 1920s.* Princeton, N.J.: Princeton University Press.

Foner, Eric. 1983. *Nothing but Freedom: Emancipation and Its Consequences.* Baton Rouge: Louisiana State University Press.

Foner, Phillip S. 1970. The IWW and the Black Worker. *Journal of Negro History* 54 (4): 45–64.

Forbath, William E. 1991. *Law and the Shaping of the American Labor Movement.* Cambridge, Mass.: Harvard University Press.

Fortunati, Leopoldina. 1995. *The Arcane of Reproduction: Housework, Prostitution, Labor and Capital.* Translated by Hilary Creek. Brooklyn, N.Y.: Autonomedia.

Foucault, Michel. 1965. *Madness and Civilization.* New York: Random House.

———. 1970. *The Order of Things: An Archaeology of the Human Sciences.* New York: Vintage Books.

———. 1975. *The Birth of the Clinic: An Archaeology of Medical Perception.* New York: Vintage Books.

———. 1977. *Discipline and Punish: The Birth of the Prison.* Translated by Alan Sheridan. New York: Pantheon Books.

———. 1982. Space, Power and Knowledge: An Interview with Michel Foucault by Paul Rabinow. *Skyline,* March, 16–20.

———. 1991. Faire vivre et laisser mourir: La Naissance du racisme. *Les Temps Modernes* 535: 37–61.

Fraad, Harriet. 1990. Anorexia Nervosa: The Female Body as a Site of Gender and Class Transition. *Rethinking Marxism* 3 (3–4): 79–100.

Fraad, Harriet, Stephen Resnick, and Richard Wolff. 1994. *Bringing It All Back Home: Class, Gender & Power in the Modern Household.* London: Pluto Press.

Franklin, H. Bruce. 1982. *Prison Literature in America.* Westport, Conn.: Lawrence Hill.

———. 1998. *Prison Writing in Twentieth Century America.* New York: Penguin Books.

Fraser, Joelle. 2003. An American Seduction: Portrait of a Prison Town.

In *Prison Nation,* ed. Tara Herivel and Paul Wright, 73–84. New York: Routledge.

Fraser, Nancy, and Linda Gordon. 1992. Contract versus Charity: Why Is There No Social Citizenship in the United States? *Socialist Review* 22 (3): 45–67.

Fraser, Steve, and Gary Gerstle, eds. 1989. *The Rise and Fall of the New Deal Order, 1930–1980.* Princeton, N.J.: Princeton University Press.

Freedman, Carl. 1992. Louisiana "Duce": Notes toward a Systematic Analysis of Postmodern Fascism in America. *Rethinking Marxism* 5 (1): 19–31.

Freedman, Estelle B. 1996. *Maternal Justice: Miriam van Waters and the Female Reform Tradition.* Chicago: University of Chicago Press.

Freeman, Richard B. 1996. The Supply of Youths to Crime. In *Exploring the Underground Economy,* ed. Susan Pozo, 57–81. Kalamazoo, Mich.: W. E. Upjohn Institute.

Fregoso, Rosa Linda. 1990. "Born in East LA" and the Politics of Representation. *Cultural Studies* 4 (3): 264–80.

Freire, Paolo. 1970. *Pedagogy of the Oppressed.* New York: Seabury Press.

Freyfogle, Eric T., ed. 2001. *The New Agrarianism: Land, Culture, and the Community of Life.* Washington, D.C.: Island Press.

Frieden, Bernard J., and Lynne B. Sagalyn. 1989. *Downtown, Inc.* Cambridge, Mass.: MIT Press.

Friedman, Lawrence M. 1993. *Crime and Punishment in American History.* New York: Basic Books.

Friedman, Sheldon, Richard W. Hurd, Rudolph A. Oswald, and Ronald L. Seeber, eds. 1994. *Restoring the Promise of American Labor Law.* Ithaca, N.Y.: ILR Press.

Friedmann, John, and Clyde Weaver. 1979. *Territory and Function: The Evolution of Regional Planning.* Berkeley: University of California Press.

Froines, Ann. 1992. Renewing Socialist Feminism. *Socialist Review* 22 (2): 125–31.

Fuller, Lisa G. 1993. Visitors to Women's Prisons in California: An Exploratory Study. *Federal Probation* 57 (4): 41–47.

Fusfeld, Daniel R. 1972. *The Age of the Economist.* Rev. ed. Glenview, Ill.: Scott Foresman.

Gabriel, Satyananda. 1990. The Continuing Significance of Race: An Overdeterminist Approach to Racism. *Rethinking Marxism* 3 (3–4): 65–78.

Galbraith, John Kenneth. 1967. *The New Industrial State.* New York: New American Library.

Gallagher, Tom. 1991. Massachusetts: Miracle to Debacle. *Socialist Review* 21 (1): 155–76.

Gang Truce Leader: From Peacemaker to Prisoner. 1992. *Los Angeles Times,* December 20, B-1.

Garcia, Matt. 2001. *A World of Its Own: Race, Labor, and Citrus in the Making of Greater Los Angeles, 1900–1970.* Chapel Hill: University of North Carolina Press.

Garland, David. 1990. *Punishment and Modern Society: A Study in Social Theory.* Chicago: University of Chicago Press.

———. 2002. *The Culture of Control: Crime and Social Order in Contemporary Society.* Chicago: University of Chicago Press.

Garnham, Nicholas. 1993. The Mass Media, Cultural Identity, and the Public Sphere in the Modern World. *Public Culture* 5 (2): 251–66.

Gay, Paul du. 1991. Enterprise Culture and the Ideology of Excellence. *New Formations* (13): 45–61.

Geiger, Roger L. 1985. *To Advance Knowledge.* New York: Oxford University Press.

———. 1993. *Research and Relevant Knowledge.* New York: Oxford University Press.

Geohegan, Thomas. 1991. *Which Side Are You On? Trying to Be for Labor When It's Flat on Its Back.* New York: Farrar Straus Giroux.

George, Alexander, ed. 1991. *Western State Terrorism.* New York: Routledge.

Gest, Ted. 2001. *Crime and Politics: Big Government's Erratic Campaign for Law and Order.* New York: Oxford University Press.

Gibbons, Don. 1990. From the Editor's Desk: A Call for Some "Outrageous" Proposals for Crime Control in the 1990s. *Crime and Delinquency* 36 (2): 195–203.

Giddens, Anthony. 1987. A *Contemporary Critique of Historical Materialism*. Vol. 2: *The Nation-State and Violence*. Berkeley: University of California Press.

Giddings, Paula. 1984. *When and Where I Enter: The Impact of Black Women on Race and Sex in America*. New York: William Morrow.

Gilbert, Melissa. 1998. "Race," Space, and Power: The Survival Strategies of Working Poor Women. *Annals of the Association of American Geographers* 88 (4): 595–621.

Gilkes, Cheryl Townsend. 1979. *Black Women's Work as Deviance: Social Sources of Racial Antagonism*. Wellesley, Mass.: Wellesley College Center for Research on Women.

—————. 1989. Dual Heroisms and Double Burdens: Interpreting Afro-American Women's Experience and History. *Feminist Studies* 15 (3): 573–90.

Gill, Richard T. 1994. The Importance of Deterrence. *Public Interest,* Fall, 51–56.

Gillespie, Ed, and Bob Schellhas, eds. 1994. *Contract with America: The Bold Plan by Rep. Newt Gingrich, Rep. Dick Armey and the House Republicans to Change the Nation.* New York: Times Books.

Gilmore, Glenda Elizabeth. 1996. *Gender and Jim Crow: Women and the Politics of White Supremacy in North Carolina, 1896–1920.* Chapel Hill: University of North Carolina Press.

Gilmore, Ruth Wilson. 1991. Decorative Beasts: Dogging the Academy in the Late 20th Century. *California Sociologist* 14 (1–2): 113–35.

—————. 1993a. Public Enemies and Private Intellectuals: Apartheid USA. *Race & Class* 35 (1): 69–78.

—————. 1993b. Terror Austerity Race Gender Excess Theater. In *Reading Rodney King, Reading Urban Uprising,* ed. Robert Gooding-Williams, 23–37. New York: Routledge.

—————. 1994. Capital, State and the Spatial Fix: Imprisoning the Crisis at Pelican Bay. Unpublished ms.

————. 1998. Globalisation and U.S. Prison Growth: From Military-Keynesianism to Post-Keynesian Militarism. *Race and Class* 40 (2–3): 171–87.

————. 1999. "You Have Dislodged a Boulder": Mothers and Prisoners in the Post Keynesian California Landscape. *Transforming Anthropology* 8 (1–2): 12–38.

————. 2002a. Fatal Couplings of Power and Difference: Notes on Racism and Geography. *Professional Geographer* 54 (1): 15–24.

————. 2002b. Race and Globalization. In *Geographies of Global Change,* ed. R. J. Johnstone, P. J. Taylor, and M. Watts, 261–74. 2nd ed. Oxford: Basil Blackwell.

Gilmore, Ruth Wilson, and Craig Gilmore. 2004. The Other California. In *Globalizing Liberation,* ed. David Solnit, 381–96. San Francisco: City Lights Books.

Gilpin, Kenneth N. 1995. Corporate Profits Are Robust, Despite Slowing Growth. *New York Times,* August 4, D-3.

Gilroy, Paul. 1987. *There Ain't No Black in the Union Jack.* London: Hutchinson.

————. 1993. *The Black Atlantic: Modernity and Double Consciousness.* Cambridge, Mass.: Harvard University Press.

————. 2000. *Against Race.* Cambridge, Mass.: Harvard University Press.

Gilroy, Paul, Lawrence Grossberg, and Angela McRobbie. 2000. *Without Guarantees: In Honour of Stuart Hall.* New York: Verso.

Ginzburg, Ralph. [1962] 1988. *100 Years of Lynchings.* Baltimore: Black Classic Press.

Glassner, Barry. 2000. *The Culture of Fear.* New York: Basic Books.

Glazer, Nathan. 1997. *We Are All Multiculturalists Now.* Cambridge, Mass.: Harvard University Press.

Glenn, Evelyn Nakano. 1985. Racial Ethnic Women's Labor: The Intersection of Race, Gender and Class Oppression. *Review of Radical Political Economics* 17(3): 86–108.

————. 2002. *Unequal Freedom: How Race and Gender Shaped American Citizenship and Labor.* Cambridge, Mass.: Harvard University Press.

Glenn, Evelyn Nakano, Grace Chang, and Linda Rennie Forcey, eds. 1994. *Mothering: Ideology, Experience, and Agency.* New York: Routledge.

Glenn, Myra C. 1984. *Campaigns against Corporal Punishment: Prisoners, Sailors, Women and Children in Antebellum America.* Albany: State University of New York Press.

Glickman, Lawrence. 1991. Wages and the Gendering of Need. *Socialist Review* 21 (2): 185–91.

Glyn, Andrew, Alan Hughes, Alain Lipietz, and Ajit Singh. 1990. The Rise and Fall of the Golden Age. In *The Golden Age of Capitalism: Reinterpreting the Post-War Experience,* ed. Stephen J. Marglin and Juliet B. Schor, 39–125. WIDER Studies in Economic Development. Oxford: Clarendon Press.

Godlewska, Anne, and Neil Smith, eds. 1994. *Geography and Empire.* Oxford: Basil Blackwell.

Goldberg, Carey. 1996. Alarm Bells Sounding as Suburbs Gobble Up California's Richest Farmland. *New York Times,* June 20, A-10.

Goldberg, David Theo. 2002. *The Racial State.* Oxford: Blackwell.

Goldberg, Eve, and Linda Evans. 1998. *The Prison Industrial Complex and the Global Economy.* Berkeley, Calif.: Agit Press.

Goldman, George. 1991. Agricultural Policy. In *California Policy Choices,* vol. 8, ed. John J. Kirlin, 181–97. Published annually by the Sacramento Public Affairs Center. Los Angeles: School of Public Administration, University of Southern California.

Goldschmidt, Walter. 1946. *Small Business and the Community: A Study in Central Valley of California on Effects of Scale of Farm Operations.* Report of the Special Committee to Study Problems of American Small Business. U.S. Senate, 79th Cong., 2nd sess. Washington, D.C.: Government Printing Office.

Goodall, Merrill R., John D. Sullivan, and Timothy De Young. 1978. *California Water: A New Political Economy.* Montclair, N.J.: Allanheld, Osmun.

Gooding-Williams, Robert, ed. 1993. *Reading Rodney King, Reading Urban Uprising.* New York: Routledge.

Gordon, David M. 1996. *Fat and Mean: The Corporate Squeeze of Working Americans and the Myth of Managerial Downsizing.* New York: Free Press.

Gordon, David M., Richard Edwards, and Michael Reich. 1982. *Segmented Work, Divided Workers.* Cambridge: Cambridge University Press.

Gordon, Diana R. 1990. *Justice Juggernaut: Fighting Street Crime, Controlling Citizens.* New Brunswick, N.J.: Rutgers University Press.

———. 1994. *The Return of the Dangerous Classes: Drug Prohibition and Policy Politics.* New York: Norton.

Gordon, Linda. 1994. *Pitied but Not Entitled: Single Mothers and the History of Welfare.* New York: Free Press.

Gorman, Tom. 1996. Lawyer Fired over "3 Strikes" Switches Sides. *Los Angeles Times,* April 25, A-3.

Gottlieb, Robert. 1988. *A Life of Its Own: The Politics and Power of Water.* San Diego: Harcourt Brace Jovanovich.

———. 1992. A Question of Class: The Workplace Experience. *Socialist Review* 22 (4): 131–65.

Gottman, Jean. 1961. *Megalopolis: The Urbanized Northeastern Seaboard of the United States.* New York: 20th Century Fund.

Gottschalk, Marie. 2000. *The Shadow Welfare State.* Ithaca, N.Y.: ILR Press.

———. 2002. Black Flower: Prisons and the Future of Incarceration. *Annals of the American Academy of Political and Social Science* 582: 195–227.

Graham, Julie. 1991. Fordism/Post-Fordism, Marxism/Post-Marxism: The Second Cultural Divide. *Rethinking Marxism* 4 (1): 39–58.

Gramlich, Edward M. 1991. The 1991 State and Local Fiscal Crisis. *Brookings Papers on Economic Activity* 2: 249–87.

———. 1994. Infrastructure and Investment: A Review Essay. *Journal of Economic Literature* 32 (September): 1176–96.

Gramsci, Antonio. 1971. *Selections from the Prison Notebooks.* New York: International Publishers.

Granovetter, Mark. 1985. Economic Action and Social Structure: The

Problem of Embeddedness. *American Journal of Sociology* 91 (3): 481–510.

Grant, David, Melvin L. Oliver, and Angela D. James. 1996. African Americans: Social and Economic Bifurcation. In *Ethnic Los Angeles,* ed. Roger Waldinger and Mehdi Bozorgmehr, 379–413. New York: Russell Sage Foundation.

Grant, James. 1992. *Money of the Mind: Borrowing and Lending in America from the Civil War to Michael Milken.* New York: Farrar, Straus & Giroux.

Greenberg, David, ed. 1981. *Crime and Capitalism.* Palo Alto, Calif.: Mayfield Publishers.

Greenberg, Michael, and Dona Schneider. 1994. Violence in American Cities: Young Black Males Is the Answer, but What Was the Question? *Social Science and Medicine* 39 (2): 179–87.

———. 1995. Gender Differences in Risk Perception: Effects Differ in Stressed vs. Non-Stressed Environments. *Risk Analysis* 15 (4): 503–11.

Greene, Judy. 2001. Bailing Out Private Jails. *American Prospect* 12 (16): 23–27.

Greenhouse, Linda. 1997. Related Acquittal Needn't Be Bar to Tougher Sentence, Court Says. *New York Times,* January 7, A1.

Greenhouse, Steven. 1997. U.S. Surveys Find Farm Worker Pay Down for 20 Years. *New York Times,* March 31, A1.

Greenwood, Peter, and Angela Hawken. 2002. *An Assessment of the Effects of California's Three Strikes Law.* Santa Monica: Greenwood and Associates.

Greenwood, Peter W., et al. 1994. *Three Strikes and You're Out: Estimated Benefits and Costs of California's New Mandatory-Sentencing Law.* Santa Monica: Rand Corporation.

Gregory, James N. 1989. *American Exodus: The Dust Bowl Migration and Okie Culture in California.* New York: Oxford University Press.

Gruchy, Allan G. 1990. Three Different Approaches to Institutional Economics: An Evaluation. *Journal of Economic Issues* 24 (2): 361–69.

Guérin, Daniel. 1994. *The Brown Plague: Travels in Late Weimar and Early Nazi Germany.* Durham, N.C.: Duke University Press.

Gutiérrez, Ramón A. 1993. Community, Patriarchy and Individualism: The Politics of Chicano History and the Dream of Equality. *American Quarterly* 45 (1): 44–72.

Gutman, Herbert. 1977. *Work, Culture and Society in Industrializing America*. New York: Vintage Books.

Haag, Ernest van den. 1996. Crime/Criminal Justice. Racism and Public Policy Conference, Rutgers University, April 19, New Brunswick, N.J.

Hadjor, Kofi Buenor. 1995. *Another America: The Politics of Race and Blame*. Boston: South End Press.

Hall, Stuart. 1980. Race, Articulation, and Societies Structured in Dominance. In *Sociological Theories: Race and Colonialism*, ed. UNESCO, 305–46. Paris: UNESCO.

———. 1986. Gramsci's Relevance for the Study of Race and Ethnicity. *Journal of Communication Inquiry* 10 (2): 5–27.

———. 1988a. *The Hard Road to Renewal: Thatcherism and the Crisis of the Left*. New York: Verso.

———. 1988b. New Ethnicities. In *Black Film, British Cinema*, ed. Kobena Mercer et al., 27–31. London: Institute of Contemporary Arts.

———. 1988c. The Toad in the Garden: Thatcherism among the Theorists. In *Marxism and the Interpretation of Culture*, ed. Cary Nelson and Lawrence Grossberg, 35–57. Urbana: University of Illinois Press.

———. 1990. The Whites of Their Eyes: Racist Ideologies and the Media. In *The Media Reader*, ed. Manuel Alvarado and John O. Thompson, 7–23. London: British Film Institute.

———. 1991. Brave New World. *Socialist Review* 21 (1): 57–64.

———. 1992. Race, Culture, and Communications: Looking Backward and Forward at Cultural Studies. *Rethinking Marxism* 5 (1): 10–18.

———. 1995. Negotiating Caribbean Identities. *New Left Review* 209: 3–14.

Hall, Stuart, with Bill Schwartz. 1988. State and Society. In id., *The Hard Road to Renewal*, 95–122. New York: Verso.

Hall, Stuart, Chas Cricher, Tony Jefferson, John Clarke, and Brian Roberts. 1978. *Policing the Crisis: Mugging, the State, and Law and Order.* New York: Holmes & Meier.

Hallinan, Joseph T. 2001. *Going up the River: Travels in a Prison Nation.* New York: Random House.

Halttunen, Karen. 1995. Humanitarianism and the Pornography of Pain. *American Historical Review* 100 (2). Read in page proofs in possession of author.

Hamel, Gary, and C. K. Phahalad. 1994. Competing for the Future. *Harvard Business Review,* July–August, 122–28.

Hamilton, David. 1991. Is Institutional Economics Really "Root and Branch" Economics? *Journal of Economic Issues* 25 (1): 179–86.

Hamm, Theodore. 2001. *Rebel and a Cause: Caryl Chessman and the Politics of the Death Penalty in Postwar California, 1948–1974.* Berkeley: University of California Press.

Hammer, Michael, and James Champy. 1993. *Reengineering the Corporation.* New York: HarperBusiness.

Hammer, Rhonda, and Peter McLaren. 1992. The Spectacularization of Subjectivity: Media Knowledges, Global Citizenry and the New World Order. *Polygraph* (5): 46–66.

Haney, Craig. 1998. Riding the Punishment Wave: On the Origins of Our Devolving Standards of Decency. *Hastings Women's Law Journal* 9: 27–78.

———. 1999a. Ideology and Crime Control. *American Psychologist* 54: 786–88.

———. 1999b. Reflections on the Stanford Prison Experiment: Genesis, Transformations, Consequences. In *Obedience to Authority: Current Perspectives on the Milgram Paradigm,* ed. Thomas Blass, 221–37. Hillsdale, N.J.: Erlbaum.

———. 2001. Afterword. In *Undoing Time,* ed. J. Evans, 245–56. Boston: Northeastern University Press.

Haney, Craig, and Philip G. Zimbardo. 1998. The Past and Future of U.S. Prison Policy: Twenty-five Years after the Stanford Prison Experiment. *American Psychologist* 53: 709–27.

Hansen, Miriam. 1993. Unstable Mixtures, Dilated Spheres: Negt and Kluge's the Public Sphere and Experience, Twenty Years Later. *Public Culture* 5 (2): 179–212.

Haraway, Donna J. 1991. Situated Knowledges: The Science Question in Feminism and the Privilege of the Partial Perspective. In id., *Simians, Cyborgs and Women: The Reinvention of Nature*. New York: Routledge.

Hardt, Michael, and Antonio Negri. 1994. *Labor of Dionysus: A Critique of the State-Form*. Translated by Michael Hardt. Minneapolis: University of Minnesota Press.

———. 2000. *Empire*. Cambridge, Mass.: Harvard University Press.

Harlow, Barbara. 1987. *Resistance Literature*. New York: Methuen.

———. 1990. Constructions of the Intifada. *Polygraph* (4): 35–38.

———. 1992a. *Barred: Women, Writing, and Political Detention*. Hanover, N.H.: University Press of New England.

———. 1992b. Drawing the Line: Cultural Politics and the Legacy of Partition. *Polygraph* (5): 84–112.

———. 1996. *After Lives: Legacies of Revolutionary Writing*. New York: Verso.

Harrington, Michael. 1972. The Invisible Mass Movement. In id., *Socialism*. New York: Bantam Books.

Harris, Cheryl. 1993. Whiteness as Property. *Harvard Law Review* 106: 1707–91.

Harrison, Bennett. 1994. *Lean and Mean: The Changing Landscape of Corporate Power in the Age of Flexibility*. New York: Basic Books.

Hart, Gillian. 2001. Development Critiques in the 1990s: Culs de Sac and Promising Paths. *Progress in Human Geography* 25 (4): 649–58.

———. 2002. *Disabling Globalization*. Berkeley: University of California Press.

Hart-Landsberg, Martin. 1993. *The Rush to Development: Economic Change and Political Struggle in South Korea*. New York: Monthly Review Press.

Hartmann, Heidi. 1981. The Family as the Locus of Gender, Class and Political Struggle: The Example of Housework. *Signs* 6 (3): 366–94.

————. 1996. How Are Women Faring in the New Economy? Keynote address at the Women Work Conference, Rutgers Institute for the Study of Women, New Brunswick, N.J.

Hartsock, Nancy C. M. 1991. Louis Althusser's Structural Marxism: Political Clarity and Theoretical Distortions. *Rethinking Marxism* 4 (4): 10–40.

Harvey, David. [1982] 1989. *The Limits to Capital.* Midway Reprints. Chicago: University of Chicago Press.

————. 1989a. *The Condition of Postmodernity.* Oxford: Basil Blackwell.

————. 1989b. *The Urban Experience.* Baltimore: Johns Hopkins University Press.

————. 1991. Flexibility: Threat or Opportunity? *Socialist Review* 21 (1): 65–77.

————. 1993. Class Relations, Social Justice and the Politics of Difference. In *Place and the Politics of Identity,* ed. Michael Keith and Steve Pile, 41–66. New York: Routledge

————. 1995. Militant Particularism and Global Ambition: The Conceptual Politics of Place, Space and Environment in the Work of Raymond Williams. *Social Text* (42): 69–98.

————. 1997. Plenary address. Socialist Scholars Conference. Borough of Manhattan Community College, New York City, March 29.

————. 2000. *Spaces of Hope.* Berkeley: University of California Press.

Healey, Dorothy Ray, with Maurice Isserman. 1993. *California Red: A Life in the American Communist Party.* Urbana: University of Illinois Press.

Heller, Matthew. 2001. The Prison Prosperity Myth. *Los Angeles Times Sunday Magazine,* September 1. Cover story.

Henwood, Doug. 1997. *Wall Street: How It Works and for Whom.* New York: Verso.

Herbert, Steve. 1997. *Policing Space: Territoriality and the Los Angeles Police Department.* Minneapolis: University of Minnesota Press.

Herivel, Tara, and Paul Wright, eds. 2003. *Prison Nation: The Warehousing of America's Poor.* New York: Routledge.

Hill, Elizabeth G. 1993. *Making Government Make Sense.* Sacramento: LAO.

————. 1994. *Crime in California.* Sacramento: LAO.

————. 1995. *Juvenile Crime: Outlook for California.* Sacramento: LAO.

————. 1996. Fiscal Impact of Corrections Master Plan. Memorandum to State Senator Bill Lockyer. Prison Reform Conference Committee. Sacramento: LAO.

Hill, Polly. 1986. *Development Economics on Trial: The Anthropological Case for the Prosecution.* Cambridge: Cambridge University Press.

Hillinger, Charles. 1987. Tiny County Has Welcome Mat for Prison. *Los Angeles Times,* 1–3.

Hillyard, Paddy. 1993. *Suspect Community: People's Experience of the Prevention of Terrorism Acts in Britain.* London: Pluto Press.

Himes, Chester. [1945] 1986. *If He Hollers Let Him Go.* New York: Thunder's Mouth Press.

————. [1947] 1986. *Lonely Crusade.* New York: Thunder's Mouth Press.

————. [1952] 1972. *Cast the First Stone.* New York: New American Library/Signet.

————. 1971. *The Quality of Hurt: The Autobiography of Chester Himes.* New York: Doubleday.

————. 1993. *Plan B.* Jackson: University Press of Mississippi.

Hirsch, Joachim. 1983. The Fordist Security State and New Social Movements. *Kapitalistate* 10/11: 75–87.

Hobsbawm, Eric J. 1959. *Primitive Rebels: Studies in Archaic Forms of Social Movement in the 19th and 20th Centuries.* New York: Norton.

————. 1982. Gramsci and Marxist Political Theory. In *Approaches to Gramsci,* ed. Anne Showstack Sassoon, 20–36. London: Writers and Readers.

Hogg, Russell, and David Brown. 1998. *Rethinking Law and Order.* Annandale, NSW: Pluto Press.

Hogshire, Jim. 1994. *You Are Going to Prison.* Port Townsend, Wash.: Loompanics Unlimited.

Holland, Stuart. 1976. *Capital versus the Regions.* London: Macmillan.

hooks, bell. 1981. *Ain't I a Woman: black women and feminism.* Boston: South End Press.

————. 1990. *Yearning: Race, Gender and Cultural Politics.* Boston: South End Press.

Hooks, Gregory. 1991. *Forging the Military-Industrial Complex: World War II's Battle of the Potomac.* Urbana: University of Illinois Press.

Hooks, Gregory, Clayton Mosher, Thomas Rotolo, and Lina Lobao. 2004. The Prison Industry: Carceral Expansion and Employment in U.S. Counties, 1969–1994. *Social Science Quarterly* 85: 37–57.

Hornor, Edith R., ed. 1988–2001. *California Cities, Towns, and Counties.* Palo Alto, Calif.: Hornwood Press. Published annually.

Horton, Myles, and Paolo Freire. 1990. *We Make the Road by Walking: Conversations on Education and Social Change.* Ed. Brenda Bell, John Gaventa, and John Peters. Philadelphia: Temple University Press.

House, Gloria. 1991. *Tower and Dungeon: A Study of Place and Power in American Culture.* Detroit: Casa de Unidad.

Howitt, Richard E., and Charles V. Moore. 1994. Water Management. In *California Policy Choices,* vol. 9, ed. John J. Kirlin and Jeffrey I. Chapman, 115–141. Annual published by the Sacramento Public Affairs Center, School of Public Administration, University of Southern California, Los Angeles.

Huet, Marie-Hélène. 1982. *Rehearsing the Revolution.* Chicago: University of Chicago Press.

Huling, Tracy. 2000. Prisoners of the Census. *Mojowire,* May 10.

————. 2002. Building a Prison Economy in Rural America. In *Invisible Punishment,* ed. Marc Mauer and Meda Chesney-Lind. New York: New Press.

Humes, Edward. 1999. *Mean Justice: A Town's Terror, a Prosecutor's Power, a Betrayal of Innocence.* New York: Simon & Schuster.

Hundley, Norris. 1992. *The Great Thirst: Californians and Water, 1770s–1990s.* Berkeley: University of California Press.

Hunt, E. K., and Howard J. Sherman. 1972. *Economics: An Introduction to Traditional and Radical Views.* New York: Harper & Row.

Hunter, Allen. 1992. Prefigurative Politics. *Socialist Review* 22 (2): 133–40.

Hurst, John. 1991a. 1.5 Billion Savings Seen as Prison Admissions Drop. *Los Angeles Times,* October 8, A-3.

———. 1991b. Drop in Prison Admissions Startles Officials. *Los Angeles Times,* September 1, A-1.

Hurst, John, and Dan Morain. 1994. A System Strains at Its Bars. *Los Angeles Times,* October 17, A-1.

Hurtado, Robert. 1995. Prices Regain Some Ground; Shorter Maturities Weaker. *New York Times,* July 25, D-9.

Hyde, Lewis. [1979] 1999. *The Gift: Imagination and the Erotic Life of Property.* London: Vintage Books.

Igler, David. 2001. *Industrial Cowboys: Miller & Lux and the Transformation of the Far West, 1850–1920.* Berkeley: University of California Press.

Ignatieff, Michael. 1978. *A Just Measure of Pain: The Penitentiary and the Industrial Revolution, 1750–1850.* New York: Columbia University Press.

International Black Women for Wages for Housework. 1992. *Legal Defense Information Sheet.* Los Angeles: International Black Women for Wages for Housework.

Irwin, John. 1985. *The Jail: Managing the Underclass in American Society.* Berkeley: University of California Press.

Isard, Walter, et al. 1960. *Methods of Regional Analysis: An Introduction to Regional Science.* Cambridge, Mass.: Technology Press of the Massachusetts Institute of Technology; New York: Wiley.

Ives, George. [1914] 1970. *A History of Penal Methods: Criminals, Witches, Lunatics.* Montclair, N.J.: Patterson Smith.

Ivy, Marilyn. 1993. (Ef)facing Culture: A Reply to Greg Urban. *Public Culture* 5 (2): 245–48.

Jackson, George. 1970. *Soledad Brother: The Prison Letters of George Jackson.* New York: Bantam Books.

Jackson, Peter, ed. 1987. *Race and Racism: Essays in Social Geography.* London: Allen & Unwin.

Jacobs, James B. 1980. The Prisoners' Rights Movement and Its Impacts, 1960–1980. In *Crime and Justice,* ed. Norval Morris and Michael Tonry, 429–70. Chicago: University of Chicago Press.

Jacobs, Jane. 1969. *The Economy of Cities.* New York: Vintage Books.

Jacobs, Paul. 1986. Sale of Property Clouds Outlook for L.A. Prison. *Los Angeles Times,* December 31, 1–1.

Jacobs, Paul, and Janet Clayton. 1987. Deukmejian Vows to Fight for Downtown Prison Site. *Los Angeles Times,* January 1, 2–1.

Jacobs, Paul, and Leo C. Wolinsky. 1986. 4 Alternative Plans Tossed into Fray in Battle over Los Angeles Prison Site. *Los Angeles Times,* September 12, 1–3.

James, C. L. R. 1980. *Fighting Racism in World War Two.* New York: Pathfinder Press.

James, Joy. 1996. *Resisting State Violence: Radicalism, Gender, and Race in U.S. Culture.* Minneapolis: University of Minnesota Press.

———, ed. 2003. *Imprisoned Intellectuals.* Lanham, Md.: Rowman & Littlefield.

James, Selma. 1986. *Sex, Race, and Class.* London: Falling Wall.

Jargowsky, Paul A. 1997. *Poverty and Place: Ghettos, Barrios, and the American City.* New York: Russell Sage Foundation.

Jaynes, Gerald David. 1986. *Branches without Roots: The Genesis of the Black Working Class in the American South, 1862–1882.* New York: Oxford University Press.

Jeffreys-Jones, Rhodri. 1978. *Violence and Reform in American History.* New York: New Viewpoints.

Jencks, Christopher. 1992. *Rethinking Social Policy: Race, Poverty and the Underclass.* Cambridge, Mass.: Harvard University Press.

Jennings, Ann, and William Waller. 1990. Constructions of Social Hierarchy: The Family, Gender and Power. *Journal of Economic Issues* 24 (2): 623–31.

Jessop, Bob. 1983. Accumulation Strategies, State Forms, and Hegemonic Projects. *Kapitalistate* 10/11: 89–111.

Jezierski, Louise. 1991. The Politics of Space. *Socialist Review* 21 (2): 177–84.

Johnson, Charles. 1986. *The Sorcerer's Apprentice.* New York: Macmillan.

Johnson, Toni E. 1999. *Handcuff Blues: Helping Teens Stay Out of Trouble with the Law.* West Hollywood, Calif.: Goofyfoot Press.

Johnston, Paul. 1994. *Success While Others Fail: Social Movement Union-ism and the Public Workplace*. New York: ILR Press.

Jones, Jacqueline. 1985. *Labor of Love, Labor of Sorrow: Black Women, Work and the Family from Slavery to the Present*. New York: Basic Books.

————. 1992. *The Dispossessed: America's Underclass from the Civil War to the Present*. New York: Basic Books.

Jones, LeRoi. 1967. The Changing Same (R&B and New Black Music). In id., *Black Music*, 180–211. New York: William Morrow.

————. 1970. *Black Music*. New York: William Morrow.

Jordan, Winthrop. [1968] 1969. *White over Black: American Attitudes to-ward the Negro, 1550–1812*. Baltimore: Penguin Books.

Josi, Don A. 1996. Site Selection and Construction of Prisons. In *The Encyclopedia of American Prisons*, ed. Marilyn McShane and Frank Williams, 446–49. New York: Garland.

Kaplan, Temma. 1982. Female Consciousness and Collective Action: The Case of Barcelona, 1910–1918. *Signs* 7 (31): 545–66.

Katrak, Ketu. 1986. *Wole Soyinka and Modern Tragedy*. Westport, Conn.: Greenwood Press.

Katz, Cindi. 1991. A Cable to Cross a Curse: Everyday Cultural Prac-tices of Resistance and Reproduction among Youth in New York City. MS.

————. 1992. All the World Is Staged: Intellectuals and the Projects of Ethnography. *Environment and Planning D: Society & Space* 10: 495–510.

————. 1997. Disintegrating Developments: Global Economic Re-structuring and the Eroding Ecologies of Youth. In *Cool Places*, ed. T. Skelton and G. Valentine. New York: Routledge.

————. 2001a. On the Grounds of Globalization: A Topography for Feminist Political Engagement. *Signs* 26 (4): 1213–34.

————. 2001b. Vagabond Capitalism and the Necessity of Social Re-production. *Antipode* 33 (4): 709–28.

Katz, Cindi, and Janice Monk, eds. 1993. *Full Circles: Geographies of Women over the Life Course*. New York: Routledge.

Katz, Cindi, and Neil Smith. 1992. L.A. Intifada: Interview with Mike Davis. *Social Text* (33): 19–33.

Katzenberger, Elaine, ed. 1995. *First World, Ha, Ha, Ha! The Zapatista Challenge.* San Francisco: City Lights Books.

Katznelson, Ira. 1985. Working Class Formation and the State: Nineteenth Century England in American Perspective. In *Bringing the State Back In,* ed. Peter B. Evans, Dietrich Rueschemeyer, and Theda Skocpol, 257–84. Cambridge: Cambridge University Press.

Kauffman, L. A. 1991. The Left vs. the Law: An Interview with Frank Deale. *Socialist Review* 21 (1): 31–39.

Kazin, Michael. 1987. Struggling with the Class Struggle: Marxism and the Search for a Synthesis of U.S. Labor History. *Labor History* 28: 497–514.

Keil, Roger. 1990. The Urban Future Revisited: Politics and Restructuring in L.A. after Fordism. *Strategies* 3: 105–37.

Keith, Michael. 1993. *Race, Riots and Policing: Lore and Disorder in a Multi-Racist Society.* London: UCL Press.

Keith, Michael, and Steve Pile, eds. 1993. *Place and the Politics of Identity.* New York: Routledge.

Kelley, Robin D. G. 1990. *Hammer and Hoe: Alabama Communists during the Great Depression.* Chapel Hill: University of North Carolina Press.

———. 1993. "We are not what we seem": Rethinking Black Working-Class Opposition in the Jim Crow South. *Journal of American History* 80 (1): 75–112.

———. 1994. *Race Rebels: Culture, Politics and the Black Working Class.* New York: Free Press.

———. 1997. *Yo' Mama's Disfunktional! Fighting the Culture Wars in Urban America.* Boston: Beacon Press.

———. 2002. *Freedom Dreams: The Black Radical Imagination.* Boston: Beacon Press.

Kent, George. 1972. *Blackness and the Adventure of Western Culture.* Chicago: Third World Press.

Kerner, Otto, et al. 1968. *Report of the National Advisory Committee on Civil Disorders.* New York: Dutton.

Keynes, John Maynard. [1936] 1973. *General Theory of Employment, Interest and Money.* London: Macmillan.

Kidd-Hewett, David, and Richard Osborne, eds. 1995. *Crime and the Media: The Postmodern Spectacle.* London: Pluto Press.

Kim, Claire Jean. 1999. The Racial Triangulation of Asian Americans. *Politics & Society.* 27 (1): 105–38.

Kinealy, Christine. 1997. *A Death-Dealing Famine: The Great Hunger in Ireland.* London: Pluto Press.

King, Ryan S., Marc Mauer, and Tracy Huling. 2003. *Big Prisons, Small Towns: Prison Economics in Rural America.* Washington, D.C.: Sentencing Project.

Kirlin, John J., ed. 1992. *California Policy Choices.* Vol. 8. Annual published by the Sacramento Public Affairs Center, School of Public Administration, University of Southern California, Los Angeles.

Kirlin, John J., and Jeffrey I. Chapman, eds. 1994. *California Policy Choices.* Vol. 9. Annual published by the Sacramento Public Affairs Center, School of Public Administration, University of Southern California, Los Angeles.

Kirlin, John J., and Donald R. Winkler, eds. 1984. *California Policy Choices.* Vol. 1. Annual published by the Sacramento Public Affairs Center, School of Public Administration, University of Southern California, Los Angeles.

———, eds. 1991. *California Policy Choices.* Vol. 7. Annual published by the Sacramento Public Affairs Center, School of Public Administration, University of Southern California, Los Angeles.

Knopp, Fay, and John Regier. [1976] 2005. *Instead of Prisons.* Oakland, Calif.: Critical Resistance.

Koetting, Mark, and Vincent Schiraldi. 1997. Singapore West: The Incarceration of 200,000 Californians. *Social Justice* 24: 44–50.

Kornbluh, Felicia. 1991. Subversive Potential, Coercive Intent: Women, Work and Welfare in the '90's. *Social Policy* 21 (4): 23–39.

Kotz, David. 2003. Neoliberalism and the U.S. Economic Expansion of the '90s. *Monthly Review* 54 (11): 15–33.

Krause, Jerrald D. 1992. The Effects of Prison Siting Practices on Community Status Awareness: A Framework Applied to Siting of California State Prisons. *Crime and Delinquency* 38 (1): 27–55.

Krier, Beth Ann. 1986. Life near a Prison: Weighing the Good, the Bad. *Los Angeles Times,* September 19, 5–1.

Kroll, Cynthia, and Mary Corley. 1994. Recovering from Defense Cuts. In *California Policy Choices,* vol. 9, ed. John J. Kirlin and Jeffrey I. Chapman, 51–94. Annual published by the Sacramento Public Affairs Center, School of Public Administration, University of Southern California, Los Angeles.

Krugman, Paul. 1994. *Peddling Prosperity.* New York: Norton.

———. 1995. *Development, Geography, and Economic Theory.* Cambridge, Mass.: MIT Press.

———. 1999. *The Return of Depression Economics.* New York: Norton.

Kugelmass, Jack. 1993. "The Fun Is in Dressing Up": The Greenwich Village Halloween Parade and the Reimagining of Urban Space. *Social Text* 36: 138–52.

Kuletz, Valerie L. 1998. *The Tainted Desert: Environmental and Social Ruin in the American West.* New York: Routledge.

Kuminoff, Nicolai V., Alvin D. Sokolow, and Daniel A. Sumner. 2001. *Farmland Conversion: Perceptions and Realities.* Agricultural Issues Brief 16. Davis, Calif.: University of California Agricultural Issues Center.

Kupers, Terry. 1999. *Prison Madness.* San Francisco: Jossey-Bass.

LaBotz, Dan. 1992. *Mask of Democracy: Labor Suppression in Mexico Today.* Boston: South End Press.

LaGuardia, Maria L. 1994. New Prisons No Panacea for Ills of Rural California. *Los Angeles Times,* October 18, A-1.

Lake, Robert W. 1992. Structural Constraints and Pluralist Contradictions in Hazardous Waste Regulation. *Environment and Planning A* 24: 663–81.

———. 1994. Negotiating Local Autonomy. *Professional Geographer* 13 (5): 423–42.

Landis, John D. 1992. Regional Growth Management Reform. *California Policy Choices*, vol. 8, ed. John J. Kirlin, 83–126. Annual published by the Sacramento Public Affairs Center, School of Public Administration, University of Southern California, Los Angeles.

Langan, Patrick A. 1994. No Racism in the Justice System. *Public Interest,* Fall, 48–51.

Langley, Winston. 1990. What Happened to the New International Economic Order? *Socialist Review* 20 (3): 47–62.

Lapido, David. 2001. The Rise of America's Prison-Industrial Complex. *New Left Review*, 2nd ser., 7: 109–23.

Lash, Scott. 1991. Disintegrating Firms. *Socialist Review* 21 (3 & 4): 99–110.

Lawson, Bill E., ed. 1992. *The Underclass Question.* Philadelphia: Temple University Press.

Lea, John, and Jock Young. 1993. *What Is to Be Done about Law and Order?* London: Pluto Press.

Lee, Benjamin. 1993. Going Public. *Public Culture* 5 (2): 165–78.

Leiman, Melvin M. 1993. *The Political Economy of Racism.* London: Pluto Press.

Lemelle, Sidney J. 1992. Ritual, Resistance and Social Reproduction. *Journal of Historical Sociology* 5 (2): 161–82.

Lemelle, Sidney, and Robin D. G. Kelley, eds. 1994. *Imagining Home: Class, Culture, and Nationalism in the African Diaspora.* New York: Verso.

LeRoy, Greg. 2005. *The Great American Jobs Scam: Corporate Tax Dodging and the Myth of Job Creation.* San Francisco: Berrett-Koehler.

Lesce, Tony. 1991. *The Big House: How American Prisons Work.* Port Townsend, Wash.: Loompanics Unlimited.

Levinas, Emmanuel. 1989. As If Consenting to Horror. *Critical Inquiry* 15 (2): 485–88.

Lewis, Mike. 2000. Economic Lockdown. *Fresno Bee,* January 9, A-1.

Lewis, W. David. 1965. *From Newgate to Dannemora: The Rise of the*

Penitentiary in New York, 1769–1848. Ithaca, N.Y.: Cornell University Press.

Lichtenstein, Alex. 1996. *Twice the Work of Free Labor: The Political Economy of Convict Labor in the New South.* New York: Verso.

Lichtenstein, Nelson. 1982. *Labor's War at Home: The CIO in World War II.* Cambridge: Cambridge University Press.

Linebaugh, Peter. 1992. *The London Hanged: Crime and Civil Society in the Eighteenth Century.* Cambridge: Cambridge University Press.

———. 1995. Gruesome Gertie at the Buckle of the Bible Belt. *New Left Review* 209: 15–33.

Linebaugh, Peter, and Marcus Rediker. 2000. *The Many-Headed Hydra: Sailors, Slaves, Commoners, and the Hidden History of the Revolutionary Atlantic.* Boston: Beacon Press.

Lipsitz, George. 1987. *A Life in the Struggle: Ivory Perry and the Culture of Opposition.* Philadelphia: Temple University Press.

———. 1994. *Rainbow at Midnight: Labor and Culture in the 1940s.* Urbana: University of Illinois Press.

———. 1998. *The Possessive Investment in Whiteness.* Philadelphia: Temple University Press.

Liu, Laura Y. 2000. The Place of Immigration in Studies of Geography and Race. *Social and Cultural Geography* 1 (2): 169–82.

Livingstone, David N. 1992. *The Geographical Tradition.* Cambridge, Mass.: Blackwell.

Lofting, Everard M., and Oliver B. Linton. 1985. *Economic and Fiscal Impacts of the Proposed State Prisons in Kings County.* Sacramento: California Department of Corrections.

Lomax, Adrian. 1998. Prison Jobs and Free World Unemployment. *Prison Legal News* 9 (5): 14–15.

Long, Charles. 1986. *Significations: Signs, Symbols, and Images in the Interpretation of Religion.* Philadelphia: Fortress Press.

Lotchin, Roger W. 1992. *Fortress California, 1910–1961: From Warfare to Welfare.* New York: Oxford University Press.

Loury, Glenn C. 1994. Listen to the Black Community. *Public Interest,* Fall, 33–37.

Lubiano, Wahneema, ed. 1997. *The House That Race Built*. New York: Pantheon Books.

Lusane, Clarence. 1991. *Pipe Dream Blues: Racism and the War on Drugs*. Boston: South End Press.

————. 2000. *We Are the World: Race and the International War on Drugs*. In *Foreign Policy and the Black (Inter)national Interest*, ed. C. P. Henry, 51–73. Albany: State University of New York Press.

Lutz, Catherine. 2001. *Homefront: A Military City and the American Twentieth Century*. Boston: Beacon Press.

Luxemburg, Rosa. 1968. *The Accumulation of Capital*. Translated by Agnes Schwarzchild. New York: Monthly Review Press.

Lynd, Staughton. 2004. *Lucasville: The Untold Story of a Prison Uprising*. Philadelphia: Temple University Press.

Lyson, Thomas A., and William W. Falk, eds. 1993. *Forgotten Places: Uneven Development in Rural America*. Lawrence: University Press of Kansas.

MacKinnon, Catherine. 1989. *Toward a Feminist Theory of the State*. Cambridge, Mass.: Harvard University Press.

Madhubuti, Haki R., ed. 1993. *Why L.A. Happened*. Chicago: Third World Press.

Makdisi, Saree S. 1992. The Empire Renarrated: Season of Migration to the North and the Reinvention of the Present. *Critical Inquiry* 18 (4): 804–20.

Males, Mike A. 1996. *The Scapegoat Generation: America's War on Adolescents*. Monroe, Maine: Common Courage Press.

————. 1999. *Framing Youth: 10 Myths about the Next Generation*. Monroe, Maine: Common Courage Press.

Mann, Michael. 1986. *Sources of Social Power*. Oxford: Blackwell.

————. 1988. *States, War, and Capitalism*. Oxford: Blackwell.

Mann, Susan A. 1989. Slavery, Sharecropping, and Sexual Inequality. *Signs* 14 (4): 774–832.

Manza, Jeff. 1992. Postindustrial Economics. *Socialist Review* 22 (1): 107–12.

Marable, Manning. 1981. The Third Reconstruction: Black Nationalism and Race in a Revolutionary America. *Social Text* (4): 3–27.

———. 1982. *How Capitalism Underdeveloped Black America*. Boston: South End Press.

———. 1991. *Race, Reform and Rebellion*. 2nd ed. Jackson: University of Mississippi Press.

Marcos, Subcomandante. 1995. *Shadows of Tender Fury: The Letters and Communiqués of Subcomandante Marcos and the Zapatista Army of National Liberation*. Translated by Frank Bardacke and Leslie López of the Watsonville Human Rights Committee. New York: Monthly Review Press.

Marks, Carol. 1989. *"Farewell—We're Good and Gone": The Great Black Migration*. Bloomington: Indiana University Press.

Markusen, Ann R. 1985. *Profit Cycles, Oligopoly, and Regional Development*. Cambridge, Mass.: MIT Press.

———. 1987. *Regions: The Economics and Politics of Territory*. Totowa, N.J.: Rowman & Littlefield.

———. 1994. American Federalism and Regional Policy. *International Regional Science Review* 16 (1 & 2): 3–15.

Markusen, Ann R., and Karen McCurdy. 1989. Chicago's Defense-based High Technology: A Case Study of the "Seedbeds of Innovation" Hypothesis. *Economic Development Quarterly* 3 (1): 15–31.

Markusen, Ann R., and Joel Yudken. [1992] 1993. *Dismantling the Cold War Economy*. New York: Basic Books.

Markusen, Ann R., Peter Hall, Scott Campbell, and Sabina Deitrick. 1991. *The Rise of the Gunbelt: The Military Remapping of Industrial America*. New York: Oxford University Press.

Markusen, Ann R., Yong-Sook Lee, and Sean DiGiovanna, eds. 1999. *Second Tier Cities: Rapid Growth beyond the Metropolis*. Minneapolis: University of Minnesota Press.

Martin, Hugo. 1994. California Elections. *Los Angeles Times,* November 10, A-26.

Martinot, Steve. 2003. *The Rule of Racialization: Class, Identity, Governance*. Philadelphia: Temple University Press.

Marvell, Thomas B., and Carlisle E. Moody. 1994. Prison Population Growth and Crime Reduction. *Journal of Quantitative Criminology* 10 (2): 109–40.

Marx, Karl. [1852] 1969. The Eighteenth Brumaire of Louis Bonaparte. In *Marx/Engels Selected Works*, 398–487. Moscow: Progress Publishers.

———. [1867] 1967. *Capital.* Vol. 1. New York: International Publishers.

Massey, Doreen. 1984. *Spatial Divisions of Labor: Social Structures and the Geography of Production.* London: Macmillan.

———. 1994. *Space, Place and Gender.* Minneapolis: University of Minnesota Press.

Massey, Douglas, and Nancy Denton. 1993. *American Apartheid: Segregation and the Making of the Underclass.* Cambridge, Mass.: Harvard University Press.

Mattera, Philip, and Mafruza Khan. 2001. *Jail Breaks: Economic Development Subsidies Given to Private Prisons.* Washington, D.C.: Good Jobs First.

Mauer, Mark. 1999. *Race to Incarcerate.* New York: New Press.

Mauer, Mark, and Meda Chesney-Lind, eds. 2002. *Invisible Punishment.* New York: New Press.

Mauss, Marcel. [1950] 2000. *The Gift.* New York: Norton.

Mayer, Margit. 1991. Politics in the Post-Fordist City. *Socialist Review* 21 (1): 105–24.

McAfee, Ward M. 1989. A History of Convict Labor in California. MS.

McClellan, Dorothy S. 2002. Coming to the Aid of Women in U.S. Prisons. *Monthly Review* 54 (2): 33–44.

McClintock, Anne. 1991. "No Longer in a Future Heaven": Women and Nationalism in South Africa. *Transition* 51: 105–24.

———. 1992. The Angel of Progress: Pitfalls of the Term "Post-Colonial." *Social Text* 31/32: 84–98.

McClintock, Anne, and Rob Nixon. 1986. No Names Apart: The Separation of Word and History in Derrida's "Le Dernier Mot du Racisme." *Critical Inquiry* 13 (1): 140–54.

McCold, Paul E. 1993. The Role of Fiscal Policy in Producing Prison

Population Dynamics: A Trend Analysis and Dynamic Simulation of Felony Offender Processing in New York State, 1975–1988. Ph.D. diss., State University of New York at Albany.

McDowell, Linda. 1999. *Gender, Identity & Place*. Minneapolis: University of Minnesota Press.

McGee, Terry G. 1991. The Emergence of Desakota Regions in Asia: Expanding a Hypothesis. In *The Extended Metropolis: Settlement Transition in Asia*, ed. N. Ginsburg, B. Koppel, and T. G. McGee. Honolulu: University of Hawai'i Press.

McGirr, Lisa. 2001. *Suburban Warriors: The Origins of the New American Right*. Princeton, N.J.: Princeton University Press.

McIntyre, Richard. 1992. Theories of Uneven Development and Social Change. *Rethinking Marxism* 5 (3): 75–105.

McIntyre, Richard, and Michael Hillard. 1992. Stressed Families, Impoverished Families: Crises in the Household and in the Reproduction of the Working Class. *Review of Radical Political Economics* 24 (2): 17–25.

McKanna, Clare V., Jr. 1997. *Homicide, Race, and Justice in the American West, 1880–1920*. Tucson: University of Arizona Press.

McLanahan, Sara S., Annemette Sorenson, and Dorothy Watson. 1989. Sex Differences in Poverty, 1950–1980. *Signs* 15 (1): 102–22.

McRobbie, Angela. 1991. New Times in Cultural Studies. *New Formations* 13: 1–17.

McShane, Marilyn D., and Frank P. Williams, eds. 1996. *Encyclopedia of American Prisons*. New York: Garland.

McWilliams, Carey. [1939] 1969. *Factories in the Field*. Hamden, Conn.: Archon Books.

———. 1946. *Southern California: An Island on the Land*. New York: Duell, Sloan & Pearce.

———. [1949] 1976. *California: The Great Exception*. Santa Barbara, Calif.: Peregrine Smith.

Mellibovsky, Matilde. 1997. *Circle of Love over Death: The Story of the Mothers of the Plaza de Mayo*. Willimantic, Conn.: Curbstone Press.

Melman, Seymour, ed. 1971. *The War Economy of the United States: Readings on Military Industry and Economy*. New York: St. Martin's Press.

————. 1974. *The Permanent War Economy: American Capitalism in Decline.* New York: Simon & Schuster.

————. 1979. *Pentagon Capitalism: The Political Economy of War.* New York: McGraw-Hill.

————. 1983. *Profits without Production.* New York: Knopf.

Meranze, Michael. 1996. *Laboratories of Virtue: Punishment, Revolution and the Transformation of Authority in Philadelphia, 1760–1835.* Chapel Hill: University of North Carolina Press.

Mészáros, István. 1995. *Beyond Capital: Toward a Theory of Transition.* New York: Monthly Review Press.

Mies, Maria. 1986. *Patriarchy and Accumulation on a World Scale: Women in the International Division of Labor.* London: Zed Books.

Milkman, Ruth. 1987. *Gender at Work.* Urbana: University of Illinois Press.

Miller, Jerome G. 1991. *Last One over the Wall: The Massachusetts Experiment in Closing Reform Schools.* Columbus: Ohio State University Press.

————. 1996. *Search and Destroy: African-American Males in the Criminal Justice System.* New York: Cambridge University Press.

Mink, Gwendolyn. 1995. *The Wages of Motherhood: Inequality in the Welfare State, 1917–1942.* Ithaca, N.Y.: Cornell University Press.

Mintz, Sidney W. 1985. *Sweetness and Power: The Place of Sugar in Modern History.* New York: Viking Press.

Mitchell, Don. 1996. *The Lie of the Land: Migrant Workers and the California Landscape.* Minneapolis: University of Minnesota Press.

Mitchell, Greg. 1992. *The Campaign of the Century: Upton Sinclair's Race for Governor of California and the Birth of Media Politics.* New York: Random House.

Moe, Nelson J. 1990. Production and Its Others: Gramsci's "Sexual Question." *Rethinking Marxism* 3 (3–4): 218–37.

Moore, Charles V., and Richard E. Howitt. 1988. The Central Valley of California. In *Water and Arid Lands in the Western United States,* ed. Mohamed T. El-Ashry and Diana C. Gibbons, 85–126. New York: Cambridge University Press/World Resources Institute.

Moore, Jack B. 1993. *Skinheads Shaved for Battle: A Cultural History of American Skinheads.* Bowling Green, Ohio: Bowling Green State University Popular Press.

Morain, Dan. 1994a. Costs to Soar under "3 Strikes" Plan, Study Says. *Los Angeles Times,* March 1, A-1.

———. 1994b. Small Investment Pays Off Big for Construction Management Firm. *Los Angeles Times,* October 16, A-17.

———. 1994c. California's Profusion of Prisons. *Los Angeles Times,* October 16, A-1.

———. 1994d. Long-Term Investments: "Three Strikes" Law Will Boost Wall Street Firms That Sell Bonds to Finance Construction. *Los Angeles Times,* October 16, A-16.

———. 1994e. Inmate Jobs Harder to Find as Prison Population Soars. *Los Angeles Times,* October 17, A-20.

Morgan, Dan. 1992. *Rising in the West: The True Story of an "Okie" Family from the Great Depression through the Reagan Years.* New York: Knopf.

Morris, Aldon D. 1984. *The Origins of the Civil Rights Movement: Black Communities Organizing for Change.* New York: Free Press.

Morris, Norval. 1995. The Contemporary Prison. In *The Oxford History of the Prison,* ed. Norval Morris and David J. Rothman, 227–62. New York: Oxford University Press.

Morris, Norval, and David J. Rothman, eds. 1995. *The Oxford History of the Prison.* New York: Oxford University Press.

Morrison, Toni. 1986. *Beloved.* New York: Knopf.

Mosley, Walter. 1990. *Devil in a Blue Dress.* New York: Norton.

———. 1991. *A Red Death.* New York: Norton.

———. 1992. *White Butterfly.* New York: Norton.

———. 1994. *Black Betty.* New York: Norton.

———. 1996. *A Little Yellow Dog.* New York: Norton.

———. 1997. *Gone Fishin'.* Baltimore: Black Classic Press.

Muhammed, Al-Hajj Idris A. 1990. *What Should You Do If You Are Arrested or Framed by the Cops?* New York: Nubian Heritage Society.

Mumford, Lewis. [1961] 1989. *The City in History.* New York: Harcourt.

Murashige, Michael S. 1995. Race, Resistance, and Contestations of Urban Space in Los Angeles. Ph.D. diss., University of California, Los Angeles.

Murphy, Craig N. 1990. Freezing the North-South Bloc(k) after the East-West Thaw. *Socialist Review* 20 (3): 25–46.

Murphy, John W., and Jack E. Dison, eds. 1983 *Are Prisons Any Better? Twenty Years of Correctional Reform*. Beverly Hills, Calif.: Sage Publications.

Murray, Charles. 1984. *Losing Ground: American Social Policy, 1950–1980*. New York: Basic Books.

———. 1990. Drug Free Zones. *Current* 326 (October): 19–24.

Murray, Charles, and Richard Herrnstein. 1994. *The Bell Curve*. New York: Free Press.

Myers, Martha A. 1998. *Race, Labor, and Punishment in the New South*. Columbus: Ohio State University Press.

Myers, Samuel L. 1992. Crime, Entrepreneurship, and Labor Force Withdrawal. *Contemporary Policy Issues* 10: 84–97.

Myrdal, Gunnar. 1957. *Economic Theory and Underdeveloped Regions*. London: Duckworth.

Naples, Nancy, ed. 1998a. *Community Activism and Feminist Politics*. New York: Routledge.

———. 1998b. *Grassroots Warriors: Activist Mothering, Community Work, and the War on Poverty*. New York: Routledge.

Narotzky, Susana. 1997. *New Directions in Economic Anthropology*. London: Pluto Press.

Nasar, Sylvia. 1994. More Men in Prime of Life Spend Less Time Working. *New York Times,* December 1, A-1.

Negri, Antonio [see also Negri, Toni]. 1989. *The Politics of Subversion: A Manifesto for the 21st Century*. Translated by James Newell. Cambridge: Polity Press.

———. 1991. *Marx beyond Marx: Lessons on the Grundrisse*. Translated by Harry Cleaver, Michael Ryan, and Maurizio Viano. Edited by Jim Fleming. New York: Autonomedia.

————. 1992. Twenty Theses on Marx: Interpretations of the Class Situation Today. *Polygraph* 5: 136–70.

Negri, Toni [see also Negri, Antonio]. [1968] 1988. Marx on Cycle and Crisis. In id., *Revolution Retrieved: Selected Writings on Marx, Keynes, Capitalist Crisis and New Social Subjects, 1967–1983*, 43–90. London: Red Notes.

————. [1980] 1988. Crisis of the Crisis State. In id., *Revolution Retrieved: Selected Writings on Marx, Keynes, Capitalist Crisis and New Social Subjects, 1967–1983*, 177–98. London: Red Notes.

————. 1988. *Revolution Retrieved: Selected Writings on Marx, Keynes, Capitalist Crisis and New Social Subjects, 1967–1983*. London: Red Notes.

Ness, Manny, and Keith Brooks. 1991. Organizing the Homeless. *Social Policy* 21 (4): 2–4.

Nevins, Joseph. 2001. *Operation Gatekeeper: The Rise of the "Illegal Alien" and the Making of the U.S.-Mexico Boundary*. New York: Routledge.

Newton, Huey P. 1996. *The War against the Panthers: A Study of Repression in America*. New York: Harlem River Press.

Nieto, Marcus. 1996. *Community Correction Punishments: An Alternative to Incarceration for Nonviolent Offenders*. Sacramento: California Research Bureau, California State Library.

Nieves, Evelyn. 2000. Storm Raised by Plan for a California Prison. *New York Times*, August 27, 1–16.

Noponen, Helzi, Julie Graham, and Ann R. Markusen, eds. 1993. *Trading Industries, Trading Regions: International Trade, American Industry, and Regional Economic Development. Perspectives on Economic Change*. New York: Guilford Press.

Nordstrom, Carolyn, and JoAnn Martin, eds. 1992. *The Paths to Domination, Resistance and Terror*. Berkeley: University of California Press.

Norris, Frank. [1901] 1987. *The Octopus*. New York: Library of America.

Notes from the Brown Underground. N.d. [1997]. *Criminalization, the Xicana/o Movement, & Decoding Mass Media*. Pamphlet.

O'Connor, James. [1973] 2000. *The Fiscal Crisis of the State.* London: Transaction Publishers.

Oden, Michael, Ann Markusen, Dan Flaming, and Mark Drayse. 1996. *Post Cold War Frontiers: Defense Downsizing and Conversion in Los Angeles.* Working Paper No. 105. New Brunswick, N.J.: Rutgers University Center for Urban Policy Research.

Odum, Howard W. [1943] 1997. *Race and Rumors of Race: The American South in the Early Forties.* Baltimore: Johns Hopkins University Press.

Odum, Howard W., and Harry Estill Moore. 1938. *American Regionalism: A Cultural History of National Integration.* New York: Holt.

Ohmae, Kenichi. 1989. The Global Logic of Strategic Alliances. *Harvard Business Review,* March–April, 143–54.

Okazawa-Rey, Margo, and Gwyn Kirk. 2000. Maximum Security. *Social Justice* 27 (3): 120–32.

Oliver, Melvin L., Jr., James H. Johnson, and Walter C. Farrell Jr. 1993. Anatomy of a Rebellion: A Political-Economic Analysis. In *Reading Rodney King, Reading Urban Uprising,* ed. Robert Gooding-Williams, 117–41. New York: Routledge.

Oliver, Melvin L., Jr., and Thomas M. Shapiro. 1995. *Black Wealth/White Wealth.* New York: Routledge.

Omi, Michael, and Howard Winant. 1986. *Racial Formation in the United States: From the 1960s to the 1980s.* New York: Routledge.

Ong, Paul, and Evelyn Blumenberg. 1996. Income and Racial Inequality in Los Angeles. In *The City: Los Angeles and Urban Theory at the End of the Twentieth Century,* ed. Allen J. Scott and Edward W. Soja, 311–35. Berkeley: University of California Press.

Ong, Paul, and Abel Valenzuela Jr. 1996. The Labor Market: Immigrant Effects and Racial Disparities. In *Ethnic Los Angeles,* ed. Roger Waldinger and Mehdi Bozorgmehr, 165–91. New York: Russell Sage Foundation.

Orland, Leonard. 1975. *Prisons: Houses of Darkness.* New York: Free Press.

Ortiz, Vilma. 1996. The Mexican-Origin Population: Permanent Working Class or Emerging Middle Class? In *Ethnic Los Angeles,* ed. Roger Waldinger and Mehdi Bozorgmehr, 247–77. New York: Russell Sage Foundation.

Oshinsky, David. 1996. *"Worse than Slavery": Parchman Farm and the Ordeal of Jim Crow Justice.* New York: Free Press.

Owen, Barbara. 1998. *"In the Mix": Struggle and Survival in a Women's Prison.* Albany: State University of New York Press.

Paddock, Richard C. 1986. Governor Risks Latinos' Support on Prison Issue. *Los Angeles Times,* September 14, 1–3.

Paddock, Richard C., and Leo C. Wolinsky. 1985. Workfare Passes. *Los Angeles Times,* September 15, 1–1.

Painter, Nell Irvin. 1977. *The Exodusters.* New York: Knopf.

———. 1979. *The Narrative of Hosea Hudson.* Cambridge, Mass.: Harvard University Press.

Pardo, Mary. 1998. *Mexican American Women Activists.* Philadelphia: Temple University Press.

Parenti, Christian. 1996. Making Prison Pay: Business Finds the Cheapest Labor of All. *Nation,* January 29, 11–14.

———. 1997. Crescent City's "Colonial Master." *San Francisco Bay Guardian,* September 10, 17–19.

———. 1999. *Lockdown America.* New York: Verso.

Parker, Eric, and Joel Rodgers. 1995. *The Wisconsin Regional Training Partnership: Lessons for National Policy.* Washington, D.C.: National Center on the Workforce.

Parker, Mike, and Jane Slaughter. 1994. *Working Smart: A Union Guide to Participation Programs and Reengineering.* Detroit: Labor Notes.

Parks, Loren L., Jill M. Weigt, Everard M. Lofting, and Oliver B. Linton. 1990. *The Economic Impacts of State Prisons in Kings County, California.* Sacramento: California Department of Corrections.

Pastor, Manuel, James L. Sadd, and J. Hipp. 2001. Which Came First? Toxic Facilities, Minority Move-in, and Economic Justice. *Journal of Urban Affairs* 23 (1): 1–21.

Patterson, Orlando. 1982. *Slavery and Social Death.* Cambridge, Mass.: Harvard University Press.

Payne, Charles. 1989. Ella Baker and Models of Social Change. *Signs* 14 (4): 885–99.

Peake, Linda, and Audrey Kobayashi. 2002. Policies and Practices for an Antiracist Geography at the Millennium. *Professional Geographer* 54 (1): 50–61.

Peery, Nelson. 1994. *Black Fire: The Making of an American Revolutionary.* New York: New Press.

Petchesky, Rosalind P. 1981. At Hard Labor: Penal Confinement and Production in Nineteenth-Century America. In *Crime and Capitalism,* ed. David Greenberg, 341–57. Palo Alto, Calif.: Mayfield.

Petersilia, Joan. 1992. Crime and Punishment in California: Full Cells, Empty Pockets, and Questionable Benefits. In *Urban America: Policy Choices for Los Angeles and the Nation,* ed. James Steinberg et al., 175–205. Los Angeles: Rand Corporation.

Phelps, Margaret Dorsey. 1992. Idled Outside, Overworked Inside: The Political Economy of Prison Labor during Depressions in Chicago, 1871–1897. Ph.D. diss., University of Iowa.

Philibosian, Robert H. 1986. Statement of the Chairman. In *California State Task Force on Youth Gang Violence: Final Report,* vi. Sacramento: California Council on Criminal Justice.

Phillips, Kevin. 1969. *The Emerging Republican Majority.* New Rochelle, N.Y.: Arlington House.

———. 1990. *The Politics of Rich and Poor: Wealth and the American Electorate in the Reagan Aftermath.* New York: Random House.

Phillips, Llad. 1992. The Political Economy of Drug Enforcement in California. *Contemporary Policy Issues* 10 (January): 91–100.

Pike, Michael S. 1985. *The Principles of Policing.* London: Macmillan.

Pincetl, Stephanie S. 1999. *Transforming California: A Political History of Land Use and Development.* Baltimore: Johns Hopkins University Press.

Piore, Michael. 1979. *Birds of Passage: Migrant Labor and Industrial Societies.* Cambridge, Mass.: Cambridge University Press.

Pisani, Donald J. 1984. *From the Family Farm to Agribusiness: The Irri-*

gation Crusade in California and the West, 1850–1931. Berkeley: University of California Press.

Piven, Frances Fox. 1992. Reforming the Welfare State. *Socialist Review* 22 (3): 69–81.

Piven, Frances Fox, and Richard A. Cloward. 1971. *Regulating the Poor.* New York: Vintage Books.

Platt, Anthony. 1971. *The Politics of Riot Commissions.* New York: Collier.

Platt, Anthony, and Lynn Cooper. 1974. *Policing America.* Englewood Cliffs, N.J.: Prentice-Hall.

Polanyi, Karl. 1944. *The Great Transformation.* New York: Farrar & Reinhart.

Police and Racial Violence Project. N.d. *Stop Police Brutality/Know Your Rights.* Brooklyn: Center for Law and Social Justice, Medgar Evers College.

Potts, Lydia. 1990. *The World Labor Market: A History of Migration.* Translated by Terry Bond. London: Zed Books.

Powledge, Fred. 1991. *Free at Last? The Civil Rights Movement and the People Who Made It.* Boston: Little, Brown.

Prashad, Vijay. 2003. *Keeping Up with the Dow Joneses.* Boston: South End Press.

Preston, William L. 1981. *Vanishing Landscapes: Land and Life in the Tulare Lake Basin.* Berkeley: University of California Press.

Pulido, Laura. 1995a. *Environmentalism and Economic Justice.* Tucson: University of Arizona Press.

———. 1995b. The Mothers of East Los Angeles. Presentation, annual meetings of the Association of American Geographers, Chicago, Ill. March.

———. 1996. The Geography of Militant Labor Organizing in Los Angeles. Paper delivered at the biannual meeting of the Association for Economic and Social Analysis, Amherst, Mass. December.

———. 2000. Rethinking Environmental Racism: White Privilege and Urban Development in Southern California. *Annals of the Association of American Geographers* 90 (1): 12–40.

————. 2002. Reflections on a White Discipline. *Professional Geographer* 54 (1): 42–49.

————. 2005. *Black, Brown, Yellow and Left: Radical Activism in Los Angeles.* Berkeley: University of California Press.

Quick, Paddy. 1992. Capitalism and the Origins of Domestic Labor. *Review of Radical Political Economics* 24 (2): 1–7.

Quinn, Tom, ed. 1999. *Maximum Security University: A Documentary History of Death and Cover-up at America's Most Violent Prison.* San Francisco: California Prison Focus.

Radhakrishnan, R. 1991. Ethnicity in an Age of Diaspora. *Transition* 54: 104–15.

Ranger, Terence O., and Eric Hobsbawm, eds. 1983. *The Invention of Tradition.* Cambridge, Mass.: Cambridge University Press.

Reagon, Bernice Johnson. 1983. Coalition Politics: Turning the Century. In *Home Girls: A Black Feminist Anthology,* ed. Barbara Smith, 343–56. Albany, N.Y.: Kitchen Table: Women of Color Press.

Reed, Deborah. 2002. *Poverty in California.* Occasional Papers. San Francisco: Public Policy Institute of California.

Reich, Robert. 1991. *The Work of Nations: Preparing Ourselves for 21st Century Capitalism.* New York: Vintage Books.

Reisner, Mark. 1986. *Cadillac Desert: The American West and Its Disappearing Water.* New York: Viking Press.

Reiss, Edward. 1997. *Marx: A Clear Guide.* London: Pluto.

Resnick, Stephen, and Richard Wolff. 1994. Between State and Private Capitalism: What Was Soviet "Socialism"? *Rethinking Marxism* 7 (1): 9–30.

Reynolds, Mike, and Bill Jones, with Dan Evans. 1996. *Three Strikes and You're Out!...a Promise to Kimber.* Fresno, Calif.: Quill Driver Books.

Richardson, Harry W. 1969. *Regional Economics.* New York: Praeger.

Richie, Beth. 1998. *Compelled to Crime: The Gender Entrapment of Battered Black Women.* New York: Routledge.

Ridgeway, James. 1990. *Blood in the Face: The Ku Klux Klan, Nazi Skin-*

heads, and the Rise of a New White Culture. New York: Thunder's Mouth Press.

Rierden, Andi. 1997. *The Farm: Life inside a Women's Prison.* Amherst: University of Massachusetts Press.

Robinson, Cedric J. 1983. *Black Marxism: The Making of the Black Radical Tradition.* London: Zed Books.

———. 1990–91. Oliver Cromwell Cox and the Historiography of the West. *Cultural Critique* (17): 5–19.

———. 1997. *Black Movements in America.* New York: Routledge.

———. 2001. *Anthropology of Marxism.* Aldershot, Hants, UK: Ashgate.

Robinson, Paul H. 1994. A Failure of Moral Conviction? *Public Interest,* Fall, 40–48.

Rocco, Raymond. 1990. The Theoretical Construction of the "Other" in Postmodernist Thought: Latinos in the New Urban Political Economy. *Cultural Studies* 4 (3): 321–30.

Rodgers, Daniel. 1974. *The Work Ethic in Industrial America, 1850–1920.* Chicago: University of Chicago Press.

Rodney, Walter. 1982. *How Europe Underdeveloped Africa.* Washington, D.C.: Howard University Press.

Rodriguez, Luis J. 1993. *Always Running: La Vida Loca: Gang Days in L.A.* Willimantic, Conn.: Curbstone Press.

Roediger, David. 1991. *The Wages of Whiteness.* New York: Verso.

———. 1994. *Towards the Abolition of Whiteness.* New York: Verso.

———. 2002. *Colored White: Transcending the Racial Past.* Berkeley: University of California Press.

Roediger, David R., and Philip S. Foner. 1989. *Our Own Time: A History of American Labor and the Working Day.* New York: Greenwood Press.

Rollins, Judith. 1985. *Between Women: Domestics and Their Employers.* Philadelphia: Temple University Press.

Rolston, Bill. 1992. "When You're Fighting a War, You've Gotta Take Setbacks": Murals and Propaganda in the North of Ireland. *Polygraph* 5: 113–35.

Rommel, Bart. 1993. *Dirty Tricks Cops Use (and Why They Use Them)*. Port Townsend, Wash.: Loompanics Unlimited.

Rooney, Ellen. 1990. Marks of Gender. *Rethinking Marxism* 3 (3–4): 190–201.

Rose, Dina R., and Todd Clear. 2002. *Incarceration, Reentry, and Social Capital: Social Networks in the Balance*. www.urban.org/uploaded pdf/410623_socialcapital.pdf (accessed November 2005).

Rose, Nancy E. 1994. *Put to Work: Relief Programs in the Great Depression*. Cornerstone Books. New York: Monthly Review Press.

Rosenblatt, Elihu, ed. 1996. *Criminal Injustice: Confronting the Prison Crisis*. Boston: South End Press.

Rosser, Paul C. 1983. Justice Technology and Architecture. *Corrections Today*, April, 122–23.

Rotman, Edgardo. 1995. The Failure of Reform: United States, 1865–1965. In *The Oxford History of the Prison*, ed. Norval Morris and David Rothman, 169–98. New York: Oxford University Press.

Rouse, Roger. 1995. Thinking through Transnationalism: Notes on the Cultural Politics of Class Relations in the Contemporary United States. *Public Culture* 7 (2): 353–402.

Ruddick, Susan. 1990. Heterotopias of the Homeless: Strategies and Tactics of Placemaking in Los Angeles. *Strategies* (3): 184–201.

————. 1995. *Homeless in Hollywood: Mapping Social Identities*. New York: Routledge.

Rude, George. 1995. *The Crowd in History: A Study of Popular Disturbances in France and England, 1730–1848*. London: Serif.

Rudman, Cary J., and John Berthelsen. 1991. *An Analysis of the California Department of Corrections' Planning Process: Strategies to Reduce the Cost of Incarcerating State Prisoners*. Sacramento: California State Assembly Office of Research.

Sabagh, Georges, and Mehdi Bozorgmehr. 1996. Population Change: Immigration and Ethnic Transformation. In *Ethnic Los Angeles*, ed. Roger Waldinger and Mehdi Bozorgmehr, 79–107. New York: Russell Sage Foundation.

Sabo, Don, Terry A. Kupers, and Willie London. 2001. *Prison Mas-culinities*. Philadelphia: Temple University Press.

Said, Edward W. 1982. Travelling Theory. *Raritan* 1 (3): 41–67.

———. 1989. Representing the Colonized: Anthropology's Interlocu-tors. *Critical Inquiry* 15 (2): 205–25.

———. 1990a. Figures, Configurations, Transfigurations. *Polygraph* 4: 9–34.

———. 1990b. Third World Intellectuals/Metropolitan Culture. *Raritan* 9 (3): 27–50.

———. 1991. Identity, Authority, and Freedom: The Potentate and the Traveler. *Transition* 54: 4–18.

———. 1993. Nationalism, Human Rights, and Interpretation. *Raritan* 12 (3): 26–51.

Samuel, Raphael. 1980. British Marxist Historians. *New Left Review* 124: 28.

Sanchez, Rosaura. 1990. Ethnicity, Ideology and Academia. *Cultural Studies* 4 (3): 295–301.

Sandmeyer, Elmer Clarence. [1939] 1991. *The Anti-Chinese Movement in California*. Urbana: University of Illinois Press.

Sarabi, Brigette, and Edwin Bender. 2000. *The Prison Payoff: The Role of Politics and Private Prisons in the Incarceration Boom*. Portland, Ore.: Western Prison Project.

Sassen, Saskia. 1988. *The Mobility of Labor and Capital: A Study in International Investment and Labor Flow*. New York: Cambridge University Press.

Sassoon, Anne Showstack, ed. 1982. *Approaches to Gramsci*. London: Writers and Readers.

———. 1990. Gramsci's Subversion of the Language of Politics. *Rethinking Marxism* 3 (1): 14–25.

Savage, David G., and Jennifer Warren. 2005. Justices Reject Segrega-tion in State's Prisons. *Los Angeles Times,* February 24, A-1.

Saxenian, Annalee. 1994. *Regional Advantage: Culture & Competition in Silicon Valley and Route 128*. Cambridge, Mass.: Harvard University Press.

Saxton, Alexander. 1971. *The Indispensable Enemy: Labor and the Anti-Chinese Movement in California.* Berkeley: University of California Press.

—. 1990. *The Rise and Fall of the White Republic.* New York: Verso.

Sayer, Andrew, and Richard Walker. 1992. *The New Social Economy.* Oxford: Basil Blackwell.

Sayer, Derek. 1989. *The Violence of Abstraction.* Oxford: Blackwell.

—. 1991. *Capitalism and Modernity: An Excursus on Marx and Weber.* New York: Routledge.

Sbragia, Alberta M. 1996. *Debt Wish: Entrepreneurial Cities, U.S. Federalism, and Economic Development.* Pittsburgh: University of Pittsburgh Press.

Scherrer, Christoph. 1994. Industrial Policy Internationalism: Maintaining the Commitment to a Liberal World Market Order. *Socialist Review* 23 (4): 79–98.

Schiraldi, Vincent, and M. Godfrey. 1994. *Racial Disparities in the Charging of Los Angeles County's Third "Strike" Cases.* San Francisco: Center on Juvenile and Criminal Justice.

Schlossman, Steven. 1995. Delinquent Children: The Juvenile Reform School. In *The Oxford History of the Prison,* ed. Norval Morris and David J. Rothman, 325–49. Oxford: Oxford University Press.

Schor, Juliet. 1991. *The Overworked American.* New York: Basic Books.

Schroeder, Rick. 1988. Alfalfa and Water Subsidies in California: The Realization of Value in Irrigated Agriculture. MS.

Schulman, Bruce J. 1994. *From Cotton Belt to Sunbelt: Federal Policy, Economic Development, and the Transformation of the South, 1938–1980.* Durham, N.C.: Duke University Press.

Scott, Allen J., and Edward W. Soja, eds. 1996. *The City: Los Angeles and Urban Theory at the End of the Twentieth Century.* Berkeley: University of California Press.

Scott, James. 1998. *Seeing Like a State.* New Haven, Conn.: Yale University Press.

Scull, Andrew. 1984. *Decarceration, Second Edition.* New Brunswick, N.J.: Rutgers University Press.

Scull, Andrew, and Stanley Cohen, eds. 1983. *Social Control and the State*. New York: St. Martin's Press.

Sechrest, Dale K. 1992. Locating Prisons: Open versus Closed Approaches to Siting. *Crime and Delinquency* 38 (1): 88–104.

Seidman, Ann. 1990. *Apartheid, Militarism, and the U.S. Southeast*. Trenton: Africa World Press.

Sengupta, Somini. 1992. $3 Million Grant to Help Authorities in Gang Crackdown. *Los Angeles Times*, October 10, B-3.

Sepúlveda, Emma. 1996. *We, Chile: Personal Testimonies of the Chilean Arpilleistas*. Falls Church, Va.: Azul Editions.

Sexton, Patricia Cayo. 1991. *The War on Labor and the Left: Understanding America's Unique Conservatism*. Boulder, Colo.: Westview Press.

S.F. Prosecutor Vows to Limit "3 Strikes" Cases. 1996. *Los Angeles Times*, January 17, A-3.

Shaikh, Anwar. [1983] 1989. *The Current Economic Crisis: Causes and Implications*. Detroit: Against the Current. Pamphlet.

———. 1996. Inflation and Unemployment. Paper presented at the Brecht Forum, New York. March.

Shakur, Abdul Olugbala. N.d. *Poverty, Crime, and Government: New Afrikan Resource Guide*. Pamphlet.

Shapiro, Bruce. 1995. One Violent Crime. *Nation*, April 3, 437–52.

Sharp, John. 1994. A Report from the Texas Performance Review: Behind the Walls: The Price and Performance of the Texas Department of Criminal Justice. Texas Comptroller of Public Accounts.

Shaylor, Casssandra, and Angela Y. Davis. 2001. Race, Gender, and the Prison-Industrial Complex: California and Beyond. *Meridians: Feminism, Race, Transnationalism* 2 (1): 1–15.

Sherman, Howard J. 1997. Theories of Cyclical Profit Squeeze. *Review of Radical Political Economics* 29 (1): 139.

Shichor, David. 1992. Myths and Realities in Prison Sitings. *Crime and Delinquency* 38 (1): 70–87.

Shihadeh, Edward S., and Graham C. Ousey. 1996. Metropolitan Expansion and Black Social Dislocation: The Link between Suburbanization and Center-City Crime. *Social Forces* 75 (2): 649–66.

Shohat, Ella. 1992. Notes on the "Post-Colonial." *Social Text* 31/32: 99–113.

Shutkin, William A. 2000. *The Land That Could Be: Environmentalism and Democracy in the Twenty-First Century.* Cambridge, Mass.: MIT Press.

Silver, Paul. 1983. Crossroads of Correctional Architecture. *Corrections Today,* April, 118–19.

Simon, Jonathan. 1993. *Poor Discipline: Parole and the Social Control of the Underclass, 1890–1990.* Chicago: University of Chicago Press.

Simonsen, William, and Mark D. Robbins. 1996. Does It Make Any Difference Anymore? Competitive versus Negotiated Municipal Bond Issuance. *Public Administration Review* 56 (1): 57–64.

Sims, Calvin. 1996. The Rock, Unyielding, of the Plaza de Mayo. *New York Times,* March 2, A-4.

Sivanandan, A. 1982. *A Different Hunger: Writings on Black Resistance.* London: Pluto Press.

———. 1990. *Communities of Resistance: Black Struggles for Socialism.* New York: Verso.

———. 1995. Fighting Our Fundamentalisms: An Interview with A. Sivanandan. *Race & Class* 36 (3): 73–81.

———. 1996. Heresies and Prophecies: The Social and Political Fallout of the Technological Revolution. *Race & Class* 37 (4): 1–11.

Sivanandan, A., and Ellen Meiksins-Wood. 1997. Globalization and Epochal Shifts: An Exchange. *Monthly Review* 48 (9): 19–32.

Sklar, Holly. 1995. *Chaos or Community? Seeking Solutions Not Scapegoats.* Boston: South End Press.

Skocpol, Theda. 1985. Bringing the State Back In: Strategies of Analysis in Current Research. In *Bringing the State Back In,* ed. Peter B. Evans, Dietrich Rueschemeyer, and Theda Skocpol, 3–43. Cambridge: Cambridge University Press.

Small, Stephen. 1994. *Racialized Barriers: The Black Experience in the United States and England in the 1980s.* New York: Routledge.

Smith, Neil. [1984] 1990. *Uneven Development: Nature, Capital and the Production of Space.* 2nd ed. Oxford: Basil Blackwell.

————. 1989. Geography as Museum. In *Reflections on Richard Hartshorne's "The Nature of Geography,"* ed. N. Entrikin and S. Brunn, 91–120. Washington, D.C.: Association of American Geographers.

————. 1992a. Contours of a Spatialized Politics: Homeless Vehicles and the Production of Geographical Scale. *Social Text* (33): 54–81.

————. 1992b. Geography, Difference and the Politics of Scale. In *Postmodernism and the Social Sciences,* ed. Joe Doherty, Elspeth Graham, and Mo Malek, 57–79. London: Macmillan.

————. 1996. *The New Urban Frontier: Gentrification and the Revanchist City.* New York: Routledge.

————. 2003. *American Empire: Roosevelt's Geographer and the Prelude to Globalization.* Berkeley: University of California Press.

Smith, Neil, and Cindi Katz. 1993. Grounding Metaphor: Towards a Spatialized Politics. In *Place and the Politics of Identity,* ed. Michael Keith and Steve Pile, 67–83. New York: Routledge.

Soja, Edward W. 1989. *Postmodern Geographies: The Reassertion of Space in Critical Social Theory.* New York: Verso.

————. 1990. Heterotopologies: A Remembrance of Other Spaces in Citadel-LA. *Strategies* 3: 6–39.

Soja, Edward W., and Barbara Hooper. 1993. The Spaces that Difference Makes: Some Notes on the Geographical Margins of the New Cultural Politics. In *Place and the Politics of Identity,* ed. Michael Keith and Steve Pile, 183–205. New York: Routledge.

Soja, Edward W., and Allen J. Scott. 1996. Introduction to Los Angeles: City and Region. In *The City: Los Angeles and Urban Theory at the End of the Twentieth Century,* ed. Allen J. Scott and Edward W. Soja, 1–21. Berkeley: University of California.

Sokolow, Alvin D., and Julie Spezia. 1992. Farmland Protection Policy. In *California Policy Choices,* vol. 8, ed. John J. Kirlin, 151–68. Annual published by the Sacramento Public Affairs Center, School of Public Administration, University of Southern California, Los Angeles.

Sonenshein, Raphael J. 1993. *Politics in Black and White: Race and Power in Los Angeles.* Princeton, N.J.: Princeton University Press.

Spalter-Roth, Roberta M., Heidi Hartmann, and Linda Andrews. 1992. *Combining Work and Welfare: An Alternative Anti-Poverty Program*. Washington, D.C.: Institute for Women's Policy Research.

Spelman, Elizabeth V. 1990. *Inessential Woman*. Boston: Beacon.

Spelman, William. 1994. *Criminal Incapacitation*. New York: Plenum Press.

Spivak, Gayatri Chakravorty. 1988. Can the Subaltern Speak? In *Marxism and the Interpretation of Culture*, ed. Cary Nelson and Lawrence Grossberg, 271–313. Urbana: University of Illinois Press.

———. 1990. Gayatri Spivak on the Politics of the Postcolonial Subject. *Socialist Review* 20 (3): 81–97.

Stabile, Carol. 1996. Media's Crime Wave: Legitimating the Prison Industrial Complex. Paper delivered at Behind Bars: Prisons and Communities in the United States, George Mason University, Fairfax, Va.

Stack, Carol. 1974. *All Our Kin*. New York: Harper & Row.

———. 1996. *Call to Home: African Americans Reclaim the Rural South*. New York: Basic Books.

Stannard, David. 1992. *American Holocaust: The Conquest of the New World*. Oxford: Oxford University Press.

Steffensmeier, Darrell, and Miles D. Harer. 1993. Bulging Prisons, an Aging U.S. Population, and the Nation's Violent Crime Rate. *Federal Probation* 57 (2): 3–10.

Steinberg, Stephen. 1995. *Turning Back: The Retreat from Racial Justice in American Thought and Policy*. Boston: Beacon Press.

Sterling, Dorothy, ed. 1984. *We Are Your Sisters: Black Women in the Nineteenth Century*. New York: Norton.

Stoll, Steven. 1998. *The Fruits of Natural Advantage: Making the Industrial Countryside in California*. Berkeley: University of California Press.

Stone, Katherine. 1981. The Postwar Paradigm in American Labor Law. *Yale Law Journal* 80 (June): 1511–80.

Storper, Michael, and Richard Walker. 1984. The Spatial Division of

Labor: Labor and the Location of Industries. In *Sunbelt/Snowbelt: Urban Development and Regional Restructuring,* ed. William K. Tabb and Larry Sawyers, 19–47. Oxford: Oxford University Press.

———. 1989. *The Capitalist Imperative: Territory, Technology, and Industrial Growth.* Oxford: Oxford University Press.

Streek, Wolfgang. 1991. On the Institutional Conditions of Diversified Quality Production. In *Beyond Keynesianism: The Socio-Economics of Production and Employment,* ed. Egon Matzner and Wolfgang Streek, 21–61. London: Edgar Elgar.

Sugrue, Thomas. 1996. *The Origins of the Urban Crisis.* Princeton, N.J.: Princeton University Press.

Summers, Lawrence. 1991. The Memo. www.gsreport.com/articles/art000171.html (accessed August 2005).

Sussman, Tina, and John Howard. 1987. 2 Idle Prisons Remain Silent Hostages in Political Fight over L.A. *Los Angeles Times,* 1–3.

Sweezy, Paul M. 1994. The Triumph of Financial Capital. *Monthly Review* 46 (2): 1–11.

Sykes, Mary. 1988. From "Rights" to "Needs": Official Discourse and the "Welfarization" of Race. In *Discourse and Discrimination,* ed. Geneva Smitherman Donaldson and Teun A. van Dijk, 176–205. Detroit: Wayne State University Press.

Tabb, William. 1992. Vampire Capitalism. *Socialist Review* 22 (1): 81–93.

Tadman, Michael. 1990. *Speculators and Slaves: Masters, Traders, and Slaves in the Old South.* Madison: University of Wisconsin Press.

Takaki, Dana Y. 1992. The Retreat from Race. *Socialist Review* 22 (4): 167–89.

Takaki, Ron. 1972. *Violence in the Black Imagination.* New York: Putnam.

———. 1979. *Iron Cages.* New York: Knopf.

Talamentez, Bato, ed. 2001. *Donny: Life of a Lifer. A Prisoner's Odyssey.* San Francisco: California Prison Focus.

Teitz, Michael B. 1984. The California Economy: Changing Structure and Policy Responses. In *California Policy Choices,* vol. 1, ed. John J.

Kirkland and Donald R. Winkler, 37–59. Annual published by the Sacramento Public Affairs Center, School of Public Administration, University of Southern California, Los Angeles.

Thelan, David. 1969. Social Tensions and the Origins of Progressivism. *Journal of American History* 56: 323–41.

Thurston, Linda M., ed. 1993. *A Call to Action: An Analysis and Overview of the United States Criminal Justice System, with Recommendations.* Chicago: Third World Press.

Tilly, Charles. 1985. War Making and State Making as Organized Crime. In *Bringing the State Back In,* ed. Peter B. Evans, Dietrich Rueschemeyer, and Theda Skocpol, 169–91. Cambridge: Cambridge University Press.

———. 1995. Contentious Repertoires in Great Britain, 1758–1834. In *Repertoires and Cycles of Collective Action,* ed. Charles Traugott, 15–42. Durham N.C.: Duke University Press.

———. 1990. The Politics of the New Inequality. *Socialist Review* 20 (1): 103–20.

Tomlins, Christopher. 1985. *The State and the Unions: Labor Relations, Law and the Organized Labor Movement in America, 1880–1960.* Cambridge: Cambridge University Press.

Tonry, Michael. 1995. *Malign Neglect: Race, Crime, and Punishment in America.* New York: Oxford University Press.

Tonry, Michael, and Richard Frase, eds. 2001. *Sentencing and Sanctions in Western Countries.* New York: Oxford University Press.

Tonry, Michael, and Joan Petersilia, eds. 1999. *Prisons.* Crime and Justice, vol. 26. Chicago: University of Chicago Press.

Traugott, Charles, ed. 1995. *Repertoires and Cycles of Collective Action.* Durham, N.C.: Duke University Press.

Travis, Kevin, and Francis J. Sheridan. 1983. Community Involvement in Prison Siting. *Corrections Today,* April, 14–15.

———. 1986. New York State Site Problems? Not Here! *Corrections Today,* April, 10–16.

Truell, Peter. 1995. Underwriting on Wall Street Remained Sluggish in Quarter. *New York Times,* April 3, D-10.

Trujillo, Charley. 1990. *Soldados: Chicanos in Viet Nam*. San Jose, Calif.: Chusma House.

Tula, Maria Teresa. 1994. *Hear My Testimony*. Translated by Lynn Stephen. Boston: South End Press.

Turgeon, Lynn. 1996. *Bastard Keynesianism: The Evolution of Economic Thinking and Policymaking since World War II*. Westport, Conn.: Greenwood Press.

Turner, Robin Lanette, and Diana Pei Wu. 2002. *Environmental Justice and Environmental Racism: An Annotated Bibliography and General Overview, Focusing on U.S. Literature, 1996–2002*. Berkeley: Institute of International Studies, University of California.

Twine, France Winddance, and Kathleen Blee, eds. *Feminism and Anti-Racism*. New York: New York University Press.

United States. Bureau of the Census. Various years. *Census*. Washington, D.C.: U.S. Department of Commerce, Economics and Statistics Administration, Bureau of the Census.

———. Various years. *County Business Patterns*. Washington, D.C.: U.S. Department of Commerce, Economics and Statistics Administration, Bureau of the Census.

———. Various years. *Statistical Abstract of the United States*. Washington, D.C.: U.S. Dept. of Commerce, Economics and Statistics Administration, Bureau of the Census.

United States. Department of Agriculture. 1977–2002. *Census of Agriculture*. Washington, D.C.: U.S. Dept. of Agriculture, National Agricultural Statistics Service.

United States. Kerner Commission. 1968. *The Kerner Report: The 1968 Report of the National Advisory Commission on Civil Disorders*. New York: Pantheon Books.

United States. National Resources Committee. 1935. *Regional Factors in National Planning*. Washington, D.C.: U.S. Government Printing Office.

Urban, Greg. 1993. Culture's Public Face. *Public Culture* 5 (2): 213–38.

———. 1993. Rube Replies. *Public Culture* 5 (2): 249–50.

Urban Strategies Group. 1992. *A Call to Reject the Federal Weed and Seed Program*. Los Angeles: Labor/Community Strategy Center.

Valle, Victor, and Rudolfo D. Torres. 1994. Latinos in a "Post-Industrial" Disorder: Politics in a Changing City. *Socialist Review* 23 (4): 1–28.

Vigil, James Diego. 1996. Youth Gang Subcultures in a Changing Los Angeles. Conference of Ford Fellows, National Research Council, Irvine, Calif. October.

Viramontes, Helena María. 1995. *Under the Feet of Jesus.* New York: Dutton.

Voorheis, Valerie. 1994. Jobs from Jails. *dollars and sense,* November–December, 16–17.

———. N.d. Decreasing Opportunity in the U.S.: Prison Policy and Unemployment. Unpublished ms.

Wacquant, Loic. 2002. From Slavery to Mass Incarceration: Rethinking the "Race Question" in the US. *New Left Review,* 2nd ser., 13: 41–60.

Wagner-Pacifici, Robin Erica. 1986. *The Moro Morality Play.* Chicago: University of Chicago Press.

Waldie, D. J. 1996. *Holy Land: A Suburban Memoir.* New York: Norton.

Waldinger, Roger, and Mehdi Bozorgmehr, eds. 1996. *Ethnic Los Angeles.* New York: Russell Sage Foundation.

Walker, Richard. 1995. California Rages against the Dying of the Light. *New Left Review* 209: 42–74.

———. 1999. Putting Capital in Its Place: Globalization and the Prospects for Labor. *Geoforum* 30: 263–84.

Wallace, Henry Scott. 1993. Mandatory Minimums and the Betrayal of Sentencing Reform: A Legislative Dr. Jekyll and Mr. Hyde. *Federal Probation* 57 (3): 9–19.

Waller, William, and Ann Jennings. 1990. On the Possibility of a Feminist Economic: The Convergence of Institutional and Feminist Methodology. *Journal of Economic Issues* 24 (2): 613–21.

Wallerstein, Immanuel. 1991a. *Geopolitics and Geoculture: Essays on the Changing World-System.* New York: Cambridge University Press.

———. 1991b. *Unthinking Social Science: The Limits of Nineteenth-Century Paradigms.* Cambridge, Mass.: Polity Press in association with B. Blackwell.

———. 1992. Post-America and the Collapse of Leninism. *Rethinking Marxism* 5 (1): 93–99.

———. 1994. The Agonies of Liberalism: What Hope Progress? *New Left Review* 204: 3–17.

Walters, Dan. [1986] 1992. *The New California: Facing the 21st Century.* 2nd ed. Sacramento: California Journal Press.

Ware, Vron. 1992. *Beyond the Pale: White Women, Racism, and History.* New York: Verso.

Ware, Vron, and Les Back. 2002. *Out of Whiteness.* Chicago: University of Chicago Press.

Wark, McKenzie. 1994. *Virtual Geography: Living with Global Media Events.* Bloomington: Indiana University Press.

Warsh, David. 1984. *The Idea of Economic Complexity.* New York: Penguin Books.

Watts, Michael. 1983. On the Poverty of Theory: Natural Hazards Research in Context. In *Interpretations of Calamity,* ed. K. Hewitt, 231–62. Boston: Allen & Unwin.

———. 1993. Development I: Power, Knowledge, Discursive Practice. *Progress in Human Geography* 17 (2): 257–72.

———. 1994a. Development II: Markets, States and the Privatization of Everything. *Progress in Human Geography* 18 (3): 371–83.

———. 1994b. Life under Contract: Contract Farming, Agrarian Restructuring and Flexible Accumulation. In *Living under Contract: Contract Farming and Agrarian Transformation in Sub-Saharan Africa,* ed. Peter Little and Michael Watts, 21–77. Madison: University of Wisconsin Press.

Wayne, Leslie. 1995. Court Upholds Donations Ban in Bond Market. *New York Times,* August 5, A-31.

Weber, Devra. 1994. *Dark Sweat, White Gold: California Farm Workers, Cotton and the New Deal.* Berkeley: University of California Press.

Welch, Michael. 2002. *Detained: Immigration Laws and the Expanding I.N.S. Jail Complex.* Philadelphia: Temple University Press.

Wells, Miriam. 1996. *Strawberry Fields: Politics, Class and Work in California Agriculture.* Ithaca, N.Y.: Cornell University Press.

West, Cornel. 1988. Marxist Theory and the Specificity of Afro-American Oppression. In *Marxism and the Interpretation of Culture*, ed. Cary Nelson and Lawrence Grossberg, 17–29. Urbana: University of Illinois Press.

West Hills Community College District. 1996–2000. *Catalog*. Published annually.

Western, Bruce, and Kathy Beckett. 2000. The Penal System and the U.S. Labor Market. *Prison Legal News* 11 (10): 1–4.

Weymouth, Toni D., and Maria Telesco. n.d. *Outsiders Looking In: How to Keep from Going Crazy When Someone You Love Goes to Jail*. Fresno, Calif.: OLINC Publishing.

Whalen, Charles J. 1989. John R. Common's Institutional Economics: A Re-Examination. *Journal of Economic Issues* 23 (2): 443–54.

What's News Worldwide. 1997. *Wall Street Journal*, August 8, A-1.

White, Deborah Gray. 1985. *Ar'n't I a Woman? Female Slaves in the Plantation South*. New York: Norton.

Wial, Howard. 1993. The Emerging Organizational Structure of Unionism in Low-Wage Services. *Rutgers Law Review* 45: 671–738.

Wicker, Tom. [1974] 1994. *A Time to Die: The Attica Prison Revolt*. Lincoln: University of Nebraska Press.

Wilentz, Sean. 1984. *Chants Democratic*. New York: Oxford University Press.

Williams, Brackette F. 1991. *Stains on My Name, War in My Veins: Guyana and the Politics of Cultural Struggle*. Durham, N.C.: Duke University Press.

———, ed. 1996. *Women out of Place: The Gender of Agency and the Race of Nationality*. New York: Routledge.

Williams, Eric. 1944. *Capitalism and Slavery*. Chapel Hill: University of North Carolina Press.

———. [1970] 1984. *From Columbus to Castro: The History of the Caribbean*. New York: Vintage Books.

Williams, Patricia J. 1988. On Being the Object of Property. *Signs* 14 (1): 5–24.

Williams, Raymond. 1961. *The Long Revolution*. New York: Columbia University Press.

———. 1980. *Problems in Materialism and Culture: Selected Essays*. London: Verso.

Willis, Paul. 1977. *Learning to Labor: How Working Class Kids Get Working Class Jobs*. New York: Columbia University Press.

Wilson, Bobby M. 2000a. *America's Johannesburg: Industrialization and Racial Transformation in Birmingham*. Lanham, Md.: Rowman & Littlefield.

———. 2000b. *Race and Place in Birmingham*. Lanham, Md.: Rowman & Littlefield.

———. 2002. Critically Understanding Race-Connected Practices: A Reading of W. E. B. Du Bois and Richard Wright. *Professional Geographer* 54 (1): 31–41.

Wilson, James Q. 1994. Prisons in a Free Society. *Public Interest,* Fall, 37–40.

Wilson, James Q., and Richard Herrnstein. 1985. *Crime and Human Nature*. New York: Simon & Schuster.

Wilson, William Julius. 1980. *The Declining Significance of Race: Blacks and Changing American Institutions*. 2nd ed. Chicago: University of Chicago Press.

———. 1987. *The Truly Disadvantaged*. Chicago: University of Chicago Press.

———. 1992. Foreword. *The Underclass Question,* ed. William Lawson, xi–xii. Philadelphia: Temple University Press.

Winant, Howard. 1990. Postmodern Racial Politics: Difference and Inequality. *Socialist Review* 20 (1): 121–47.

Winslow, George. 1999. *Capital Crimes*. New York: Monthly Review Press.

Wirt, Frederick M. 1997. *"We ain't what we was": Civil Rights in the New South*. Durham, N.C.: Duke University Press.

Wisely, Willie. 2003. Corcoran. In *Prison Nation,* ed. Tara Herivel and Paul Wright, 245–51. New York: Routledge.

Wolch, Jennifer. 1989. *The Shadow State: Government and Voluntary Sector in Transition*. New York: Foundation Center.

Wolff, Richard D. 1984. David Harvey, Marxist Economics, and Geography—A Review Essay. *Economic Geography,* Summer, 81–85.

Wolinsky, Leo C. 1987. '82 Prison Law Symbolizes Distrust between
L.A. and Rest of California. *Los Angeles Times,* January 18, 1–3.

Wood, Ellen Meiksins. 1991. *The Pristine Culture of Capitalism: A Historical Essay on Old Regimes and Modern States.* New York: Verso.

————. 1994. From Opportunity to Imperative: The History of the
Market. *Monthly Review* 46 (3): 14–40.

————. 1995. *Democracy against Capitalism: Renewing Historical Materialism.* Cambridge: Cambridge University Press.

Wood, Ellen Meiksins, and Neal Wood. 1997. *A Trumpet of Sedition: Political Theory and the Rise of Capitalism, 1509–1688.* London: Pluto
Press.

Woodiwiss, Michael. 2001. *Organized Crime and American Power: A History.* Toronto: University of Toronto Press.

Woods, Clyde. 1998. *Development Arrested.* New York: Verso.

————. 2002. Life after Death. *Professional Geographer* 54 (1): 62–66.

Woodward, C. Vann. [1955] 2002. *The Strange Career of Jim Crow.* Oxford: Oxford University Press.

Wright, Gwendolyn, and Paul Rabinow. 1982. Spatialization of Power:
A Discussion of the Work of Michel Foucault. *Skyline,* March, 14–15.

Wright, Paul. 2003. "Victims' Rights" as a Stalking-horse for State Repression. In *Prison Nation,* ed. Tara Herivel and Paul Wright, 60–64.
New York: Routledge.

Yates, Michael. 1994. *Longer Hours, Fewer Jobs: Employment and Unemployment in the United States.* Cornerstone Books. New York:
Monthly Review Press.

Yee, Min S. 1973. *The Melancholy History of Soledad Prison.* New York:
Harper's Magazine Press.

Yogi, Stan, ed. 1996. *Highway 99: A Literary Journey through California's
Great Central Valley.* Berkeley: Heyday Books/California Council
for the Humanities.

Youth Force. N.d. *Yo! On the Serious Tip/If You Get Stopped by a Cop.*
New York: Youth Force Pamphlet.

Zedlewski, Edwin. 1987. *Making Confinement Decisions*. Washington, D.C.: U.S. Department of Justice, National Institute of Justice.

Zimring, Franklin E. 1993. Research on the Death Penalty: On the Liberating Virtues of Irrelevance. *Law & Society Review* 27 (1): 9–17.

Zimring, Franklin E., and Gordon Hawkins. 1997. *Crime Is Not the Problem: Lethal Violence in America*. New York: Oxford University Press.

Zimring, Franklin, Sam Kamin, and Gordon Hawkins. 1999. *Crime and Punishment: The Impact of Three Strikes and You're Out*. Berkeley, Calif.: Institute for Governmental Studies Press.

Zinn, Maxine Baca. 1989. Family, Race and Poverty in the Eighties. *Signs* 14 (4): 856–74.

INTERVIEWS

Conrad Andrews, Los Angeles, 1995, 1996

Constance Andrews, Los Angeles, 1995, 1996

Francie Arbol, Los Angeles, 1995, 1996, 1997, 1999, 2000, 2002

Berndt Beutenmueller, Sacramento, 1995

Gwynnae Bird, Sacramento, 1999, 2000, 2002, 2003

Pearl Daye, Los Angeles, 1995, 1996

Tom Dumphy, Sacramento, 1996

Mona Estrada, Los Angeles, 1995, 1996

June Fernandez, Los Angeles, 1995, 1996

Gilda Garcia, Pomona, 1995, 1996

Belle Gillespie, Los Angeles, 1996

Leticia Gonzales, Los Angeles, 1995, 1996

Melissa W. Harriman, Avenal, 1996

Bernice Hatfield, Covina, 1995, 1996

Paris Jackson, Los Angeles, 1995, 1996

John C. Lum, Sacramento, 2003

Barbara Meredith, Los Angeles, 1995, 1996, 1997, 1998, 2000

Dan Morain, Sacramento, 1995

R. Bernard Orozco, Sacramento, 1995, 1996

Andrew Parks, Modesto, 1995

Frederic Prager, San Francisco, 1996
J. Edward Tewes, Modesto, 1995
Jeanette Todd, Corcoran, 1995
Charley Trujillo, San Jose, 1999
Graciela Vega, Claremont, 1995, 1997

INDEX

activists, 29, 241–42, 245–48; antiracist, 37, 39, 89, 168–69, 170,
190–91, 192, 244, 246–47; antitax,
42–43, 49, 62, 80–84, 95, 97, 101,
126, 147, 258n16; campus, 38;
civic elites, 12, 22, 188; Corcoran,
152–54, 168; vs. criminalization
and imprisonment as solutions to
social problems, 1–5, 109, 172,
185, 229, 249–51; criminalization
of, 89, 90–91; for dispossessed,
12; environmentalist, 142,
258n16; environmental justice,
178, 249–51; extremist, 233; governmental, 135; grassroots organization, 178, 184, 186, 231, 251;
for "kids," 177, 178; lawyers,
210–11; and Los Angeles upris-
ings, 39, 50, 196–97, 203–4; "maternal," 195; "moral panics," 90–
91, 93; Mothers ROC, 5–6, 181–
240, 241; vs. police brutality, 50,

190, 196, 202, 203, 212; and
power, 222, 238, 247–48; prisoner, 244–45; vs. prison siting,
103–4, 152–54, 175, 176–80, 227–
28, 266n31, 272–73n29; professionalization of, 242; rural people
vs. prisons, 152–54, 175, 176–80,
249–51, 266n31, 272–73n29;
scholar, 5–6, 27, 183–84, 241; ten
theses for, 29, 245–48; urban
people vs. prisons, 103–4, 180,
249–51; vs. "Weed and Seed"
funding by DOJ, 277n19;
women, 181–240. *See also* coalitions; labor activism; Mothers
ROC; Progressives; strikes; voter
propositions; voting power
aerospace industry, 36–37, 40, 60,
125–26
affirmative action, 50, 118, 160–61
Africa, activist women, 181, 184,
239

killing, 13; as permanent problem, 122; and prisoner risk classifications, 265–66n27; public anxiety number one, 18, 116; status offense, 261n9; theft, 13, 19, 112–13, 112 *table;* "wobblers," 108, 224–27, 264n22; workfare-warfare state vs., 85–86. *See also* crime rates; criminalization; drugs; felonies; police; "three strikes"; violence
Crime and Delinquency, 174
crime rates: change in method of calculating, 9; Corcoran, 173; declining, 7, 8 *fig,* 9 *fig,* 18, 19, 95, 114, 115–16, 173; drug, 19, 108; and prison growth, 7, 15–20, 24, 114; property, 19; "three strikes" and, 15, 112–13
criminalization: of activists, 89, 90–91; activists vs., 2, 172; decriminalization and recriminalization of controlled substances possession (1970s–80s), 108; deindustrialization and welfare state decline creating, 232; Gilbert Jones, 203, 204; and imprisonment as solutions for social problems, 1–5, 109, 172, 185, 229, 249–51; legal, fiscal, and programmatic linkages, 124; new laws passed, 6, 12, 96, 107–8, 110–12, 122, 221, 227, 263n20; politics of "law and order"/"tough on crime" and, 40, 53–54, 88, 95–112; racist, 64, 110–11, 224–25; sentence enhancement, 107–12; Stick Hatfield, 212–14; of youth, 172, 173. *See also* prison; sentencing; "three strikes"
criminal justice: as state power, 174. *See also* trials
crises, 40–51, 54–86; agribusiness, 145; defined, 26, 54; farm debt, 48, 67–68, 134, 147; fixes, 26, 129, 179; micro and macro, 186–87; Mothers ROC responding to, 181, 185, 196–97; political economy, 26–28, 54–86, 88, 195–96, 256–58n12; and prison construction, 96–97; state, 26, 78–84, 86; surpluses and, 54–84, 86, 88, 124, 147–48, 179. *See also* state of emergency

dams, 138–39; Peripheral Canal and, 142, 258n16
Davis, Angela Y., 181
Daye, Harry, 223–24
Daye, Pearl, 223–27
deaths: crimes causing, 13; genocide, 32, 243; Noyes, 196–97, 202, 203, 206; prisoners shot by guards, 121; sociospatial apartheid and, 74
debt: farm, 48, 67–68, 134, 147. *See also* public debt
dehumanization, 243
deindustrialization, 7, 14, 185, 204, 232, 259n20, 274n8
Delano: Delano II prison 266n31; "megaprisons," 125; prison employment, 176–77, 273n30

364   INDEX

Del Norte County, prison siting, 104
Democrats: Bradley, 48; Jerry Brown, 49, 93; California governors, 49, 81, 93; elections (1970s), 40–41; and GOB debt, 97–98; vs. LRBs for CDC, 121; regional relationships, 79
Denny, Reginald, 206, 273n1
Department of Defense (DOD). See U.S. Department of Defense
depressions: Great, 25, 34–35, 79, 80, 116, 141, 205–6; rural, 22, 69, 149, 176; welfare state, 25, 52. See also recessions
deterrence, imprisonment as, 14, 107
Deukmejian, George, 48–49, 53–54, 62, 94–95, 97, 267n36
development: exurban, 69–70; prison as antidevelopment problem, 179, 272n25; prison-related, 148–49, 157, 165–66; suburbanization, 68–70, 147; water, 137–38, 142–43. See also building
devolution, federal, 22, 81, 245
disinvestment, 88; agricultural land, 53, 65, 68–70, 105–6, 126–27, 155–57, 162, 258n17; anticipatory, 68; enforced, 258n17; Proposition 13 and, 260n25; surplus land and, 63, 64, 65, 68
dispossessed, 42, 106–7; activists standing up for, 12; Black workers, 141; farmers, 32, 192, 268–69n1; Mexicanos, 32, 132, 141; mothers of, 185; Okies, 135;

prison and, 12; white homesteaders, 32; World War II racial-ethnic, 35–36, 141, 244. See also hierarchical relationships
District of Columbia, highest per capita income and highest poverty in U.S., 30
diversity: California's, 30–32. See also class; immigrants; race
DOD. See U.S. Department of Defense
DOJ (U.S. Department of Justice), "Weed and Seed" funding, 231–32, 277n19
Doolittle, Marvin, 204
Downey, Sheridan, 138–39
drought, 126, 270n11; agriculture and, 41, 67, 68, 141–43, 147, 155; and groundwater, 141–42, 162
drugs, 87; controlling offense, 112–13, 112 table; decline in illegal use, 19, 108; decriminalization (1970s), 108; diversion for first- and second-time drug convictions, 267n37; laws, 96, 265n24; legal/illegal, 13, 96; prison growth explained by epidemic of, 18–19; recriminalization (1980s), 108; treatment programs, 101
Dumphy, Tom, 97, 99, 100–101, 120

economics, 6, 7; arms buildup, 43; booms, 19–20, 43, 48, 49, 125–26, 199, 269n6; business cycle, 55–56; California as "principal en-

politics *(continued)*
229, 236; prison siting, 156–57,
164; U.S. governmental power,
242–43. *See also* activists; communism; Democrats; power;
Progressives; Republicans; restructuring; social movements
population: CDC workforce, 8;
Central Valley, 69; Corcoran,
130, 150, 152, 158; Kings
County, 130; relative surplus,
70–78, 73–74*table,* 111, 113, 184–
85, 240; taxation based on, 150,
163. *See also* California population
postsecondary education: antiracist
admissions policies, 167; California Master Plan for, 37, 49,
254n3; CO training, 118–20,
266n30; finance, 49, 98–99,
267n35; Morrill Act funding, 37;
private, 98–99, 254n3; tuition
and scholarships, 49, 98–99, 147,
254n3
poverty, 30, 43–44, 70, 179; Black,
38–39; child, 52, 57, 148; Corcoran, 129, 145, 146, 148, 155, 160;
Mothers ROC and, 224–25, 228,
229, 230–31, 237; relative, 30;
Sinclair's End Poverty in California (EPIC) campaign, 35; tax
changes and, 43, 44, 95, 246; underclass, 259n20; white, 15. *See
also* welfare state; working poor;
workless poor
power, 247–48; balance of, 78–80,
84; criminal justice, 174; gun

control and, 255n6; Mothers
ROC meditating on, 222, 238;
planning, 175; prison sitings
and, 154, 156; social change, 29;
status determinations used to
concentrate, 110; and surplus
state capacity, 113–14, 126. *See
also* politics
Prager, Frederic, 97–98, 99, 100–101
prayers: Mothers ROC, 221–22, 227.
See also churches
Presley, Robert, 97–98, 107
prices: land for prison siting, 106;
near prison sites, 157–58; Southern Pacific Railroad land, 268n5;
wages and, 72
prime rate: decline (1989), 60, 61 *fig;*
savings and loans reaction, 48;
and unemployment, 44–45
prison, 21–22, 353; as deterrence, 14,
107; as incapacitation, 14–15, 16,
21, 95, 185; measure of capacity,
261n4; "megaprisons," 125,
267n36; percentage of public, 21;
privatized, 21–22, 124–25, 227–
28, 253n1, 267n35; for public
safety, 18, 94, 122; as punishment, 91, 95; purposes of, 11–17,
18, 91, 94, 95–96, 242; as rehabilitation, 14, 88–93; as retribution,
14; as solution to social problems, 1–5, 172, 229, 249–51;
three spheres of sanction, 173.
See also California prisons; jails;
prisoner labor; prisoner populations
"prison alley," Central Valley, 129

prison construction, 4–8, 54, 85, 88–
89, 92–126, 246–47, 253n1; crime
rate decline and, 7, 15–20, 24,
114, 115–16; finances, 7, 88, 93–
94, 97–102, 114–23, 125, 126;
Folsom replacement, 92; JL-
CPCO, 94, 95, 106, 121–22, 127,
150, 162–63; land, 88, 102–7,
149–50, 155–57; Legislative Analyst's report (1986), 114–15, 120;
local labor for, 149; prisoner
labor for, 125, 151; for rehabilitation, 92–93; San Quentin replacement, 92, 103. *See also*
prison siting
Prison Construction Bond Act
(1982), California, 97
prison employment, 88, 149–50, 246;
Black, 276n12; Corcoran, 130–
31, 149, 150, 152, 154, 158–61,
165–66, 168, 171, 175–76; Delano, 176–77, 273n30; East Los
Angeles, 103; job classifications,
270–71n15; population of workforce, 8; rural areas, 22–23, 104,
106–7; South Central Los Angeles, 228; training, 118–19,
266n30. *See also* COs (correctional officers); prisoner labor
prisoner labor: cheap, 12–13, 21;
Corcoran public works, 166,
168; free, 185; prison construction, 125, 151
prisoner populations: relative
poverty and, 30. *See also* California prisoner population; prison
construction

prison growth. *See* prison construction; prisoner populations
prison guards. *See* COs (correctional officers)
prison labor. *See* prison employment; prisoner labor
Prison Reform Conference Committee (PRCC), California,
123
prison siting, 102–7, 129–30, 148–
66, 174–79; activists vs., 103–4,
152–54, 175, 176–80, 227–28,
266n31, 272–73n29; Avenal, 104,
148, 157–58, 162, 272n25; CDC
Office, 103–4, 105, 148–66; class
and, 155, 177; Corcoran, 104,
129–30, 148–66, 175–76; Costa
politically key in, 157, 264n21;
economics, 146–52, 155, 157–66,
168, 174, 175–76, 247, 271–
72nn22,23; "fear" vs. "finances,"
174–78; land, 88, 102–7, 149–50,
155–57, 175; Los Angeles
County, 103–4, 227–28, 250,
263nn15,18; politics, 156–57,
164; race and, 154, 155, 177; Susanville experience, 151, 158,
164, 166, 271n16; water supply
concern, 153, 162, 177, 272n25
private colleges and universities,
public finances for, 98–99,
254n3
private irrigation districts, 268–
69n5
private prisons, 21–22, 124–25, 227–
28, 253n1, 267n35
private security industry, 125

135–36; Black-white coalitions,
216; California settlement
(1800s), 31; class-based strife between, 35; colonizers, 32; Corcoran chiefs of police scandal,
170; Corcoran dominance, 146,
169; dispossessed homesteaders,
32; employers, 34–35; femi-
nist/gender politics, 188; gangs,
204–5, 217; guards with prisoners of color, 22; labor activists,
32–33, 135–36, 146, 192; majority status lost in California, 42,
52, 57; male employment, 76;
Mothers ROC, 184, 207, 209;
Okies, 34–35, 135, 146–47,
271n17; poor, 15; prisoner population, 110–11, 111table, 204–
5, 244–45, 275n11, 277n18; and
prison sitings, 154; Progressive
women, 187–88; "reserve army
of whiteness," 244; supremacy
of, 33–37, 42, 135, 204–5; third
strike prisoners, 113; wealth
controlled by, 26, 34; "wobbler"
charges, 225. See also European
immigrants
Williamson Act (1965), 258n17,
268n2
Wilson, Pete, 49, 53–54, 62, 121, 123
"wobblers," 108, 224–27, 264n22.
See also felonies
women: activists, 181–240; Argentina's presumptions about,
194; Black club women, 187–91;
employment declines among

Black, 75–76; feminist/gender
politics, 188; income/asset per-
centages (world), 279n24; inequalities, 26, 279n24; prisoner
population, 7; Progressive, 187–
90; social parenting, 74; struggles, 184, 195–96, 201–8, 218,
238, 276n12; unemployment, 75;
visibility of, 190–92, 238–39;
workfare programs, 49;
working-class, 187–91, 194, 199,
239. See also mothers
workers. See labor
workfare-warfare state, 79, 85–86
workfare, 48–49, 86
working class, 119; bus riders for
freedom, 2; Corcoran, 148, 156;
criminalization, 110; education,
181; Mothers ROC, 187–91, 194,
199, 211, 224–25, 239; and prison
siting, 103. See also labor; prison
employment; working poor
Workingmen's Party, 33
working poor: Mothers ROC, 237;
prisoner population, 7, 15, 237;
relative surplus population, 77;
underclass, 259n20; welfare state
and, 45; workfare programs, 48–
49
workless poor, prisoner population,
7, 15
World War I, 134
World War II, 80; "creative destruction," 35; defense boom in Los
Angeles County, 199; farmworkers and, 136, 141; golden

AMERICAN CROSSROADS
EDITED BY EARL LEWIS, GEORGE LIPSITZ, PEGGY PASCOE, GEORGE SÁNCHEZ,
AND DANA TAKAGI

TEXT
11/15 Granjon
DISPLAY
HTF Knockout; Akzidenz Grotesk
COMPOSITOR
Binghamton Valley Composition, LLC
PRINTER AND BINDER
Maple-Vail Manufacturing Group
INDEXER
Barbara Roos
CARTOGRAPHER/ILLUSTRATOR
Bill Nelson